ANALYTIC THEISM, HARTSHORNE, AND THE CONCEPT OF GOD

SUNY Series in Philosophy
Edited by George R. Lucas, Jr.

Analytic Theism, Hartshorne, and the Concept of God

Daniel A. Dombrowski

STATE UNIVERSITY OF NEW YORK PRESS

Published by
State University of New York Press, Albany

Printed in the United States of America

For information, address State University of New York Press,
State University Plaza, Albany, N.Y., 12246

Production by Cathleen Collins
Marketing by Fran Keneston

Library of Congress Cataloging in Publication Data

Dombrowski, Daniel A.
Analytic theism, Hartshorne, and the concept of God / Daniel A. Dombrowski.
p. cm. — (SUNY series in philosophy)
Includes bibliographical references and index.
ISBN 0-7914-3099-5 (alk. paper). — ISBN 0-7914-3100-2 (pbk. : alk. paper)
1. Hartshorne, Charles, 1897—Contributions to doctrine of God.
2. God. 3. God—History of doctrines—20th century. 4. Theism.
5. Process theology. I. Title. II. Series.
BT98.H26D66 1966
211′.092—dc20 95-47051
CIP

10 9 8 7 6 5 4 3 2 1

Contents

List of Schemata vii

Acknowledgments ix

Abbreviations of Works by Hartshorne xi

Introduction 1

Chapter One
Must a Perfect Being Be Immutable? 13

Chapter Two
Method and Polar Equality in Dipolar Theism 39

Chapter Three
Divine Embodiment 77

Chapter Four
Alston and Morris on the Concept of God 121

Chapter Five
Describing God 143

Chapter Six
The Concept of God and the Moral Life 173

Notes 219

Bibliography 233

Index of Names 245

Schemata

Schema 1	8
Schema 2	20
Schema 3	50
Schema 4	50
Schema 5	51
Schema 6	51
Schema 7	62
Schema 8	86
Schema 9	90
Schema 10	90
Schema 11	125
Schema 12	128
Schema 13	156

Acknowledgments

There are three groups of people I would like to thank for their help in the development and publication of this book. First, much of the work for this book was made possible by a sabbatical I received from Seattle University, my first after sixteen years of teaching (only the last seven of which were at Seattle University). I would like to thank those who made this sabbatical possible. Second, I would like to express appreciation to George Lucas, Lois Patton, three anonymous readers, and others at SUNY Press who have been most generous and helpful to me. And third, I would like to thank several analytic theists who have carefully read parts of this manuscript: William Alston, Richard Creel, Colin Gunton, Brian Leftow, and James Ross. Through their efforts I came to appreciate more deeply than I had before the important idea found in Mill and Popper that rational criticism not only makes one aware of what one's dialectical partner thinks, it also makes one more aware of the content and implications of one's own ideas.

Abbreviations of Works by Hartshorne

AD	*Anselm's Discovery*
AW	*Aquinas to Whitehead*
CA	*Creativity in American Philosophy*
CS	*Creative Synthesis and Philosophic Method*
DL	*The Darkness and the Light*
DR	*The Divine Relativity*
EA	*Existence and Actuality*
IO	*Insights and Oversights of Great Thinkers*
LP	*The Logic of Perfection*
MV	*Man's Vision of God*
NT	*A Natural Theology for Our Time*
OO	*Omnipotence and Other Theological Mistakes*
PC	*The Philosophy of Charles Hartshorne*
PS	*Philosophers Speak of God*
RS	*Reality as Social Process*
UB	"An Outline and Defense of the Argument for the Unity of Being in the Absolute or Divine Good"
WM	*Wisdom as Moderation*
WP	*Whitehead's Philosophy*
WV	*Whitehead's View of Reality*

Introduction

From the time of Philo and the Church Fathers until the seventeenth century the concept of God for the most part remained, from a philosophical point of view, fixed. Although there was disagreement regarding theological questions (like whether or not Jesus was divine), there was general agreement among Jewish, Christian, and Muslim thinkers that God was omnipotent, omniscient, omnibenevolent, and that God was eternal in the sense of being outside of time altogether and hence was immutable. The Protestant reformers did not reform this concept of God, and Kant, who did alter questions regarding the epistemology of religious belief, nonetheless held on to this traditional concept of God. But Spinoza, Hume, Voltaire, Feuerbach, Marx, Nietzsche, Freud, and the positivists, among others, have in various ways attacked belief in God, and this often because of inconsistencies in the above concept of God. Some of the key questions that should continue to be asked by contemporary theists are whether or not there is some legitimacy to these attacks on the concept of God and whether or not it is acceptable to continue with the pre-Enlightenment concept of God. One of the theses of this book is that analytic philosophers who are theists tend to take Hume and the rest seriously regarding questions in the epistemology of religious belief but not seriously enough regarding the problems found in the traditional concept of God.[1]

It is one of the great ironies of twentieth-century philosophy that the greatest defender of process philosophy and perhaps the greatest analytic philosopher were initially collaborators. Paul Kuntz and especially George Lucas have done excellent work in detailing both the lifelong commonality of intellectual interests in Whitehead and Russell as well as their divergent ways of responding to those interests (see Lucas 1988, 1989; Kuntz 1988). The well-known jibes these two delivered to each other (Whitehead thought Russell simpleminded and Russell thought Whitehead muddleheaded) are due to many factors. For example, Whitehead and the philosophers he influenced have always been mystified as to why Russell revitalized the worst features of Hume's philosophy: a theory of purely external relations or atomicity, on the one hand, and determinism, on the other. Hume and Russell (the latter with a more sophisticated logic at his disposal) both radically disconnect and radically connect reality. There is some evidence to suggest that the same sort of antipathy as that between Russell and Whitehead is at work in contemporary philosophy of religion. I do not know if Charles Hartshorne has ever explicitly referred to analytic theists as simpleminded, but he has been known to speak in terms that have perhaps hindered dialogue. It is clear that he is bothered by the fact that analytic theists generally have returned (somewhat uncritically) to the traditional concept of God without feeling the full force of the criticisms of that concept. He is also bothered by the persistence of Humean-Russerlian nominalism in their thought, for instance, in an antipathy to systematically considering alternative conceptions of God. And I do not know if any analytic philosopher has ever explicitly referred to Hartshorne as muddleheaded, but their general neglect of him is at least indicative of the fact that they do not think—rightly or wrongly—that he meets certain criteria regarding what philosophy ought to be, and this despite the fact that Hartshorne has been dealing in published writings with the concept of God for seventy years, almost fifty of which were during a period when analytic philosophers ignored or denigrated the concept. It is true that one can feel the full force of a person's criticisms of an idea without agreeing that those criticisms discredit the idea, but only a few analytic theists (e.g., Alston, Ross) have shown published evidence that they continue with the traditional concept of God because they have concluded that the process criticisms are insufficient to justify abandoning that concept.

The purpose of the present book is to attempt to initiate a dialogue where one does not exist, and to continue a dialogue where one has been tentatively initiated, regarding the concept of God in Hartshorne and that found in analytic theism (or more precisely, in analytic theists who adhere to classical theism). Most defenders of the latter are latter-day Boethians or Augustinians or Thomists. It is admittedly odd that a Catholic like myself would defend Hartshorne as opposed to these Boethians, Augustinians, and Thomists, but the matter can be explained when it is understood that Hartshorne's view, which he refers to as neoclassical theism, is as much "classical" as "neo," as I will try to show in this book. That is, Hartshorne's concern is both that the great achievements of the defenders of the traditional concept of God be preserved and that the flaws in this concept be eliminated. It is the latter part of Hartshorne's philosophical project in religion that is controversial. I should also make it clear that I will be concentrating on the relationship between Hartshorne and analytic theists regarding the concept of God and not on the proofs for the existence of God or the epistemology of religious belief, the latter having already received a great deal of well-deserved attention by commentators who are analytic philosophers. Likewise, I will be concentrating only on those aspects of the thought of analytic theists that relate to the concept of God, in general, or to Hartshorne's approach to the concept of God, in particular.

In chapter 1 I ask what I take to be a crucial question in the effort to locate the similarities and differences between Hartshorne and analytic theists: must a perfect being be immutable? I allege that many analytic theists (e.g., Paul Helm, Norman Kretzmann, William Mann, D. Z. Phillips, Alvin Plantinga, Eleanore Stump) *assume* that a perfect being is immutable without offering reasons to counter Hartshorne's partially negative response to this question. Richard Creel, however, offers a response to this question that at least in part takes Hartshorne's view into consideration. Although I am not entirely convinced by Creel's approach, he is nonetheless to be commended for at least making an attempt to argue against Hartshorne on this basic issue. Many of the topics to be treated in detail later in the book are introduced in this initial chapter. It should be noted that the above-mentioned analytic theists do an excellent job of arguing for the way in which God *is* immutable, even on neoclassical grounds. We will see that the neoclassical view is that God is immutable in existence, but preeminently mutable in actuality or in the mode of divine existence.

Chapter 2 consists in a treatment of method in Hartshorne's thought (including a comparison with some thoughts on method by A. O. Lovejoy), the purpose of which is to respond in detail to the criticism of Hartshorne's thought by Colin Gunton. This criticism alleges that there is a lack of equality in Hartshorne's dipolar theism, that Hartshorne, for example, devotes too much attention to divine relativity at the expense of divine absoluteness. I hold that Hartshorne's method includes at least these three features, features which make it possible to respond in a fruitful way to Gunton: (1) the development of position matrices to determine the available options regarding a particular problem; (2) the use of the history of philosophy to see which options have been carefully examined before; so as to (3) moderately choose among the most promising options, with "moderately" referring at the very least to a consideration of both the question of logical consistency and to the pragmatic implications of each promising option. Both chapters 1 and 2 end with a consideration of Plato; these uses of Plato are intended to illuminate the similarities and differences between analytic, classical theism and neoclassical theism. It will be seen that I have a strong commitment to the belief that philosophical views, in general, and concepts of God, in particular, grow out of their historical predecessors, and that a consideration of Plato and Aristotle is crucial for any adequate treatment of the concepts of God found in the contemporary philosophers examined in this book.

In chapter 3 the issue of divine embodiment is treated. William Alston indicates the need for something other than the traditional view of pure divine immateriality, even if he does not commit to belief in divine embodiment. Richard Swinburne does commit to such a belief, albeit in a very limited way. After briefly treating Keith

Ward, Robert Oakes, and William Wainwright, I move to Hartshorne, who has a much stronger commitment to divine embodiment than either Alston or Swinburne. Plato and the history of philosophy will once again be examined in this chapter through three scholars in particular: Jurgen Moltmann and Friedrich Solmsen, who are treated favorably, and Richard Mohr, who is criticized. That is, one of the aims of this book is to show that many of the inadequacies of analytic theism stem from its uncritical appropriation of the Aristotelian tradition in theology. Readers who are only interested in the Hartshorne-analytic theism debate over the concept of God, and not in the historical roots to these two views, can skip sections G–I of this chapter as well as section I in chapter 1 and section E in chapter 2.

Chapter 4 starts with a treatment of the distinction between pantheism and panentheism, a distinction that is crucial in the effort to criticize certain classical theists in analytic philosophy. Two such thinkers treated in this chapter are Alston and Thomas Morris. The former carefully treats Hartshorne's concept of God and makes several concessions to Hartshorne's concept of God, but we will see that ultimately he takes back with one hand what he gives with the other. That is, Alston, like Morris, is for the most part a monopolar, classical theist. Both of these thinkers are saddled with the inconsistencies which have traditionally been associated with this position.

In Chapter 5 I examine two more analytic theists—James Ross and Michael Durrant—who have insightfully commented on Hartshorne's concept of God. Both of these thinkers are instructive (intentionally or not) regarding Hartshorne's approach to religious language, which has not received sufficient attention from scholars, and regarding the inadequacies of classical theism when certain issues in philosophy of language are considered. At the end of the chapter I treat the connection between mysticism and the concept of God. Specifically I try to show how the great Christian mystics support Hartshorne's distinctions among the different sorts of religious language: literal-1 and literal-2, analogical, and symbolic.

Throughout Hartshorne's work one gets the impression that his metaphysics and philosophy of religion are based on certain aesthetic principles or tendencies that also have an impact on how we should think about the moral life. The purpose of the final chapter of the book is to make some of these implications explicit. That is, the two concepts of God treated throughout the book—the classical one used by most analytic theists and the neoclassical one—will be brought to bear on the moral life. Chapter 6 will have three foci. First, I will look at the thought of Thomas Nagel from the perspective of Hartshorne's thought. I will claim that in three key areas—death and the absurdity of life, the concept of freedom, and the mind-body problem—Nagel is paradoxically both very close to, yet far from process philosophy's treatment of these problems. Throughout this chapter I will be showing some of the problems created by a view of things *sub specie aeternitatis*, a view made famous by classical theists, and showing how a view *sub specie temporalis* resolves or avoids these problems. Second, I will also argue that taking polytheism seriously, as does Stephen R. L. Clark, even though polytheism must ultimately be rejected, acts as a corrective to classical theism's emphasis on the view of things *sub specie aeternitatis*. Third, I will apply classical and neoclassical concepts of God to the abortion debate; the former, I will claim, leads to a misguided opposition to the moral permissibility of abortion in the early stages of pregnancy. Once again, I will argue that the classical theistic view of things *sub specie aeternitatis* is the cause of error both regarding theoretical issues and those in applied ethics.

I should note at the outset of this book that I do not think there is any *necessary* connection between classical theism and analytic philosophy, but the latter's (nominalistic) tendency not to consider position matrices of the sort illustrated later in this Introduction and described in chapter 2, so as to map out the possible solutions to an intellectual problem, may well have as one of its effects a too easy acceptance of classical theism. The razor-sharp tools of analytic philosophy can, I think, be put to better use. Throughout the book I will point out what I take to be the strengths as well as the weaknesses in the concept of God employed by analytic theists. It should be clear, I hope, that my criticisms are nonetheless conducive to a healthy dialogue in that for rational criticism to do its (Popperian) work then each party has to be willing not only to give ground when a legitimate criticism is received, but also to stand firm until such criticism is received. At this stage in the conversation, it seems to me, it is necessary for neoclassical theists to stand firm until they are engaged more explicitly by analytic theists.

There are some analytic theists like Robert Cook and Brian Leftow who detect a growing consensus among philosophical theists in favor divine sempiternity. I wish this were the case! There are still those like Paul Helm (and others to be treated in chapter 1) who defend divine eternity. And there are others, like Richard Swinburne, who appear to have gradually moved away from the Boethian view of divine eternity, but they have done so only slightly. That is, analytic philosophers like Keith Ward, who does, in fact, defend a modified process view, are few in number.

Consider the case of Alan Padgett, who defends a view of God as "relatively timeless"; or better, he defends a view where God is not within measured time. He rightly points out that neither Old Testament *olam* nor New Testament *aion* or *aidios* are to be equated with Boethian eternity, and that the biblical passages cited by Stump and Kretzmann (who will be treated in chapter 1)—Malachi 3:6, John 8:58, and James 1:17—refer to *moral* steadfastness, which is indeed a divine attribute, rather than to eternity. But Padgett's view does not support Cook's and Leftow's assessment, and for the following reasons. First, according to Padgett, God *chooses* to be dynamic, which seems to indicate that behind divine *dynamis* there lies an immutable God that is not dynamic. And second, God *is* immutable, he thinks, but is not absolutely immutable. What is needed here, I suspect, is a more careful examination of the ways in which God is characterized by *aseity*, in that God does not owe the divine existence to others. But we also need to avoid the stasis view of time (McTaggert's B-series), as Padgett rightly suggests. (1992, 35, 122–23, 125, 133, 140). Until these matters are cleared up, it will be difficult to determine in detail just how much of an effect process thinkers have had on analytic theists. My suspicion is that it has thus far been less of an effect than Cook or Leftow think.

The concept of God has a rich past, the best elements of which deserve preservation. It is also to be hoped that this concept will have a rich future. Analytic theists are obviously not to be blamed for the fact that, from the seventeenth century until the present, defenders of the concept of God have indeed been on the defensive. However, analytic theists do deserve criticism to the extent that they have recently analyzed in detail almost every issue in the philosophy of religion *except* the possibility that the neoclassical concept of God is superior to the classical one. It is the purpose of this book to explore this possibility.

Not all analytic theists have ignored the neoclassical concept of God; although most have, in fact, largely ignored it, even those who have been more concerned with the concept of God than with the epistemology of religious belief or the practical consequences of religious belief. My hope is that the reasons in favor of the neoclassical concept developed in this book are sufficiently strong so as to at least: (1) initiate a dialogue with those analytic theists who have not yet commented on the neoclassical view; and (2) fruitfully continue a dialogue already in progress with Alston, Creel, Durrant, Gunton, Morris, Ross, and a few others. Philosophical theists in the English-speaking world swim in a pond that is not too large; we would have to try hard not to periodically bump into each other.

Perhaps a good place to start such a dialogue is to see what analytic, classical theists and neoclassical theists can make of a very recent effort on the part of Hartshorne to develop a position matrix (schema 1) regarding divine and worldly necessity and contingency, a matrix which is a refinement of previous matrices developed by Hartshorne that have been left unanalyzed by philosophical theists (see Hartshorne 1993). The matrix looks like this:

SCHEMA 1

	I	II	III	IV
1.	N.n	C.n	NC.n	O.n
2.	N.c	C.c	NC.c	O.c
3.	N.cn	C.cn	NC.cn	O.cn
4.	N.o	C.o	NC.o	O.o

Key

Columns: I. God is in all respects necessary (or absolute, etc.).
II. God is in all respects contingent (or relative, etc.).
III. God is in diverse respects necessary and contingent.
IV. God is impossible or has no modal status.

Rows: 1. World (what is not God) is in all respects necessary.
2. World is in all respects contingent.
3. World is in diverse respects necessary and contingent.
4. World is impossible or has no modal status.

At least six of these sixteen items can be termed theistic: the first three in columns I and III. And the first and third items in row 4 might also be theistic; they seem to fit varieties of acosmism or mystical monism found in Hinduism (although a pluralistic Hinduism is sometimes defended in different terms).

In column IV are the explicitly atheistic theoretical possibilities. "N" can be interpreted as meaning that God, as a single being, exists necessarily, whether all God's qualities are necessary (N standing alone) or whether there are also contingent divine qualities (NC). And "n" can be interpreted as meaning that the world is necessary. That is, if "c" is the case this does not mean that there might have been no world at all. In "cn" we have the view that there might have been a different world, but there could not have been no world at all. As Hartshorne (1993, 298) puts the point, "I am among those who see nothing glorious in an ability to do nothing." "C" or "c" mean *could* have been otherwise, and "N" or "n" mean *could not* have been otherwise. Once again, to defend "c" is compatible with the view that God is not merely contingently creative but essentially so: yet just *how* God creates is another matter.

Hartshorne himself defends NC.cn, but this defense has been developed dialectically over his career in a constant give and take with the other fifteen options that have been defended in the history of philosophy. For example, there are both strengths and weaknesses in Aristotle's view, N.cn, that are well known to classical theists. But not so well known to classical theists are the weaknesses that are inherited by them from Aristotle. In fact, most medieval thinkers fell into classical theism, N.c, somewhat unwittingly, with Cusanus and Scotus Erigena the exceptions to the rule in that they came close to NC.cn. The point here is that even a defensible version of classical theism, if there is such, depends on such a position matrix in that one can only know that one's own position is the best if one is thoroughly aware of the alternatives. And there *are* alternatives to classical theism other than that offered by Spinoza and the Stoics, N.n.

It is understandable that classical theists would not agree to any of the positions in column II, positions that some (not Hartshorne) might defend in terms of a strictly finite God. C.c, for example, may fit William James. Perhaps only the great mystics can abandon all use of abstractions in their understanding of God, and it is doubtful if even they can do so completely. (St. Teresa of Avila brought St. John of the Cross into the Carmelite order *because* he was an intellectual.) Philosophy is, as Whitehead urges, the critique of abstractions, but we need to know what the available abstractions are before we can assume that our critiques are moving us in the right direction. Hartshorne sees a jagged path from Plato to a few medievals, to Faustus Socinus and Jules Lequier, Otto Pfleiderer, Bernardino Varisco, and W. P. Montague, to Bergson and Whitehead in defense of the abstract view NC.cn. (Hartshorne also agrees with Bergson [1977 (1932), 255] that the Christian mystics unanimously bear witness that God needs us, in a way, just as there is an obvious sense in which we need God.) Hartshorne thinks it wise to follow *this* path rather than the classical theistic one in large part because N.c and N.cn (classical theism and Aristotelian theism, respectively) are both self-contradictory unless it is false that God knows contingent things or truths. This is exactly why Aristotle himself denied divine knowledge of the contingent. And this is exactly why Spinoza denied the contingency of the world. The illogicality of classical theism is attested to not only by neoclassical theists, but also by Spinoza and, paradoxically, by Aristotle, the greatest predecessor of classical theism.

At times Hartshorne gets into trouble with classical theists by at least implying, if not by stating explicitly, that they are "simple-minded." Hartshorne's intent here, however, is not to deliver an *ad hominem* attack, but to claim that N.c (classical theism) and N.n (deterministic pantheism) are, in fact, defective views because they are too simple. N.cn is somewhat more complex, but it, too, is overly simple. The simplicity of classical theism, in particular, consists in the fact that it caters to the human tendency to react to danger and fear by seeking an escape into a realm in which there are no changes, hence no change for the worse. That this might also mean no concrete good is not often noticed.

One of the reasons why there has not been as much rapprochement as possible between classical theists and neoclassical ones is the fact that Hartshorne's distinction between existence and actuality has been insufficiently digested by philosophers of religion. Has anyone yet argued (convincingly or not) against this distinction? For Hartshorne "actual" contrasts with "possible," not with "existent." Existence, as employed in philosophy of religion, is less concrete than actuality or *how* God exists. As long as the essence-existence dichotomy is taken as exhaustive in philosophy of religion, as opposed to the essence-existence-actuality trichotomy, neoclassical theism will continue to be either largely ignored or misunderstood. Without this trichotomy a theist who rightly thinks that God's existence is necessary has a tendency to think of "necessity" as being an unequivocal term of praise. But neither "necessary" nor "contingent" are good or bad without qualification, as I hope I will demonstrate in this book. To deny God contingency altogether is to have the asymmetrical, directional order of God's life collapse. Life *is* asymmetrical; and asymmetry is more beautiful than mere symmetry. Indeed, the most symmetrical of all the options is O.o, the most objectionable of the sixteen possibilities from the perspective of theism.

It should also be noted that the topic of the present book should be of interest not only to analytic theists and to process philosophers, but also to atheists and agnostics. In order for them to feel secure about their view (one of the positions in columns II or IV) they, too, would have to be aware of the available options and of the differences among these options; very often atheists and agnostics assume without argument that classical theism just *is* theism. Or again, atheists and agnostics should be interested in the topic of this book because very often their positions are reactions against classical theism, reactions which process theists find quite understandable if not justifiable.[2]

The point to such a position matrix is *not* that logic or abstract reasoning is sufficient in metaphysics or philosophy of religion, but rather that it is necessary to do the job well. Without this and other position matrices we are more likely to rely on uncritical common sense or unquestioned tradition than we should. By *questioning* the tradition of classical theism we are more likely to take advantage of the vast laboratory of the history of philosophy (including some lesser-known thinkers who glimpsed great truths), wherein each of these sixteen options is evidenced at least once. That is, from the perspective of neoclassical theism, analytic philosophers who are classical theists tend at once to be too much dependent on the history of philosophy (in assuming that the concept of God was, for the most part, correctly discovered in the early Middle Ages—as before, most analytic theists strike me as latter-day Augustinians or Boethians or Thomists), and too much removed from the history of philosophy (in failing to consider carefully the options listed in the above position matrix, especially NC.cn). As Hartshorne emphasizes: "Fragments that we are, what we can know is also fragmentary—except for the uttermost abstractions that enable us to make some sense in principle of our place in that besouled cosmos apart from which (*per impossible*) we and the creatures which we know would indeed be as 'nothing.'" (Hartshorne 1993).

CHAPTER ONE

MUST A PERFECT BEING BE IMMUTABLE?

A. INTRODUCTION

One would think that philosophical theists would have a great deal in common with each other, yet it is surprising how little theists read across the various boundaries in contemporary philosophy. In this book I will try to cross one such divide, that between analytic and process theism. George Lucas has appropriately chided process philosophers for not paying careful enough attention to current debates in analytic philosophy, if for no other reason than the fact that Whitehead's thought can contribute significantly to those debates.[1] But Lucas' door can swing both ways. In this chapter I am going to suggest that analytic theists (in particular, Mann, Stump, Kretzmann, Plantinga, and Creel) have not paid careful enough attention (or, in some cases, any attention at all) to the thought of a thinker who many think is the most profound philosophical theist of the twentieth century, Charles Hartshorne. I allege that they could learn from Hartshorne, just as Hartshorne could learn from them, as is evidenced by his regret that he does not know more about the details of modal logic.

For example, two widely cited articles in the philosophy of religion have appeared whose theses hinge on the assumption that a perfect being is not subject to change—Eleonore Stump and Norman

Kretzmann's "Eternity" (1981) and William Mann's "Simplicity and Immutability in God." (1983) Because both of these important articles are carefully argued, it is surprising that such a fundamental assumption should go unnoticed.[2] In both articles, the authors make Herculean efforts to show that the traditional conception of God does not lead to incoherence when the following issues are considered: the logical relationship between eternity and time, the problem of showing how an eternal and immutable God can act in time, and whether God's immutable omniscience precludes human freedom. Anyone familiar with these issues realizes that Herculean efforts are the only ones that could be successful when such difficult matters are considered from the perspective of the traditional conception of God.

Now that many analytic philosophers are showing an interest in questions about God, it is surprising that many of them should do so on the assumptions of old-style metaphysics. One such assumption is precisely that a perfect being is not subject to change. Since the 1920s Hartshorne has been challenging this assumption, but his work has hardly received detailed criticism from most analytic philosophers. One generation of analytic philosophers apparently dismissed his work as meaningless just because it was metaphysical. It is to be hoped that another generation will not ignore him merely because he is not thought to write in one of the styles considered appropriate by analytic philosophers. This hope is intensified when one notices Hartshorne's eminent clarity.

The general purpose of the next few sections of this chapter is to show why analytic philosophers should examine Hartshorne's work in detail, even though he is not usually thought of as an analytic philosopher. Because one way to view Hartshorne's philosophy is as a lifelong, consistent search for a coherent *meaning* to the term "God," his thoughts should be of special interest to contemporary analytic philosophers of religion. One interpreter even goes so far as to call him a revisionary metaphysician in the Strawsonian sense. (Gunton 1978, II). Eventually I will also treat in this chapter the thought of Alvin Plantinga and Richard Creel. My hope is that many of the basic issues to be treated in this book will surface in this chapter and that, even if these issues are not fully resolved in this chapter,

Hartshorne's approach to them will be seen as so strong that a philosopher of religion can ignore them only at her peril.

B. MANN AND IMMUTABILITY

This author's article opens with the statement that:

> Steadfastness is a virtue we prize in persons. All other things being equal, we disapprove of those who break their promises, forsake their covenants, or change their minds capriciously. We regard as childish those who are easily deflected from the pursuit of their goals. We pity those who suffer radical transformations of character. It is not surprising, then, that many theists believe that no such fickle flickerings of human inconstancy could characterize God. Many theists—especially those infected with a bit of philosophy—carry these speculations a step further. God is supremely steadfast, but he is also insusceptible to ceasing to be the being he is. A steadfast mortal is still mortal. . . . Many orthodox theologians and philosophers have taken yet a further step. For example, the great medieval philosophers argued that God is utterly and completely immutable, that no change of any kind can befall him. (267)

It is this most extreme form of the doctrine of divine immutability (DDI), held by St. Thomas Aquinas and others, that Mann defends.

The defense proceeds by way of showing that an immutable God can be a personal and active being. Mann is not deterred by those who accuse him of building the temple of Elea in Jerusalem (268). He argues that God can be both immutable and active through an appeal to another doctrine, that of divine simplicity (DDS). God has no parts, nor does God have temporal extension. The divine attributes are coextensive: the omniscience of God *is* the omnipotence of God, and so on. This is what makes God simple, and it is also what makes it possible for Mann to argue that God is immutable and active. God's immutability *is* God's activity. Likewise, it is possible for God to be immutable and a person because God's immutability *is* God's eternal knowing and willing. This means that, although God can know and will, God cannot come to know, forget, calculate, have *fore*knowledge, or engage in inductive reasoning; nor can God fall in love, grow in love, become angry, or the like, for these entail divine change.

Mann admits that his list of divine attributes is a "curtailed repertoire" (270), but this does not bother him. Some peculiar conclusions follow from his views. The activity by which God wills punishment at what is from a human perspective time-1 *is* the activity by which God is "reconciled" to the punished ones at what is from a human perspective time-2. One is led, on Mann's reasoning, to conclude that divine anger, expressed in hailstorms and locusts, *is* divine joy. One is also led to believe that if God's care is equally present "from" eternity to time-1 and time-2, then there is no increase in God's love when human beings respond to God's call, nor does God *respond* to our sufferings. All of this is on the assumption that a perfect being does not change or respond. What unresponsive love is like we are not told. Presumably, for Mann, God eternally knows and cares about our sufferings even before, from a human perspective, they occur. Why, since divinity is also omnipotent for Mann, God does not *do* something to prevent human suffering is a question that Mann does not treat. That is, theodicy is as much a problem as ever; traditional assumptions still yield traditional problems.

What is to be noticed is that all of Mann's efforts are needed *only if* one starts, as he does, with an analysis of the virtue of steadfastness to the exclusion of an analysis of other virtues. None of the four objections to his views that he considers even implicitly raise the possibility that a perfect being may be allowed to (or better, be required to) change. Mann is intent on refuting the views that:

1. DDI can be established without DDS.
2. Divine foreknowledge of proposition P cannot be identical to knowledge of proposition L.
3. DDS is incompatible with human freedom.
4. DDS precludes God's freedom of will.

The degree to which Mann succeeds in refuting these four views is not my prime concern here (although it is hard to see how he overcomes 3 and 4). The point I want to make is that the very need to respond to these sorts of objections (not to mention the theodicy problem, et al.) is worthy of our attention. Paradoxically, Mann says that it is "the logic of perfection" (272) (the phrase Hartshorne popularized in the title of one of his books) that leads Mann to his conclusions. On Hartshorne's view, as we will see shortly, it is the logic of perfection that should lead us to be suspicious of the doctrine of divine immutability rather than to assume it, as Mann does.

C. STUMP AND KRETZMANN ON ETERNITY

Although Stump and Kretzmann's article (1981) antedates Mann's (1983), and supplies the basis for many of Mann's views (although not DDS), it is not as obvious that these authors share the assumption that a perfect being is not subject to change. But the assumption is made nonetheless. The authors ably distinguish sempiternity (or what Hartshorne would call everlastingness) from eternity. The former consists in limitless duration in time (1981, 430). The latter, as developed primarily by Boethius, but also by St. Thomas and others, and defended by Stump and Kretzmann, consists in "the complete possession all at once of illimitable life" (431). The authors initially state that they are not claiming that if God exists God must be eternal; they are only elucidating what the concept of eternity means (431). But later they are not so indirect (455–56). In an analysis of an argument which has as its first three premises the following:

1. A perfect being is not subject to change.
2. A perfect being knows everything.
3. A being that knows everything always knows what time it is.

Stump and Kretzmann state that "it is clear that *the* weak point in the proof is premise (3)" (my emphasis). Premise 1 is assumed to be true and is operative throughout their article. It is the assumption of premise 1 that requires them to defend the following views: that there is only an apparent incoherence between divine eternity and temporality, or between divine atemporality and divine life; that God knows simultaneously that Nixon is alive and dead; and that:

> If such an entity (God) atemporally wills that Hannah conceive on a certain day after the day of her prayer (to get pregnant), then such an entity's bringing it about that Hannah conceives on that day is clearly a response to her prayer. (451)

Once again, my prime intent here is not to evaluate these defenses, but to question the authors' unargued assumption that a perfect being is not subject to change. It is worth mentioning, however, that this assumption forces them to make some questionable claims. Consider the Hannah example. If God eternally wills that the woman conceive, can she freely engage in the sexual relation which brought about her pregnancy? Is it really *her* prayer? Should not the word "respond" above be put in scare quotes, at the very least, if not dropped altogether? And how can God's "response" to the woman's prayer be an expression of God's concern for *her*, if God's decision were made eternally? The authors make it clear that their aim is to show the plausibility of the attributes given to God by orthodox theology, a God who is immutable (457–58), and to show the plausibility of Christ eternally having both a divine and a human nature (453). What eternally having a *human* nature is I do not know, but once the drive for permanence gets rolling it is quite hard to stop.

The authors do an excellent job of making what sense can be made of the doctrine of divine immutability and eternity. Stump and Kretzmann in particular are ingenious in their use of Einstein's theory of simultaneity to explain relations between the eternal and the temporal. But they should have paid attention to the assumption on which these relations rest, that a perfect being must be immutable. Because Hartshorne is a prolific writer, only a few of his insights on the topic of this chapter will be treated,[3] but they should be sufficient to point out what the analytic philosophers of religion under consideration here could learn from him. At the very least I will show that one must *argue* for the claim that a perfect being is not subject to change; the claim cannot be assumed with equanimity, as the aforementioned authors do.

Perhaps, it will be objected, thinkers like Kretzmann are engaged in a conceptual exploration of certain divine attributes, rather than an attempt to give reasons for accepting them. If this is the case then I am not criticizing Kretzmann's position so much as I am pointing out problems with his conceptual exploration. John Moskop's treatment of Kretzmann is instructive here because Moskop points out that in an earlier article Kretzmann himself gives good reasons why an immutable being cannot know facts about the passage of time:

1. A perfect being is not subject to change.
2. A perfect being knows everything.
3. A being that knows everything always knows what time it is.
4. A being that always knows what time it is is subject to change.
5. A perfect being is subject to change.
6. A perfect being is not a perfect being.

From this argument Kretzmann should have been pushed closer to Nelson Pike's view that if God creates then God cannot timelessly bring about a temporal state of affairs: 'creates' is a production verb that has temporal relation as part of its essence. Rather, if I understand Kretzmann correctly, he has stayed close to R. M. Martin's view that God's desires must remain timeless, whatever timeless desire might be.[4]

D. HARTSHORNE'S DIPOLAR THEISM

One of the major complaints that Hartshorne has with traditional theism, or, as he refers to it, classical theism (in philosophy and theology, as opposed to biblical theism) is that it either explicitly or implicitly identifies God as permanent and not changing. St. Thomas's unmoved mover is the most obvious example of this tendency, but, in general, classical theists see God as a timeless, supernatural being who does not change.

For Hartshorne, the term "God" refers to the supremely excellent or all-worshipful being. As is well known, Hartshorne has been the most important defender of the ontological argument in this century, and his debt to St. Anselm is evident in this preliminary definition. It closely resembles St. Anselm's "that than which no greater can be conceived." Yet the ontological argument is not what is at stake here.

Even if the argument fails, which Hartshorne would doubt, the preliminary definition of God as the supremely excellent being, the all-worshipful being, or the greatest conceivable being seems unobjectionable. To say that God can be defined in these ways still leaves open the possibility that God is even more excellent or worshipful than our ability to conceive. This allows one to avoid objections from Thomists or Wittgensteinian fideists who fear that by defining God we are limiting God to human language. All Hartshorne is suggesting is that when we think of God we must be thinking of a being who surpasses all others, or we are not thinking of God. Even the atheist or agnostic would admit this much. When the atheist says, "There is no God," he is denying that a supremely excellent, all-worshipful, greatest conceivable being exists.

The contrast excellent-inferior is the truly invidious contrast when applied to God. If to be invidious is to be injurious, then this contrast is the most invidious one when applied to God because God is only excellent. God is inferior in no way. Period. To suggest that God is in some small way inferior to some other being is no longer to speak about God, but about some being that is not supremely excellent, all-worshipful, or the greatest conceivable. Hartshorne criticizes classical theism because it assumes that all contrasts, or most of them, when applied to God are invidious.

Let me assume from now on that God exists.[5] What attributes does God possess? Consider the following two columns of attributes in polar contrast to each other:

SCHEMA 2

permanence	change
one	many
activity	passivity
necessity	contingency
self-sufficient	dependent
actual	potential
absolute	relative
abstract	concrete

Classical theism tends toward oversimplification. It is comparatively easy to say "God is strong rather than weak, so in all relations

God is eternally active, not passive." In each case, the classical theist decides which member of the contrasting pair is good (on the left) then attributes it to God, while wholly denying the contrasting term (on the right). Hence, God is one but not many, permanent but not changing, and so on. This leads to what Hartshorne calls the monopolar prejudice. Monopolarity is common to both classical theism and pantheism, with the major difference between the two being the fact that classical theism admits the reality of plurality, potentiality, and becoming as a secondary form of existence "outside" God (on the right), whereas in pantheism God is equated with reality. Common to both classical theism and pantheism is the belief that the above categorial contrasts are invidious. The dilemma these two positions face is that either the deity is only one constituent of the whole (classical theism) or else the alleged inferior pole in each contrast (on the right) is illusory (pantheism).

For Hartshorne this dilemma is a pseudo-problem. It is produced by the assumption that excellence is found by separating and purifying one pole (on the left) and denigrating the other (on the right). That this is not the case can be seen by analyzing some of the attributes on the right side. At least since St. Augustine, classical theists have been convinced that God's eternity meant not that God endured through all time, but that God was outside of time altogether and did not, could not, be receptive to temporal change. St. Thomas identified God, following Aristotle, who was the greatest predecessor to classical theism, as unmoved. Yet both activity and passivity can be either good or bad. Good passivity is likely to be called sensitivity, responsiveness, adaptability, sympathy, and the like. Insufficiently subtle or defective passivity is called wooden inflexibility, mulish stubborness, inadaptability, unresponsiveness, and the like. Passivity per se refers to the way in which an individual's activity takes account of, and renders itself appropriate to, the activities of others. To deny God passivity altogether is to deny God those aspects of passivity which are excellences. Or again, to deny God altogether the ability to change does avoid fickleness, but at the expense of the ability to *react* lovingly to the sufferings of others.

The terms on the left side have both good and bad aspects as well. Oneness can mean wholeness, as Mann notices, but also it can mean monotony or triviality. Actuality can mean definiteness, but it can mean nonrelatedness to others. What happens to divine love when God, according to St. Thomas, is claimed to be *pure* actuality? God ends up loving the world, but is not internally related to it, whatever sort of love that may be. Self-sufficiency can, at times, be selfishness.

The task when thinking of God, for Hartshorne, is to attribute to God all excellences (left *and* right sides) and not to attribute to God any inferiorities (right *and* left sides). In short, excellent-inferior or good-evil are invidious contrasts; that is, they cannot be applied (both terms) to supreme goodness because it makes no sense to bifurcate evil into good-evil (a contradiction, not a contrast) and evil-evil (a redundancy). But permanence-change, being-becoming, and so on, are noninvidious contrasts. Unlike classical theism and pantheism, Hartshorne's theism is dipolar. To be specific, within *each* pole of a noninvidious contrast (e.g., permanence-change) there are invidious elements (inferior permanence or inferior change), but also noninvidious, good elements (excellent permanence or excellent change).

E. SOME OBJECTIONS

It may be helpful at this point to respond to some possible criticisms from Mann, Stump, and Kretzmann. First, Hartshorne does not believe in two gods, one unified and the other plural, and so on. Rather, he believes that what are often thought to be contradictories or contraries are really mutually interdependent correlatives: "The good as we know it is unity-in-variety; if the variety overbalances, we have chaos or discord; if the unity, we have monotony or triviality" (PS, 3).

Supreme excellence, if it is truly supreme excellence, *must* somehow be able to integrate all the *complexity* there is in the world into itself as one spiritual whole. The word "must" indicates divine necessity, along with God's essence, which is to necessarily exist. And the word "complexity" indicates the contingency that affects God through creaturely decisions. But in the classical theistic view God is solely identified with the stony immobility of the absolute. For Hartshorne, in God's abstract nature—God's being—God may in a way escape from the temporal flux, but a living God is related to the world of becoming, a fact which entails divine becoming as well, if the world in some way is internally related to God. The classical theist's alternative to this view suggests that all relationships to God are external to divinity, once again threatening not only God's love, but also God's nobility. A dog's being behind a particular rock affects the dog in certain ways, thus this relation is an internal relation to the dog. But it does not affect the rock, whose relationship with the dog is external to the rock's nature. Does this not show the superiority of canine consciousness, which is aware of the rock, to rocklike existence, which is unaware of the dog? Is it not therefore peculiar that God has been described solely in rocklike terms: unmoved, permanent, only having external relations, being not becoming?

It might be wondered at this point why classical theism has been so popular among theists, yet has these defects. Hartshorne suggests at least four reasons, none of which establishes the case for classical theism:

1. It is simpler to accept monopolarity than dipolarity, that is, it is simpler to accept one pole and reject the other of contrasting (or better, correlative, noninvidious) categories rather than to show how each, in its own appropriate fashion, applies to an aspect of the divine nature. Yet the simplicity of calling God "the absolute" can come back to haunt the classical theist if absoluteness precludes relativity in the sense of relatedness to the world. That is, the simplicity of accepting monopolarity eventually leads to Herculean efforts to save it.
2. If the decision to accept monopolarity has been made, it is simpler to identify God as the most permanent than to identify God as the most changing. Yet the acceptance of God as most permanent need not imply a denial of divine change, nor a denial of the fact that God, who loves all, would therefore have to change with respect to all. That is, God may well be the most permanent of all as well as the most changing of all, in the sense that, and to the extent that, both of these are

excellences. God is permanent and changing in different aspects of the divine. There is a crucial distinction between God's permanent, necessary *existence* (the fact *that* God exists) and God's contingent *actuality* (*how* God exists), a distinction that Hartshorne has spent a great deal of time defending, and which analytic theists have largely ignored.

3. There are emotional considerations favoring divine permanence, as found in the longing to escape the risks and uncertainties in life. But even if these uncertainties obtain they should not blind us to other emotional considerations, like those which give us the solace which comes from knowing that the outcome of our sufferings and volitions makes a difference in the divine life which, if it is all-loving, would not be unchanged by the suffering of creatures.
4. Monopolarity is seen as more easily made compatible with monotheism. But the innocent monotheistic contrast between the one and the many deals with God as an individual, not with the claim that the divine individual itself cannot have parts or aspects of relatedness to the world.

In short: "God's being and becoming form a single reality: there is no law of logic against attributing contrasting predicates to the same individual, provided they apply to diverse aspects of this individual" (PS, 14–15). The remedy for "ontolatry," the worship of being, is not the contrary pole, "gignolatry," the worship of becoming: "God is neither being as contrasted to becoming nor becoming as contrasted to being; but categorically supreme becoming in which there is a factor of categorically supreme being, as contrasted to inferior becoming, in which there is inferior being" (PS, 24). The divine becoming is more ultimate than the divine being in neoclassical theism only for the reason that it is more inclusive.

To the rather simple objection that if God changed God would not be perfect, for if God were perfect there would be no need to change, Hartshorne makes this reply: to be supremely excellent God must at any particular time be the greatest conceivable being, the all-worshipful being. But at a later time, or in a new situation in which some creature that previously did not suffer now suffers, God has new opportunities to exhibit supreme excellence. That is, God's perfection does not just allow God to change, but requires God to change.[6]

Finally, it might be objected that God is neither permanent nor changing, neither one nor many, and so forth, because no human concept whatsoever applies to God literally or univocally, but at most analogically. The classical theist would say, perhaps, that God is more unitary than unity, more permanent than permanence as humanly known. Yet one wonders how the classical theist, once she has admitted the insufficiency of human conceptions, can legitimately give a favored status to one side (the left) of conceptual contrasts at the expense of the other. Why, Hartshorne asks, if God is more simple than the one, is God not also more complex—in terms of relatedness to diverse actual occasions—than the many? Analogical predication and negative theology can just as easily fall victim to the monopolar prejudice as univocal predication.

F. SOME PRELIMINARY CONCLUSIONS

To sum up, Hartshorne's theism is:

1. *Dipolar*, because excellences are found on both sides of the above contrasting categories.
2. *Neoclassical*, because it relies on the belief that classical theists (especially St. Anselm) were on the right track when they described God as the supremely excellent, all-worshipful, greatest conceivable being, but they did not think through carefully enough the logic of perfection, nor did they adequately test their ideas against the experience of those who had perceived God, to use William Alston's phrase.
3. A *process theism*, in that it posits a need for God to become in order for God to be perfect, but not at the expense of God's always (i.e., permanently) being greater than all others.
4. A theism properly called *panentheism*, which literally means "all in God." God is neither completely removed from the world, nor identified with the world, as in pantheism. Rather, God is world-inclusive in the sense that God cares for

> all the world and has sympathy for it; and all feelings in the world—especially suffering feelings—are felt by God. And God is transcendent in the sense that God is greater than any other being, especially because of God's necessary existence and eminent changeability.

Although it would obviously be too much to hope that analytical classical theists would be "converted" to dipolar theism as a consequence of what I have said thus far, I hope that I have at least established two points. First, the case made above for dipolar theism is at the very least strong enough to encourage the classical theist to *argue* for the belief that God is immutable. To assume monopolarity without argument, as Mann, Stump, and Kretzmann do, is inadequate. One would hope that they would contend not only with their fellow analysts, but also with neoclassical thinkers like Hartshorne. And second, the case made above for dipolar theism is strong when divine attributes are considered. In that the weight of classical theistic tradition is on the side of our three authors, it might seem that the burden of proof is on Hartshorne.[7] But since Hartshorne has assiduously tried to incorporate *all* excellences into his theory of God, both those associated with divine permanence and those associated with divine change, should not the burden of proof lie with those who would like to treat the supremely excellent being as *only* possessing the excellence of permanence or the excellence of change?[8]

G. PLANTINGA, "ASEITY," AND CONTROL

Perhaps it will be claimed that, although most analytic theists have simply assumed divine immutability, there is nonetheless good reason for such an assumption because if God were not immutable God's *aseity* would be compromised. Alvin Plantinga seems to make just this point. In *God and Other Minds* Plantinga (1967, 174–80) rightly notes that two demands of the "religious attitude" are that God exists necessarily and that God should possess "various qualities in some necessary manner." Hartshorne would agree, at least he would agree *if* one of these qualities, say, is the ability always to respond to the momentary sufferings of creatures (n.b., "always" *and* "respond"). But from this demand that God's character be *a se*, Plantinga (1967, 78) emphasizes the necessary absence of *certain* kinds of change in God.

It might seem that Plantinga is not as committed to divine immutability as the authors previously considered, since he says that it is "surely clear" that God does undergo change, as in the change from not being worshipped by St. Paul in 100 B.C.E. to being so worshipped in 40 C.E. But this change for Plantinga is a relational or logical one (more precisely, an external relation); God's eternal being, he thinks, is not merely changeless but unchangeable. Plantinga sides with St. Augustine in denying Hartshorne's fundamental distinction between divine necessary existence (that God exists) and divine contingent actuality (how God exists); that is, he denies dipolarity in God.[9] The reason Plantinga sides with the classical theistic tradition is that there is an essential connection, as he sees it, between divine *aseity* ("his uncreatedness, self-sufficiency and independence of everything else") and omnipotence (his control over all things).

Hartshorne would agree with Plantinga that God does not depend on us for divine existence, nor does God depend on us in particular for omnibenevolence. But, if not us in particular, then some creatures or other would be needed for God to love in order for God to have the properties of omniscience and omnibenevolence. This divine dependence, as Hartshorne sees it, is more than what Plantinga (1980) would claim is "Pickwickian" in *Does God Have a Nature?* To claim rightly, as Plantinga does (1980, 2–3), that even the rebel's existence is dependent on God does not establish the case, as Plantinga thinks, that the rebel has no significant effect on God.

For various reasons, Plantinga (along with Stump and Kretzmann) disagrees with Mann's thesis regarding divine simplicity, but this denial also, he thinks, poses a threat to divine *aseity* because if abstract objects of a Platonic sort (e.g., necessary truths) are different from God's nature they threaten the notion of divine control. But it is important to notice that Plantinga himself admits that *his* notion of sovereignty-*aseity* is (merely) an intuition (34, 68), or as I have used the term, an assumption.

There are, at the very least, plausible grounds for believing that abstract objects do not threaten God's *aseity*, hence do not conflict with the denial of divine immutability. That is, one can criticize divine immutability and still preserve some sense of *aseity* (see again the terms on the left side of Schema 2 on p. 20), as well as allow for the sorts of abstract objects Plantinga believes in. "X is independent of Y" minimally implies that it could be the case that X exists while Y does not, which implies that Y is contingent. If X stands for abstract objects and Y for God, then the nonexistence of God is being taken as possible. But this "possibility" conflicts not only with Hartshorne's defense of arguments in favor of God's existence but also with Plantinga's. If one asks Hartshorne whether abstract objects have supremacy over God, he would respond that the issue is secondary and largely verbal (PS, 56–57) because both abstract objects and God are everlasting and independence has no clear meaning between everlasting things.

In two significant respects Plantinga's theism is like that of Richard Swinburne.[10] First, he assumes that God could not be embodied in any sense; he thinks that theists have always held that God is immaterial. (Swinburne's modified version of this view will be treated in a later chapter.) Because if God were material God would change, there is no apparent need to argue any further for divine immateriality. But on historical grounds Plantinga is in trouble here. David of Dinant and Hobbes are not, as he thinks, the only philosophers who have defended divine embodiment. As Plutarch attests, almost all of the ancient philosophers, including Plato, believed in God as the World-Soul who animates the world-body. These examples, along with Hartshorne's lifelong defense of the Platonic World-Soul, are noteworthy omissions in Plantinga's historical gloss.[11] My point here is not yet to demonstrate the strength of the belief in divine embodiment, but rather to show the intellectual and historical thinness of the assumption made by analytic theists, in this case by Plantinga, that God must be completely immaterial, in order that they might preserve belief in divine immutability. The neoclassical theist suggests that by taking Hartshorne seriously, and by thinking carefully about holy change and about nature as sacramental, one may treat the theodicy problem, the environmental crisis, and so on, in more fruitful ways than is possible in even the most technically proficient varieties of classical theism defended by analytic theists. Most of the traditional problems in classical theism are found in analytic theism, problems that stem in large part from the belief in God as a supernatural being who does not change. For pragmatic reasons alone, there should be an incentive to examine the assumption that God is this sort of being.

Second, Plantinga agrees with Swinburne (against St. Thomas, Stump, Kretzmann, and Mann) that God's eternity is not timeless, but rather consists in endless and beginningless duration, that is, in sempiternity or everlastingness. (Perhaps it is this sort of evidence that leads Cook and Leftow to suggest, as mentioned in the Introduction, that there is a growing consensus among analytic theists in favor of divine sempiternity.) From this claim, however, Plantinga does not make the understandable move toward neoclassical theism, but tries to hold on to the classical theistic belief in a God whose knowledge is not "temporally limited" (1980, 45). God, for Plantinga, right now knows even the remote future in minute detail, *but* God is not timeless, whatever that means. God in some peculiar way acts in time and does some things before others, but is not affected by time or change (1980, 45–46).

Plantinga has a very strong sense of God as absolutely omnipotent, of God as in control of everything, or as Hartshorne would put it in a way that very often angers other theists, of God as despot. Hartshorne would agree with Plantinga that the notion of God as maximal power is "non-negotiable" (1980, 134) from the perspective of theism, but what it means to have maximal power differs in the two thinkers, with Hartshorne (see OO) claiming that *omni*potence in the classical theistic sense conflicts with belief in human freedom, the statistical nature of scientific laws (à la Peirce), and creates the nastiest problem of evil. The point I want to make here, again, however, is that Hartshorne has spent a great deal of energy criticizing in detail the concept of omnipotence and analytic theists have spent a great deal of time ignoring these efforts. Moreover, from Hartshorne's point of view, their unquestioned assumption that immutability is integral to theism is connected to their overly strong view of divine omnipotence. For, in their view, if God were not omnipotent He (the masculine pronoun is needed here) would not be in control and could be pushed around (i.e., changed) by others.

H. THE BEGINNINGS OF A DIALOGUE

Whereas Mann, Stump, and Kretzmann assume *simpliciter* that God is immutable, Plantinga (with Swinburne and Wolterstorff) offers at least some indication, however inadequate, of why immutability should be attributed to God. Richard Creel, in his book *Divine Impassibility* (1986), is one of the few analytic theists who argue in depth for classical theistic assumptions regarding immutability. It should be noted that Creel is primarily concerned with God as "impassible" (*apathes*), which is not necessarily the same as "immutable," in that an immutable being must be impassible but an impassible being does not have to be immutable, for example, if it changes itself. Because much of Creel's analysis affects immutability as well as impassibility, his book is one of the most fruitful signs that bridges can be built between neoclassical theism and analytic theism. But these are difficult bridges to build when one considers that for Hartshorne it is only the dead (or the insentient aggregates of sentient constituents) that truly can be said to be impassible.[12]

The dialogue is facilitated by distinguishing four senses of "impassibility" used by Creel.

1. Regarding the impassibility, indeed the immutability, of God's *nature*, there is no disagreement between Hartshorne and Creel. God always exhibits maximal power, goodness, and wisdom; and God exists necessarily and hence not contingently. In this sense Hartshorne agrees that God is immutable.

2. There is some agreement also in Creel's account of impassibility of *will*. He correctly notes (1986, 60–61, 87) that in Hartshorne's theory God's memory of the past, although all-embracing, must change due to the influence of later stages of process, just as each new generation of human beings must rewrite their history books, that is, God's knowledge of the past is in a way passible for Hartshorne. For

the most part, however, there is quite a distance between Creel and Hartshorne on impassibility of will. Creel wants to hold that God's response to creatures does not entail that God change; it is perhaps more accurate to call these responses "presponses" or "indesponses" (1986, 16, 209). There is no real re-sponse on the part of God because God decides independently of our actions what he will do. God has already decided what the divine "indesponse" will be when we choose. This is what allows Creel to hold the oxymoronic (Hartshorne would say inconsistent) classical theistic claim that God is both *apathes* and loving (18, 26).

It should be obvious that Creel's position regarding impassibility of will depends on God knowing the future. God knows all possibilities (34, 62), according to Creel, but to know a possibility thoroughly is to know what an actuality will be like that instantiates that possibility (46). This is what allows Creel to hold that God not only knows all possibilities, but also all actualities, *including* future actualities (35), hence allowing God to be impassible in will in that God can will his "indesponse" before the creature acts.

But this view sidesteps altogether Hartshorne's critique of Whitehead's theory of eternal objects as well as Hartshorne's claim that omniscience consists in knowing all actualities as actual and all possibilities as possible. To know a future contingency as actual is to misunderstand the meaning of contingency and is thus not consistent with maximal knowledge. Hartshorne would wonder how a future event could be actual, for if it were actual it would be here already. Future events, he thinks, must be potential (even those for which there is a very high degree of probability) for them to remain future. This is not to say that God was once ignorant of anything actual. God has *always* known the actual, but future contingencies are not actual.

One gets the suspicion that Creel, despite his wishes, is defending an eternal duplicate of this world in God's mind which will eventually be actualized exactly as God's knowledge indicates it must. This odd version of Platon*ism* differs from Hartshorne's more judicious use of Plato,[13] and it leaves the analytic theist with most of the traditional problems of classical theism. Creel's concessions leave the major problems about divine immutability and impassibility untouched.

3. Creel's position regarding impassibility of *knowledge* is similar to that regarding will. But it is here that the fundamental tension (or contradiction) in his thought surfaces most clearly. On the one hand, he holds that God is impassible and immutable since God knows the realm of possibility (the plenum) *exhaustively* (1986, 80, 86), hence he knows how every possibility, if chosen, will be actualized (35, 46). On the other hand, God's knowledge of "concrete possibilities," that is, of actual individuals, is temporal, passible, and mutable (86–87). The latter part is a concession to Hartshorne, the former to classical theism.

One wonders if Creel can have it both ways. Consider this quotation from him: "Hence even if his knowledge of what I *will* do is impassible, his knowledge of what I *am* doing must be passible, that is, subject to influence by what I am doing" (88). Clearly, Creel *thinks* he can have it both ways, but if he is correct in saying that by virtue of knowing a possible world God knows what I will do if he actualizes that world (179), then there simply is little or no room for his concession to Hartshorne that God's knowledge of actual individuals is mutable. In short, Creel has not met the neoclassical theist halfway; rather, he has taken a step or two in the direction of neoclassical theism, whereas if Hartshorne were to agree with Creel's position regarding impassibility of knowledge he would have to jog several miles.

This same tension can be found in Creel's view of eternity. On the one hand, he criticizes the Boethian "eternalism" found in Peter Geach (as well as in Mann, Stump, and Kretzmann) because, as we have seen, he thinks God's knowledge in *some* sense is passible. That is, he agrees with Hartshorne that there are no individual determinables, that there are no individuals apart from determinateness. Relying on Nicholas Wolterstorff as well as on Hartshorne, Creel holds that God only knows possible individuals before they become actual (1986, 96–99). On the other hand, Creel admits that he is closer to the classical theistic stance on divine eternity than to process theism because he believes that "time can pass without change" occurring (102–03). This is an odd position, to say the least. It does not suffice merely to *say* that God has (temporal) duration but not a successive existence; one must, in addition, indicate how this could be so without stretching human concepts of time to the (Boethian) breaking point.

At other points in his book Creel quite explicitly states that God is unchangeable, atemporal rather than temporal. "He simply is," without past or future (104). But this is precisely the Boethian view which Creel earlier criticized. Creel's only concession to neoclassical theism here is that we can make temporal statements about God, for example, that "God existed" (105–6). But God has all of *his* life at once (106-107). Hartshorne would wonder how, on Creel's view, God could have all of his *life* at once if living entails temporal change and adaptation from moment to moment: responding to at least the immediate past, savoring the fleeting present, and anticipating at least the immediate future. Creel is quite understandably forced into the old Thomistic trap of claiming that all relations are external to God (109). I find unintelligible his own novel formulation of this: "changes in God's knowledge of actuality make a difference *in* him [Then why not say that God has internal relations?] but not *to* him" (111—my insert).

4. Creel believes that God is impassible in *feeling* for several reasons. First, in response to the claim that *personality* requires passibility he uses Stoic *apatheia* as an example of a type of personal awareness which de-emphasizes passibility. Stoic "impassibility," however, is obviously a mask (literally one of several *personae*) worn by a passible, feeling, human animal. That is, not even an Epictetus could, strictly speaking, be impassible. Second, Creel rejects the idea that *love* requires passibility, as when he claims that: "I see no problem with assuming that an emotionally impassible being could *feel* about and be disposed toward the welfare of someone else" (1986, 117—my emphasis). But if the Greek word *pathe* by definition means feeling in the sense of being passive with respect to something, how can there be a feeling being who is *apathes*? Creel's view seems to be that divine feeling is merely a disposition to feel rather than the ability to have feelings in a strong sense, that is, really to react to

creatures. Further, Creel's rejection of divine passible love is integrally connected, as we will see, with the traditional classical theistic theodicy, which has made the case for theism so untenable for many thinking (and feeling) people over the last several centuries. He says that: "We cannot, then, rule out the possibility that God knows something about our destiny that renders it unnecessary and inappropriate for him to be disturbed by our suffering in this life" (121). But this plays right into the hands of a Humean or Camus-like thinker who would accuse God of sadism.

Third, Creel does not think that *omniscience* requires passibility; he does not think that to know suffering is, in a way, to suffer. Creel's view here is based, however, on the view that God does not know any of our feelings directly (129); and this view is based on the (again, as in Plantinga's case, unexamined) assumption that divine embodiment makes no sense (Creel 1986, 25, 85). It also denies that God can be "sympathetic" in the strongest sense of the word. Creel is correct that there is a difference between one's own feelings and those of others, but if God is sympathetic with creatures (literally, sym-pathy), as he sometimes admits, then the gap between divine and creaturely feeling is bridged, as in my feeling pain because cells in my finger have been burned.[14]

And fourth, Creel does not think that morality or *theodicy* requires passibility. He admits that on his view God is omnipotent pure activity (1986, 68), and because of God's omnipotence God is directly or indirectly responsible for all suffering; but suffering, he thinks, is an instrumental ingredient in redemption (147). That is, God can "counter-balance or cancel out" any evil (189). Hartshorne, by way of contrast, agrees with Wordsworth that "what having been, must ever be." There is no way that innocent suffering can be completely canceled out, as Creel thinks (149), because any being with memory, especially the greatest conceivable memory, would be pained to recall, for example, that some innocent being sometime before had been tortured. In that Hartshorne's God is not omnipotent (although Hartshorne's God does have the most power logically compatible with free creatures) it is not his God who can be accused of cooperating with the Holocaust (138), because the concrete pole of the divine nature is not entirely up to God, as Creel incorrectly alleges of Hartshorne's view (1986, 166).

Yet if God is, as Creel alleges, an omnipotent pure activity, then one can quite legitimately accuse this "God" of cooperating with the Holocaust. It is easy to allege this cooperation because of Creel's claim that God does not take pleasure in, nor is God pained by, each creature intensively but only extensively (144). What this means is that God merely counts the number of beings who experience pain without divinity being pained. Is *this* a morally supreme being? Creel thinks so, comparing his God's impassibility to Buddhist compassion (158), but exactly what sort of compassion could this be? An incomprehensible compassion, I think, just as incomprehensible as the claim made by Creel that God did not choose this world because it is the best possible one, but rather this is the best possible one *because* an omnipotent and impassible (in effect, immutable) God "chose" it (203). Here Creel is open to a charge similar to the one made by many readers of the *Euthyphro* to the effect that there is something arbitrary about the claim that this is the best possible world *because* God made it.

I. PLATO

As indicated in the Introduction, this chapter is an attempt to start a dialogue with those analytic theists who have assumed with equanimity that God is immutable. It is also an attempt to continue the beginnings of a dialogue already in progress between Creel and neoclassical theists, a dialogue which has only scratched the surface of the differences between the two, and perhaps of some similarities as well, as when Creel emphasizes divine impassibility of existence or nature. The differences, however, are not due, as some would think, to Creel and other classical theists inheriting the Greek tradition of immutability while Hartshorne and other neoclassical theists eschew this Greek tradition in theology. Rather, the differences seem to be due to two separate modes of appropriating the Greeks, particularly Plato.

There are two significant ways in which Plato talks about God (*theos*). First, he inherited from Parmenides the notion that being is eternal, immutable, and self-same. This notion was the starting point for the tradition of classical, monopolar theism, a tradition kept alive, with few changes made, by the analytic theists I have treated in this chapter. "The extent to which Plato is committed to such an absolute schism between *being* and *becoming* . . . would seem to dictate for him a similar exclusion from divinity of all shadow of change." (Eslick 1982, 244). This tendency is evidenced in Book 2 and elsewhere in the *Republic*, in the *Phaedo* (78–80), and in the *Symposium* (202–3).

Second, however, there is no textual foundation for the popular identification of Plato's God with the transcendent form of the good, nor even with the world of forms, either as a whole or in part.[15] Even when talking about divine eternity and immutability (in the limited dipolar sense) the Platonic locus for divinity is *psyche* or *nous*. It comes as a shock to some readers of Plato who have read only the *Republic, Phaedo*, and *Symposium* that in the *Phaedrus* (245, etc.) Eros is claimed to be divine. Here Plato discovers, according to Leonard Eslick, a new, dynamic meaning for perfection, similar to the one Hartshorne defends. The perfection that is dynamic is the perfection of life itself, treated not only in the *Phaedrus* but in book 10 of the *Laws* as well.

In the *Timaeus* and the *Sophist* both poles in Plato's theism are brought together: the perfection of divine immutability and the perfection of divine life. The former is identified in the *Timaeus* with the Demiurge, who eternally and without change contemplates, but is not identical with, the archetypal models, the eternal forms. The latter is identified with the World-Soul, whose essence is self-motion, but whose motions include both actions and passions. In fact, in the *Sophist* reality is identified with *dynamis* or power, specifically the power to affect or to be affected by others. Aristotle (Metaphysics A) attests to the fact that reality (even divine reality) for Plato is the joint product of the One and the Indefinite Dyad. Unfortunately, Aristotle's own notion of God as completely unmoved loses the second tendency in Plato's theism, and the mesmerizing influence that

Aristotle has had on the history of theism (through the neo-"platonists"—who are in many respects really neo-Aristotelians—and St. Thomas, etc.) has prevented progress from being made in the Platonic project of bringing the two poles or tendencies in God's nature together.

It is the appropriation of the former tendency in Plato, as filtered through Aristotle and the classical theistic tradition, which supports analytic theism's denigration of divine change and divine embodiment.[16] And it is Hartshorne's appropriation of both tendencies in Plato (not the latter tendency only)—tendencies that represent the mature Platonic metaphysics—that supports Hartshorne's defense of God as the World-Soul of the body of the world, a World-Soul that is nonetheless happy in the midst of the tragedy it experiences (contra Creel, 1986, 137). Perhaps some agreement can be found here with Creel's comparison of God with Buddhist compassion. And perhaps the best way to explore the extent to which analytic theism's version of classical theism and neoclassical theism can agree is for both analytic theists and neoclassical theists to reread the *Timaeus* and *Sophist*. In these dialogues, the two tendencies in Plato's theism are brought together, a synthesis that underlies these profound lines from Whitehead (1961 [1933], 381), lines which indicate in a short space how a mutable, tragic God is nonetheless a perfect being worthy of worship:

> At the heart of the nature of things there are always the dream of youth and the harvest of tragedy. The Adventure of the Universe starts with the dream and reaps tragic Beauty. This is the secret of the union of Zest with Peace:—That the suffering attains its end in a Harmony of Harmonies. The immediate experience of this Final Fact, with its union of Youth and Tragedy, is the sense of Peace. In this way the World receives its persuasion towards such perfections as are possible for its diverse individual occasions.

The belief in divine immutability is often a veiled theodicy, as is made explicit in Creel, but is implicit in all of the authors I have treated in this chapter: there is ultimately no need to be troubled by evil and pain in the world because God, who is not changed by these, makes everything turn out fine in the end. Hartshorne and Whitehead, however, in their mode of appropriating Plato, as opposed to that of the classical theists, are also interested in appropriating the Greek sense of life, even divine life, as tragic but worth living nonetheless.

CHAPTER TWO

Method and Polar Equality in Dipolar Theism

A. INTRODUCTION

In the previous chapter we have seen that many analytic theists have made assumptions that are questionable from a Hartshornian point of view, hence there is need to request that these thinkers supply counterarguments to Hartshorne's own arguments. To the list of those in this category in chapter 1 can be added Paul Helm, Edward Wierenga, and D. Z. Phillips. (The unbeliever Richard Gale also seems to assume that theism is synonymous with classical theism.)[1] We have also seen that some other thinkers, like Richard Creel, are to some extent in dialogue with Hartshorne. In this chapter I would like to treat another theist in this latter category, Colin Gunton, whose stance is much like Creel's. My procedure will be to discuss the question of method in Hartshorne's thought so as to counteract the claim made by Gunton and others that there is polar inequality in Hartshorne's thought, and that, hence, his thought provides an unbalanced or tendentious view of the concept of God. By presenting Hartshorne's view as a moderate one I will be able to make explicit in chapter 2 what was implicit in chapter 1. That is, the Hartshornian question is not so much "Must a perfect being be immutable?," but rather, more precisely, "Must a perfect being be immutable in every respect?" In some respects God is obviously immutable.

On my count there are three primary working principles or methods at work in Hartshorne's philosophy. (1) Hartshorne likes the method of systematic exhaustion of theoretical options in treating philosophical problems, or again, the development of position matrices to determine the available options regarding a particular problem. (2) He uses the history of ideas to see which options have been carefully examined before (see especially PS, IO, and CA). This method has been alluded to in chapter 1 regarding Plato. Hartshorne typically emphasizes a neglected philosopher (like Jules Lequier[2]) or a neglected aspect of a famous philosopher (say Plato's dipolar theism or Plato's dynamism) so as to make it more difficult for contemporary thinkers to rest content with views they incorrectly think are time honored. Just as belief in creation *ex nihilo* as the traditional theistic view can be seen as at least somewhat problematic when it is realized that it is not found in Genesis, so also belief in divine immutability is based on a Platon*ism* never held by Plato. And (3) he uses the principle that philosophical wisdom is best seen in defense of moderate views with pragmatically sane consequences (see WM). Whereas Aristotle was correct in saying that virtue consists in a judicious mean between two contrary extremes, Hartshorne wants to expand this method so as to apply it to all, or almost all, philosophic issues. In this chapter I will concentrate on methods 1 and 3, but in the conclusion to the chapter I will return to (2).

I will first examine Hartshorne's method of systematically exhausting theoretical options, and this with the aid of A. O. Lovejoy, whose thought helps to illuminate Hartshorne's view, as Hartshorne himself has indicated as recently as 1990. Eventually I will also treat the method of looking for a moderate and pragmatic view among the plausible options. The point to looking at these two methods is to put me in a position to respond to Gunton's view of neoclassical theism, a mistaken view that seems to be a popular one among analytic theists.

B. SYSTEMATIC EXHAUSTION OF OPTIONS

In 1990 Hartshorne, at the age of 93, published his intellectual autobiography, titled *The Darkness and the Light*. Because he has been intellectually active for a longer period of time than almost any other of the great philosophers of the twentieth century, Hartshorne is in an enviable position when responding to the questions, "Is it possible for philosophy to progress?" and "If it is possible for it to progress, what prevents it from doing so?" The purpose of this section of the chapter is not to detail Hartshorne's belief, which he has held for several decades, that philosophy can, in fact, progress. Rather, granting Hartshorne's assumption that philosophy can progress, I will concentrate on the second question regarding why it has not progressed to the degree that it should have. He thinks that perhaps the best thing we could do *now* to respond to questions regarding progress in philosophy is to read A. O. Lovejoy's (1917) Presidential Address to the American Philosophical Association in 1916.[3]

This recommendation will no doubt strike some as rather odd in that, it will be claimed, Lovejoy's *Weltanschauung* would, of necessity, be radically different from that of any philosopher operating in the cacophonous and polysemic world of contemporary academe. In this section of the chapter I will show that this objection does not hold water, that Lovejoy is indeed instructive regarding why philosophy has not progressed to the extent that it should have, and that Hartshorne's own attempt to bring about progress in philosophy largely rests on a modified Lovejoy-like methodology.

Lovejoy's recommendations, or better, his "partial remedy," for what he conceived to be the ills of philosophy in 1916, was not that we have more philosophic argumentation, or at least not more argumentation for its own sake. The problem with philosophic argumentation is that it often aims to arrive at unanimity of opinion due to a sort of intellectual coercion whereby one *cannot help* but succumb to the logical rigor in a particular position. The Rortean sound to this criticism of intellectual coercion should not hide the fact that Lovejoy has a quite unRortean goal (Lovejoy 1917, 126, 131, 133).

Philosophy, he thinks, has for a long time been trying to perform two incongruous functions: impressive personal reaction to life and depersonalized "science." Yet both of these have been expected at once from the same sources. Lovejoy (1917, 134) also refers to these two functions as the desire to edify and the desire to verify, respectively:

> It is to be hoped that the truth, when found, will be found edifying. But the soul habitually on fire with a passionate conviction which it is eager to impart is scarcely of a temperature favorable to the cool and deliberate processes of severe inquiry.

That is, whereas Rorty throws out the notion of philosophy as a science which verifies and encourages the notion of philosophy as a nonrepresentational effort at edification, Lovejoy is intent on doing the reverse. Lovejoy would rather us be sceptical inquirers than preachers. Not even a hybrid of the edifying prophet and the professor will be likely to avoid paradox or contradiction. The split between these two functions of philosophy can also be seen in the distinction between the conversational teacher of philosophy, on the one hand, and the scholarly lover of wisdom, on the other, with Lovejoy's point being that the former gets in the way of, if it does not actually contradict, the latter.

Unfortunately, he thinks, one's reputation as a philosopher is more often than not determined by the prophetic or edifying character of one's remarks rather than by their "scientific" character. As we will see below, we may learn a great deal from Lovejoy even if we have come to be suspicious of what appears to be his positivism. The most rigorous logician, he hopes, is still impassioned with certain ideals. The danger arises when a person is judged to be a good philosopher *merely* because he or she is a good philosophical poet or preacher. (Obviously Hartshorne is sometimes a "preacher" in this sense, but he is far more often occupied with pointing out inconsistencies in classical theism.) Lovejoy has Royce in mind just as we may think of Rorty or Derrida. But Lovejoy's hope that the confusion between philosophy and edification was waning itself seems to be a waning hope. In any event, *if* progress is to occur in philosophy, we will not need greater rhetorical skills, or greater cognizance of our use of metaphor, so much as a progressive clarification of our problems (1917, 136–39). The following quotation should be of interest to those interested in the clash between classical and neoclassical theism: "If two astronomers, observing the same object, get variant results, neither of them insists that his own (uncorrected) observation is the true one, no matter how clearly and distinctly he saw what he reports" (140). Lovejoy is obviously no Cartesian, as his remark regarding clear and distinct ideas indicates, nor is he *guaranteeing* philosophic progress if his recommendations are taken seriously. Rather, he is suggesting that we may very well benefit if we clarify our problems in a "scientific" way.

We cannot adopt in philosophy the method sometimes used in science to mitigate error, that is, the application of the law of averages to conflicting opinions. Rather, error in philosophy seems to be due to a generic cause, to a constant fault in the general procedure used. Lovejoy offers six suggestions as to how to ameliorate this cause of error:

1. The philosopher's task should be to observe as completely and exactly as possible all of the "considerations" pertinent to the issue involved. In effect, Lovejoy is recommending that there is nothing in the generic nature of the philosopher's procedure which is not analogous to the procedures of the other sciences. The "considerations" which Lovejoy has in mind are not neatly spread out before us, but must be gathered, collated, and focused with a great deal of effort. Scientists are trained to guard against errors in enumeration or oversight, training which is integrally connected to progress in their disciplines. Lovejoy (1917, 141–43) asks rhetorically: "Can we honestly say that philosophy has as yet developed any such precautionary technique?"

Philosophers need to provide themselves with *checks and precautions* and with the production of a habit of mind conducive to that eternal vigilance which is the price of sound philosophizing. Too many philosophers, Lovejoy thinks, still practically endorse Bergson's trope to the effect that no philosopher ever says more than one thing for he or she never sees more than one point. But philosophy does not have to rely on dazzling flashes of illumination on the road to Damascus. In fact, the inebriety which comes at these moments is part of the problem. (Even Wordsworth, the greatest defender of these "spots of time," believed that wisdom was gained through flashes of genius *recollected in tranquility.*) These moments of insight are both the chief rewards of the philosopher's life and also its chief dangers. One of these dangers lies in the fact that these insights often present themselves to philosophers as necessities of thought or as self-evident truths (1917, 144–47). Lovejoy's first recommendation, therefore, is the following:

> The first thing needful, then, for the secure progress of philosophical inquiry—after the business of inquiry has been separated from the business of edification—is the development, or the very great intensification among us of a certain habit of mind—of the caution, and the sense of probable multiplicity and elusiveness of the circumstances to be taken account of. . . . The motto of philosophy should be the reverse of Danton's: not boldness, but circumspection. (148)

2. A corollary of the first point is Lovejoy's emphasis on a *deliberate and methodical attempt at exhaustiveness* in the enumeration of the elements of a problem, an attempt which is honored more in the breach than in the observance, he thinks. That is, philosophical problems are more likely to be of the enumerative type than most philosophers are willing to admit, hence philosophers are notorious for failing to draw up a complete list of the attributes of a problem. If one contents oneself with taking merely a few attributes of a problem seriously which just happen to come to mind, then even after an acute and ingenious analysis of the problem one can only expect glaringly incomplete results (149–50). Lovejoy was not offering a prolegomenon for what was to become logical positivism.

3. The method which Lovejoy is defending is none other than the dialectical method, which, of necessity, requires two or more minds at work. It is scarcely possible for one mind alone to make the exhaustive enumeration of the aspects of a problem which are requisite for philosophical progress, hence *cooperation in philosophizing is indispensible.* If one of the principal sources of error in philosophy is oversight, or the too cursory regard of pertinent considerations, then we should be cognizant of "the inevitable limitations of the logical sensitivity of any individual mind" (151). Philosophers have learned innumerable things, both true and false, from the Platonic dialogues, but we are just now in this century learning the truth which is exhibited in the form of those writings: "that real philosophizing is a collective process" (150). In a confused way this is recog-

nized in the current practice of presentations and responses, publications and replies.

Once again, Lovejoy thinks that philosophers could learn from the *organized* reciprocity in the sciences, a reciprocity which is at least in part designed to check the peculiarities of vision of individual intellects. Lovejoy's point here is related to his first recommendation regarding the dangers posed by flashes of illumination. The disposition to take *one's own* reasoning as final, if it impresses one powerfully, does great harm in philosophy. Indeed, there is now a great deal of philosophical discussion and criticism, but most of it comes too late for it to make much of a difference (152–53). (This point applies to analytic and process thinkers alike; Hartshorne has at times changed his mind due to criticism he has received, but these are the exceptions to the rule in his thought.)

4. Perhaps the most common complaint among philosophical writers regarding their reviewers is that they have been misunderstood. In addition to philosophical criticisms before publication (and in addition to what is now commonly called "collaborative learning"), Lovejoy suggests the adoption among philosophers of a *common and unambiguous terminology.* He laments the fact that: "terms which to some specialists seem indispensible and full of weighty import convey to others no intelligible meaning whatever" (154). The agreement needed does not have to be ad hoc, but even stipulative agreement for the sake of a particular argument would be an improvement over deliberate obfuscation of language or use of indirect discourse so as to parade before others the fact that there is no particular meaning which one wishes to convey. (Several deconstructionists I have read seem to do precisely this.) Lovejoy has no illusions regarding the results attainable even by the means he recommends. But he does anticipate that we could "secure a more precise joining of issue," and that we might witness that "rare and admirable spectacle" of a mature philosopher converted by way of argument to a new opinion (155).

5. None of the above should be taken to imply that Lovejoy wished for a return to systematic philosophy of the seventeenth-century variety. On the contrary, he thinks we should treat *philosophic*

problems in isolation and deal with each in enumerative fashion (again, as is the case in science), so as to avoid the Hegelian superstition that every philosophical issue is inextricably intertwined with every other. Eventually it may turn out that Hegel is correct (although Lovejoy is doubtful that he is), but we should not *assume* a doctrine of pure internal (or external, à la Hume or Russell) relations at the outset. We are more likely to progress in philosophy through a "linked sequence of provisionally limited and hypothetical discussions." If none of us can view the world *sub specie aeternitatis* (even if we must, at times, speak about the world as if it were a cosmic whole, a uni-verse), then we should not be ashamed of acquiring understanding bit by bit (155, 157–58).

6. And eventually there is value to be found in a *comprehensive catalogue of "considerations"* involved in each philosophic problem, a modern *Summa* of an undogmatic and nonpartisan kind. We will find, he promises, that: "The number of really distinct 'considerations' discoverable in the history of philosophy is vastly less than the unsophisticated reader of that kaleidoscopic record usually supposes" (160). This encyclopaedia of problem items or map of philosophy may help to prevent us from forgetting "considerations" and it would force us to at least consider these considerations before refuting them. The aims of this comprehensive catalog would be exhaustiveness in enumeration, obviously enough, and the avoidance of discursiveness in expression. The latter aim makes it possible for Lovejoy to highlight the fact that his modern *Summa* would state no final conclusions, but would make it possible for the judicious reader to conclude for himself. And rather than trying to systematize philosophy as a whole, Lovejoy would rather, through a proper use of cross references, exhibit the limited interdependence of seemingly distinct questions (161–63).

Lovejoy's suggestions in his 1916 version of a *Discours de la Methode* are much more practical than Descartes' version, a practicality which impressed Hartshorne in the ninetieth year of his life, when he first read Lovejoy's presidential address. There are some features of Lovejoy's recommendations which Hartshorne obviously will not accept, as in Lovejoy's claim that the gathering of pertinent considerations to a problem is "inductive." But Lovejoy's positivism is nonetheless appropriated by Hartshorne for the purpose of defending, ironically enough, Hartshorne's own bold metaphysical aspirations:

> As I have emphasized exhaustiveness in searching the possible answers to a philosophical question, he stresses the exhaustiveness of pertinent considerations. Perhaps both maxims come to much the same, I am not yet sure of this. How does one find the pertinent or relevant considerations to a philosophical question or issue? How does one know that one's list is exhaustive? My answer is, by the mathematics of combinations of concepts, either ignoring permutations, or definitely including them. Otherwise I see no way. Lovejoy barely mentions mathematics in the article. (DL, 390)

This "mathematics of combinations" aids in the discovery of chance elements in the formation of philosophical "systems," systems which do not usually exhibit consistency in the way problems are combined because, lacking position matrices which map out all of the possible positions to be taken, philosophers often end up pushing views together that do not fit with each other.

Our concern should be with problems or doctrines, not systems in the traditional sense:

> The question is not, are you a Platonist, Aristotelian, Kantian, or Humean? On some issues, each of these will be admirable enough, but on some others perhaps seriously mistaken. Richard McKeon, another learned man, took almost the contrary position. The great philosophers, he held, are consistent enough, and all of them in their way understand reality. Selecting one of them is a personal or political action, not demonstrably uniquely right. I hold with Lovejoy that we must deal with issues, not systems tied to historical names. I have been called a "semi-Whiteheadian," also, in effect, a semi-Peircean, also a Platonist. I quarrel with none of these. I am also a semi-Popperian, something of a Bergsonian, Socinian, Epicurean, and Fechnerian. (DL, 391)

Hartshorne appreciates the fact that Lovejoy is one of the few historians who give us a history of important ideas, not important figures. The connection between concern for an adequate history of ideas and concern for exhausting all of the mathematical possibilities is seen in the following quotation from Hartshorne regarding the way most historians (not Lovejoy) operate:

> Minor points by great philosophers are dealt with, often with loving care, but major points by minor philosophers are missed. One reason for this is that the historians have not sufficiently considered beforehand what the important ideas might be. In doing general history good common sense, shrewdness, and broad culture enable the historian to know what the important possibilities for human action are, but in doing history of philosophy more than this is required. One must have in mind some carefully worked-out system of possible positions on various problems in order to decide what in intellectual history is most worth knowing. Here position matrices, made exhaustive by formal logical means, are valuable. With such schemes in mind the historian can ask himself, who has held position (1) out of a set of, say, three possible positions arising from a given matrix, and who has held positions (2) or (3)? It may then turn out that all the major philosophers missed one position, while some minor philosophers did not. This in my view has actually happened. (CS, 86-87)

Obviously some of Lovejoy's and Hartshorne's criticisms of the methods of many philosophers do not apply to analytic theists. The latter seldom rely on what Lovejoy refers to as flashes of genius, nor do they engage in "edifying" philosophy, as he uses the term. For these reasons they are to be commended. But it has been my contention in the present chapter and in the previous one that analytic theists may well be guilty of starting to philosophize by assuming that certain concepts, like divine immutability or creation *ex nihilo*, are nonnegotiable and then trying to determine the meaning and implications of these concepts. That is, analytic theists are in need of the sort of enumerations or position matrices discussed by Hartshorne regarding, say, the issue of divine permanence, as I tried to show in chapter 1. No doubt process theism also needs to have its methods kept honest, and it is to be hoped that some analytic theists will continue to perform precisely that function. It should be emphasized that Lovejoy's concern that philosophers use relatively unambiguous terms is also a concern for analytic thinkers, but it is a traditional sore spot for Whiteheadians in that *Process and Reality*, in particular, is, at times, extraordinarily dark. Hartshorne, by way of contrast, is almost always clear. The question for analytic theists, I suppose, is whether Hartshorne is clearly wrong in his concept of God.

It is my contention in this book that philosophical progress can occur regarding the concept of God when:

1. Analytic, classical theists and process, neoclassical theists confront one another more directly and perhaps even more cooperatively than they have thus far.
2. Careful enumerations or position matrices regarding the options are used regarding the concept of God.
3. The history of philosophy is treated regarding the origin of certain concepts, like divine immutability, that are not themselves divinely revealed.
4. Moderation is used in the choices we have to make among those options that are not illogical or implausible.

Hartshorne's contention regarding method is that once we have developed enumerations we should criticize and eliminate illogical or untenable views, the latter for theological or pragmatic reasons, and then calibrate toward a mean among those options that remain. This calibration of one's beliefs toward a mean is not the result of an unreflective "technique." It takes a wise person to know how to achieve moderation in philosophy or to know how to choose among options that are drawn up through position matrices which plot the mathematically possible options. Lovejoy and Hartshorne agree that progress in philosophy can only occur through careful "enumeration" of "considerations," but Hartshorne does not assume that boldness will lead a philosopher to become, as Lovejoy seems to think, a latter-day Danton or Robespierre. Rather, Hartshorne is convinced, along with Popper (1972), that there is a great deal to be gained by *bold position matrices* as long as these devices are accompanied by *severe attempts at criticizing* each option.

C. ABSOLUTENESS AND RELATIVITY

In chapter 1 I alleged that regarding a contrast like that between absoluteness and relativity the classical theist basically thinks of the two terms

absolute relative (SCHEMA 3)

in polar opposition to each other such that one should determine which is good (on the left), so as to attribute it to God, and which is bad (on the right), so as to eliminate it from the list of divine attributes. My claim was that a more careful enumeration of the options would have revealed that relativity, in the sense of being really related to others, is not in every respect a bad thing, and absoluteness, in the sense of possessing *aseity*—or being *a se*—is not in every respect a good thing. In effect, the diagram should be at least this complex:

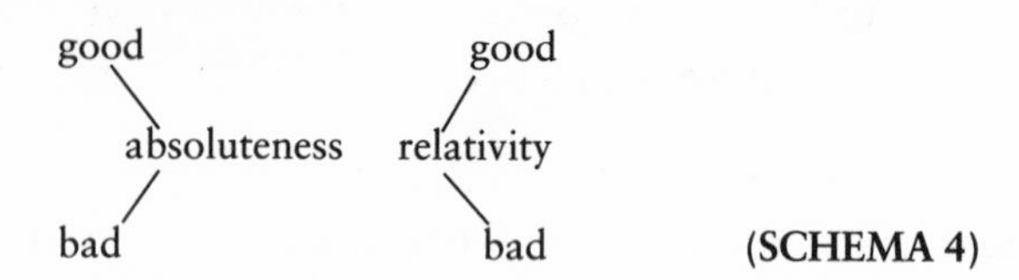

In the present chapter I would like to once again "enumerate" the "considerations" or options regarding divine absoluteness and divine relativity in a way that is more expansive than that exhibited by most analytic theists. The purpose of this enumeration is to eventually criticize Gunton for claiming that there is polar inequality in Hartshorne's concept of God. Gunton's view is that the relativity of Hartshorne's God precludes divine absoluteness or *aseity* altogether; he thinks that Hartshorne's God only has the attributes on the right side of Schemata 2–4. But in order to criticize Gunton it is necessary not only to engage in a Lovejoy-like or Hartshornian "enumeration," but also in a full-fledged effort at developing mathematicized position matrices.

Classical theists, including analytic classical theists, see two alternatives to choose from (I and III, in schema 5), whereas Hartshorne, in his careful enumeration, sees three alternatives (he prefers a version of II).

SCHEMA 5 (MV, 11–12)

I. There is a being in *all* respects absolutely perfect or unsurpassable, in no way and in no respect surpassable or perfectible. (Theism of the First Type; absolutism, Thomism, most European theology prior to 1880.)

II. There is no being in all respects absolutely perfect; but there is a being in *some* respect or respects thus perfect, and in some respect or respects not so, in some respects surpassable, whether by self or others being left open. Thus it is not excluded that the being may be relatively perfect in all the respects in which it is not absolutely perfect. (Theism of the Second Type; much contemporary . . . theology, doctrines of a "finite-infinite" or perfect-perfectible God.)

III. There is no being in *any* respect absolutely perfect; all beings are in all respects surpassable by something conceivable, perhaps by others or perhaps by themselves in another state. (Doctrines of a merely finite God, polytheism in some forms, atheism.)

Given the choice between I and III it is no wonder that classical theists have chosen I; not to do so on the basis of their attenuated list would be to give up on the greatest conceivable being altogether. One looks in vain in the writings of most analytic, classical theists for careful refutation of (or, in some cases, mention of) II.

But not even the list of three alternatives in schema 5 is expansive enough. These three options can, under a more powerful lens, be seen to contain at least seven cases (see schema 6).

SCHEMA 6 (MV, 8–9)

Group	Case	Symbol	Interpretation
I	1	A	Absolute perfection in *all* respects.
II	2	AR	Absolute perfection in *some* respects, relative perfection in all others.
	3	ARI	Absolute perfection, relative perfection, and "imperfection" (neither A nor R), each in *some* respects.

SCHEMA 6 (MV, 8–9) (*continued*)

Group	Case	Symbol	Interpretation
	4	AI	Absolute perfection in *some* respects, imperfection in all others.
III	5	R	Absolute perfection in *no* respects, relative in all.
	6	RI	Absolute perfection in *no* respects, relative in some, imperfection in the others.
	7	I	Absolute perfection in *no* respects, imperfection in all.

Explanation of symbols: A stands for absolute perfection; R for relative perfection; I for imperfection, or the joint negation of A and R.[4]

In order to understand this schema, two sets of distinctions are crucial. When it is claimed that there is "none greater" than God, the term "none" can refer to "no entity other than the being said to be perfect as it actually is" (A perfection) *or* to "no entity other than that as it is or else could become" (R perfection). According to the second meaning a perfect being is unsurpassable except by itself. And "greater" can mean "in all respects whatever" or "in some but not all respects" or "in no respect whatever." Combining the two meanings of "none" with the three of "greater" allows us to derive the seven possible cases. The question "Is there a perfect being?" is really six questions rather than one, as cases 1–6 indicate. Once again, one looks in vain for detailed argumentation for case 1 as opposed to case 2 in the writings of most analytic, classical theists, who assume that case 1 *is* theism.

No less than four of the cases in schema 6 are included in the class of "absolute" beings. Yet within groups II and III the differences are at least as important as the similarities, and in this regard it is important to notice that cases 3 and 4 are hard to see as versions of the greatest conceivable being because of the presence of imperfection. Case 2 *is* a version of God as absolute (contra Gunton) and it avoids attributing any imperfection to God. Hence the key choice lies between cases 1 and 2, but cases 3–7 are nonetheless important to show that there is nothing extreme in Hartshorne's defense of case 2 (once again, contra Gunton). Neoclassical theism is committed to the view that God is absolutely perfect "without shadow of turning" in those things that depend by their nature upon divine excellence alone, in contrast to those things that do not depend on the divine excellence alone, as in divine bliss. God knows all that goes on in the lives of a good and a bad person, but only the former contributes to divine bliss. That is, perfect power and wisdom and goodness do not insure absolute bliss (MV, 10, 13–15, 21–22).

A perfect universe, to the extent that this is conceivable, could not be an absolutely controlled universe. Individuals, concrete instances of reality, must to some degree be self-managed in that acting to some extent on one's own is inherent in concrete reality, in contrast to the reality of lifeless abstractions, as we will see. "Absoluteness" does apply to God, but only on the condition that the correlative term "relativity" also applies. Contradiction results only if no qualification, such as "in some respect," is attached to the attributes: "The classical error was one of over-trust in extremely simple ways of characterizing God. It was a kind of learned simple-mindedness" (CS, 40). Some analytic theists will take this as an insult, but the question remains: Have analytic theists sufficiently explored the historical roots of, and the reasons for, monopolarity? I think not. The monopolar prejudice originated due to several factors, including the discovery of pure mathematics and the one-sided enthusiasm for abstract ideas that this discovery understandably encouraged. But this prejudice can be escaped in a Peircian way when it is realized that the contrast between absolute terms, associated with abstract independence and external relatedness (Peirce's Firsts), and relative terms, associated with concrete dependency and internal relatedness (Peirce's Seconds or Thirds), does not point to a contradiction: the former are included in the latter. Dichotomies are cruder than trichotomies, on Peirce's view. To contrast "abstractness" with "concreteness" is in itself to fail to notice that the concept of "concreteness" is itself an abstraction. An instance of concreteness is by no means the concept all over again. Both "concreteness" and "abstractness" can be teased out of the actuality of God at any particular time. An abstraction like "absoluteness" (i.e., nonrelativity) of course refers to some specific context, unless one intends to defend the most indefensible sort of Platon*ism*. Since absoluteness is merely the negation of relativity, the more basic principle is relativity. "The real absolute is relativity itself" (CS, 104). The absolute is in the relative just as an abstraction resides in the concrete as an element that can be teased out; once again, extreme Platon*ism* aside (CS, 30, 44, 100, 118).

Relativity per se, positive and negative, is the absolute (i.e., nonrelative) principle. Or in different terms, the neoclassical theist's God is eternal not in the sense of being outside of time altogether, but rather in the sense of existing through *all* of time, hence Hartshorne's preference for the term "everlasting." A God who exists in time is also a God who suffers; indeed, neoclassical theists influenced by biblical theism may very well view the denial of divine suffering as a profanation. Let us stipulate that X loves Y. If Y, who previously did not suffer, starts to suffer, then X could hardly remain unmoved and independent (absolute) to Y's plight if X's love is in *any* way analogous to human love (CS, 120, 263).

Many theists make a mistake by *identifying* God with the absolute (or with immutability), by confusing the divine fulness with an abstraction called *the* absolute that does not change in any way. This abstraction can in fact be an object of intellectual amazement, but it cannot be the all-loving, all-worshipful being. What is truly absolute is divine relativity/love; the everlasting being *is* the ultimate type of becoming. The concept of God as all-loving (and hence as all-related) was always at odds with the concept of God as the absolute in every respect because divine absoluteness (or *aseity*) constitutes indifference to others (CS, 35, 46–47, 56, 157). For these and other reasons it makes sense to say in schema 6 that case 1 is inferior to case 2. Hartshorne follows Barth in designating the identification of the absolute (or immutability) with God a pagan idea. If Hartshorne is correct that there is more to God than the absolute, independent aspect of God (e.g., that aspect whereby God does not need us in order to sustain the divine existence), then calling God "the absolute" does not exalt God but limit (paganize) the divine nature (NT, 24). (In another sense, however, Hartshorne sees God as more absolute than many analytic, classical theists are willing to admit in that God's necessary existence cannot be proved through appeal to any empirical, contingent fact, hence Hartshorne's—in this peculiar sense, Kantian—belief that all of the proofs for God's existence are a priori and "ontological"—NT, x.)

If negation is parasitic on affirmation (as must be the case if Bergson, among others, is correct when he claims that "absolutely nothing" is unintelligible, in that whenever we try to understand the concept we end up talking about somethingness rather than "absolutely nothing"), then it is crucial to notice that absoluteness or independence are not opposed to relativity but are aspects of it. For example, the greatest conceivable being interacts with whatever individuals there are; God is absolute or independent in the sense that divine sympathy is not restricted to any historical epoch or any particular place. God is *not* absolute or independent in the sense that Plotinus' relationless One, devoid of inner plurality, is absolute or independent. (All classical theists are, to some extent, Plotinians in this regard.) There is something idolatrous in love seeking something more than Love, say in the classical theistic belief that beyond loving relations there is the relationless absolute (NT, 69–70, 106, 128).

It is a grand leap to go from the necessary existence of God to God being necessary in every aspect. Classical theists are correct in claiming that the *absolute* does not change, but the neoclassical theist would add that *God* changes. God is absolute and self-sufficient *in existence* in that God does not need us in particular in order to continue to exist, but if not us in particular then some creatures or other are needed by God if God is all-loving. Self-sufficient love is a contradiction in terms if love, by definition, is some sort of concern for others. Hence there is a need to see God as dipolar: in God's A perfection God surpasses all things, in God's R perfection God surpasses all things including previous stages of divine life (LP, 64, 67, 268, 323). As Hartshorne puts the point:

> According to the neoclassical idea, what is eternally fixed or absolute in God is exactly the unlimited flexibility of His capacity to know and value, and thus to relativize Himself. He is immutably capable, to an ideal degree and in an ideal manner, of self-enrichment through anything that may become real. (LP, 101)

But to depend for one's very *existence* on another is indeed a mark of mediocrity (LP, 136).

The analytic, classical theist at least *says* that human beings serve God, but if God *is* the absolute, concerning which there can be no increase or decrease, then it seems we can only irreligiously serve ourselves and one another (CA, 185). Once again, Hartshorne's view is a moderate one between classical theism (AA—God is absolute or self-sufficient both in existence and actuality) and the view that there is nothing absolute or self-sufficient either in existence or actuality. His moderate view (AR—God exhibits absolute or self-sufficient perfection in existence and is perfectly related to creatures in the divine *mode* of existence or actuality) consists in the belief that in one respect God is the un-self-transcending-transcender-of-all-others (A) and in another respect is the self-transcending-transcender-of-all-others (R). No growth at all (AA) and growth in every respect are the Scylla and Charybdis among concepts of God that a moderate theism tries to avoid (WP, 66, 71, 78).

No mind, not even a divine mind, could be completely "absolute." The plausibility of this claim can be seen when the classical theistic view of the divine mind is considered. On this view God's mind is not the supreme example of mind but its antithesis: God derives nothing from the object known but in fact gives the object known its reality. By way of contrast, in neoclassical theism God's mind is absolute in the sense that it is always related to all objects that can be known; it is independent of any factors which would prevent it from knowing some actuality or other. It is not the case that it is the fact that our knowledge is relative to the object known that makes our knowledge inferior to God's. Rather, our knowledge is inferior to God's because we are indistinctly related to the objects known and because we are related to so few objects. As Hartshorne puts the point regarding God's knowledge: "The concrete knowledge is relative, the generic abstract property of being-all-knowing is strictly absolute" (DR, 11). An oddity of the classical theistic view can be seen if the following question is asked: If God is absolute in both respects how can we know God as causally related to the world (à la St. Thomas or à la Swinburne)? That is, how can God be causally related to the world if

God is not really (i.e., internally) related to the world at all, if God has no relative being? A *purely* absolute God is a thing, not a person, even if absoluteness is an essential constituent of the supreme person (or persons, as in Trinitarian theology). The *religious* meaning of the absolute—the fact that God is completely reliable—is preserved in neoclassical theism. But what this reliability means is that God cannot fail to be related to creatures in a loving way (DR, 8, 15, 17, 21–22).

God is social in the sense that it is the union of the absolute and relative that constitutes the divine nature. The senses in which God is absolute are unique to God, but they are not all of God. The absolute (or nonrelative or independent or nontemporal) is God with something left out; it is not more but less than God in the sense that the abstract is less than the concrete. God's everlasting purpose is analogous to the underlying general purpose a human being may have throughout life, a "character" that a person exhibits throughout diverse circumstances. But, of course, a human being's character sometimes wavers and eventually comes to an end. To get rid of invidious absoluteness one need not get rid of God's absolute character (DR, 28, 32, 61, 80, 83):

> God himself is a supreme relativist, his absoluteness consisting in the ideally exhaustive way in which he relativizes his evaluations to all factors in the concrete actual world. This ideal relativity, absolute in its immutable adequacy, is the standard of all. (DR, 129)

The greatest conceivable being cannot suffer in the sense of being extinguished or being forced to be an inferior being, contra Patripassionism, even if the Patripassionists were correct in claiming that God's mode of existence at any particular time would include suffering if the creatures are suffering or, as is surely the case, if they have previously suffered. Divine memory of previous sufferings of creatures insures that there is always a tragic element in divinity. In effect, the option AR is no more contradictory than ar. For example, I constantly change and I am related to others through these changes, yet I retain some sort of identity and permanence through these changes; but God does so supremely. Consider the relations that God has if God knows. It is not a mere inability on our part to imagine a knowing so radically different from our knowing as that found in the God of classical theism. Rather, there is a plain contradiction in claiming that, on the one hand, the things known could have been different and, on the other, all is as it must be because God's knowledge cannot be an accident of the divine if God is absolute or *a se*, devoid of accidents (PS, 509–10). In the AR option (i.e., option II in schema 5 or case 2 in schema 6):

> the one and the many are reconciled, at the same time that the idea of perfection is given intelligible meaning. What is purely absolute cannot be relative, even in any part or factor of itself. But what is super-relative (reflexively transcendent) can be absolute in one aspect or abstract element of its being, and can also contain a world of relative things as its concrete parts. The parts determine, in interaction with the radically superior determining power of the whole-being, the accidental *de facto* state of that being (the contingent content of its experience). (RS, 122–23)

If religious believers persist in telling us, as many analytic theists encourage them to do, that God is eternally complete in all respects, so that no contribution can be made to divine experience, then we should continue to expect human beings to look elsewhere for the significance of their contributions, say to some version of a nondivine group mind like nationalism or communitarianism (RS, 66). We would be better served to notice in religion that an honest person can be equally honest at all times even though this honesty is exhibited in diverse circumstances: "Possibilities being inexhaustible (not all being compossible), perfection can be 'absolute,' non-reflexive, or a sheer maximum, only in those dimensions of value which are neutral to the distinction between actual and possible" (RS, 121). That is, it is possible to make a contribution to the divine life that has not yet been actualized.

D. THE ALLEGATION OF POLAR INEQUALITY

Some of what is claimed in Hartshorne's dipolar theism is acceptable to Gunton, but he objects to what he thinks is the priority

Hartshorne gives to the terms listed above on the right side of schema 2 (p. 20), including relativity. What we have seen Hartshorne say above in a positive way regarding absoluteness at the very least makes it easy to discredit Gunton's implied stance that Hartshorne concentrates almost exclusively on one pole. But Gunton's position (1978, 11–55) seems to be that even if Hartshorne *claims* some sort of polar equality in his dipolar theism, he cannot do so consistently.

Hartshorne admits that in concrete aspects God is relative, contingent, passive, and so forth. This logical and ontological "priority" given to God's relativity, arrived at primarily on the evidence of Hartshorne's admission that divine becoming is more inclusive than divine being, makes the absolute, as Gunton sees it, an empty abstraction. But there is nothing trivial in the fact that God is absolute because God is relative to the *whole* of reality, whereas other beings can have at best a limited relatedness to the world. God's all-embracing relativity is God's absoluteness. So also it is crucial to note that God's necessity consists in God's contingency, which means that God *always* has the possibility for change. God's contingent mode of existence must always be. God is eternal not by virtue of creating time but because God *always* exists in time; God's being consists in God's becoming; God "is" only in abstraction from the becoming that takes place in God. God is immutably mutable; divine immutability consists in God's always being uniquely mutable.

All of this shows at the very least that absoluteness plays an important role in Hartshorne's thought. That God is supremely passive, or supreme effect, Hartshorne would not deny. All that has happened or is happening is experienced by God; God includes, through divine knowing, the whole of process to date. The question is: Can Hartshorne's God also be supremely active, or the supreme cause? Gunton thinks not. God's supreme passivity or relativity makes God exclusively a God of the past and present in that it is only the past and present that have so far exerted an influence on God. God's causal "power" with respect to the future is of the weakest sort, according to Gunton; that is, God's causation lacks agency. Hartshorne's God only acts as an abstract cause, a lure, like Aristotle's gods or Plato's Form of the Good (as opposed to Plato's World-Soul or Demiurge). Ironically, despite Hartshorne's intentions he is accused of having returned to something similar to the abstract deity of classical theism or deism: rather than an unmoved mover, Hartshorne has a moved unmover, according to Gunton.

God's causality can either be efficient, in the sense that the past contains the possibilities for future action, or final, in the sense of God acting as an ideal model. But both types of causality are merely abstract, according to Gunton. Hartshorne has made God's activity into a mere divine map or statue. In schema 2 (p. 20) we can see absoluteness, activity, cause, and abstraction on the same side. More than a visual connection is to be found here for Gunton because Hartshorne's God is essentially passive, that is, effect; God's causal power is an abstraction from God's passivity or relativity. For example, God listens to us and feels our sufferings, and then if we pay attention to God's loving passivity or relativity, we are "caused" to lead better lives in imitation of God. Gunton seems to ask: Is that all there is? The weaker God's activity, the closer Hartshorne gets to Spinozistic pantheism; and exclusively abstract activity is indeed weak.

An immediate response to Gunton might be: Even if the absolute is an abstraction, that does not mean God is an abstraction in that absoluteness is only one pole of God's nature, and is not to be identified with God. Hartshorne is not a Hegelian, nor a Spinozist, as he makes abundantly clear in *Philosophers Speak of God*. And even if God does have abstract causality that does not necessarily exhaust God's causal power. In addition to the points made above and in this preliminary response, the following three points are in order.

1. Supposing Gunton to be correct that for Hartshorne God is merely an abstract agent, it should be noted that it is no small feat to be an abstract cause of supreme excellence. Even St. Augustine would admit that God's full knowledge of the Platonic forms is significant, and unique to God. Nor is it a small accomplishment to act as a perfect lure or map. Good lures (or maps, as any traveller knows!) are hard to come by, perfect ones harder still. It must be admitted that the initial subjective aim of the universe provided by Whitehead's God has been somewhat trimmed by Hartshorne, who believes that only the *most* abstract possibilities are nonemergent and

evidenced on the divine map. These would include, I think, the structure of creativity itself, and the more formal properties in mathematics, among other things. But I think it is premature to conclude that God as a lure or map in Hartshorne is of no consequence. An example may help. It is much easier for us in the West to be moved religiously by a Crucifixion scene painted by a Renaissance master than by the lines and shapes of Mondrian. Yet some might say that the terrible historical clarity of Western religious art could learn something from the complex geometrical patterns which are found in Islamic art, where art remains the felicitous handmaiden of contemplation of the divine, rather than its master. Plato's treatment of art in the *Philebus* is instructive in this regard.

2. But does God do anything else?, Gunton will ask. Yes. Disorder without limit would be unintelligible, severe disorder would be intelligible but ugly. Inflexible order may entice some, but divine decisions made in minute detail for creatures produces not beauty but monotony; chaos is avoided but freedom precluded. That is, what God does, according to Hartshorne, in addition to exerting divine abstract causality, is to limit disorder as an efficient cause to such an extent that beauty and freedom are possible for creatures. As Hartshorne often says, some of us do not wish for more than that. Once again, *making* it possible for human beings (and other creatures) to be free is no small accomplishment. It should be emphasized that God's concrete reality, as can be seen in schema 2, is potential, and the future is the only region for the potential to become actualized. God's *freedom* works against Gunton's belief that Hartshorne's God must be merely a God of the already actualized past and present. Becoming, change, and contingency are all fundamental features of God's concrete reality for Whitehead and Hartshorne, and these features presuppose the ability to *act* in some non-abstract way. (God's efficient causality here reminds us somewhat of that found in classical theism, but, as is well known (see OO) God is not omnipotent for Hartshorne in the same way that God is omnipotent for classical theists.)

3. Nevertheless, Gunton forces Hartshorne or his defender to be more precise with respect to the active-passive contrast. Given Hartshorne's claim that passivity refers to the way in which an indi-

vidual's activity takes account of, and renders itself appropriate to, the activities of others (PS, 2), one suspects that the need for a more precise use of language on Hartshorne's part is called for, otherwise the contrast will turn into an active-active redundancy. I will make some friendly amendments to Hartshorne's thought so as to defend him against Gunton's charges.

What Hartshorne is trying to do is incorporate excellent receptivity into the divine life, which most analytic, classical theists, including Gunton, still fail to do. The correlative to receptivity is not activity, for being excellently receptive *is* a type of activity. For example, one must work hard to listen to the argument of another, or sense her subtle pains, or hear the counterpoint in a difficult symphony. As Hartshorne makes clear, receptivity is passive *and* active. The correlative to excellent receptivity can perhaps be described as excellent impassibility *in the sense that* God prevents anything bad from happening which would stop God's excellent receptivity. Further, God acts abstractly as a lure for Hartshorne, but also concretely as a persuader, as in Whitehead. Excellent persuasion is active, but also passive because persuasion, as opposed to authoritarian dictation, is engaged in within the confines of a conversation where one must also listen. Dropping active-passive from the list in schema 2, we may refine it by adding:

impassibility	receptivity	
lure	persuader	(SCHEMA 7)

Gunton comes close at several places to points 1 and 2, and actually flirts with, but eventually rejects, what I suggest in point 3.[5] I suspect that the reason why he would still persist in asking "Is that all there is to divine activity?," is his own residual classical theistic belief regarding what meaningful divine activity is, although he would surely reject the designation as a classical theist. To use his own metaphors, he wants to hold out for a God who has the power and activity of a general over an army, the judiciary over a prisoner, or a lion over an antelope (44–46). But this falls precisely into classical theism, for generals and lions are not known for their receptivity in that they, along with the courts, are receptive only intermittently and imperfectly. No doubt, Gunton would also like to say that such a God is a God of peace, which is analogous to the classical theist's inconsistent desire for a God of love who yet remains an unmoved mover. A constant theme in Hartshorne's writings has been the connection between the worship of God as absolute/indifferent and the glorification of sheer force in politics. And this glorification of coercive power is not unconnected to male bias in theology.

One is reminded here of Whitehead's famous lines in "Peace" from the very end of *Adventures of Ideas*, quoted in chapter 1: "The *immediate* experience of [the union of the dream of youth and the harvest of tragedy] is the sense of Peace" (my emphasis). The sense of peace consists in an immediate experience. Mediation through brute power always keeps us at least one additional step away from peaceful, Godlike becoming-being. But it is just such mediation that Gunton wants God to exhibit, as in the military and carnivore metaphors. The dipolar process theist need not consider it a defect if God does not act in this way.[6]

In sum, there is polar equality in Hartshorne's dipolar theism because:

1. The abstractness of God as absolute is not to be *identified* with God, because God is also concrete.
2. Even God's abstract causality is not to be denigrated in that God is the only supremely excellent abstract cause.
3. God acts by concretely limiting disorder so as to avoid chaos, but not to the extent that such ordering leads to an aesthetic monotony or to the establishment of the notorious problems surrounding the possibility of human freedom found in classical theism.
4. God acts so as to prevent anything from happening which would stop God's excellent receptivity.
5. God acts as both a lure and a persuader, with neither attractiveness nor persuasion being purely passive.
6. God orders the world by giving free creatures an awareness, however dim, of their place in the cosmos.

Hartshorne makes it clear in "A Logic of Ultimate Contrasts" in *Creative Synthesis and Philosophic Method* that the two poles of each contrast in schema 2 (p. 20) stand or fall *together.* If either pole is real the contrast itself (both poles) is real. Though polarities are ultimate, it does not follow that the two poles are equal in *every* sense, as I have indicated previously regarding the more inclusive character of becoming in contrast to being. In *this* sense polar inequality is involved, but this polar inequality is part of a larger scheme wherein polar equality is the rule. Consider that Hartshorne finds the position of Plotinus and the classical theists inadequate in that, although it is true that without unity, simplicity, and absoluteness there is no sense to be made of multiplicity, complexity, and relativity, it is *equally* true that without multiplicity, complexity, and relativity there is no sense to be made of unity, simplicity, and absoluteness.

As was mentioned in the Introduction, it is a mistake to focus exclusively on the "neo" part of Hartshorne's neoclassical theism. Keith Ward provides a useful antidote to Gunton's tendency in this regard by emphasizing the "classical" element in neoclassical theism (although it must be admitted that Ward, unlike Hartshorne, is only willing to ascribe dipolarity to the way we talk about God and not necessarily to God):

> The notion of God as the creator, the necessary, omnipotent, omniscient ground of all finite beings, develops by reflection upon disclosures of transcendence in the general facts of continuous change, causality and order in the universe; and it functions to specify appropriate attitudes of dependence, reverence, awe and thankfulness in the believer throughout all his experience. The classical (Thomist) Christian concept of God belongs to this tradition of thought; and while it has sometimes seemed arid and abstract, over-concerned with purely intellectual considerations, and over-awed by the intellect of Aristotle, it does express a legitimate insight into the dependence of all things upon a transcendent reality. If the Thomist concept is modified by the doctrine of the dipolarity of God, and complemented by theistic insights drawn from other areas of experience, it remains as a compelling and perennially valid expression of the

> interpenetration of all things by a sustaining and incomprehensibly mysterious unconditioned reality.[7]

Although the "incomprehensibly mysterious" part of God can itself be overemphasized, as we will see in a later chapter, Ward is moving in the sort of direction that would make dialogue between analytic, classical theists and neoclassical theists fruitful.

E. PLATO, AGAIN

Thus far in this chapter I have tried to show that the options listed in schema 4 (p. 51) are an improvement over the attenuated list found in schema 3 (p. 50). Further, I have tried to show in schema 5 (p. 51) that the omission of option II by most analytic theists is not a trivial oversight. Schema 6 (p. 51) indicates that there is an option (case 2) in addition to that defended by classical theists (case 1) wherein God's absoluteness and God's status as the greatest conceivable being are preserved, an option largely (in some philosophers, entirely) ignored by classical theists, in general, and analytic, classical theists, in particular. The purpose of this final section of the chapter is to return to Plato to show that the views defended by analytic classical theists to the effect that God *is* the absolute, or is *a se* in every respect, or is *totaliter aliter*, or is independent in every respect, or is immutable in the classical theistic sense, and so on, are defective. (I take it that there is a family resemblance among all of these descriptions, along with case 1 in schema 6 and option I in schema 5.) That is, it is odd that analytic, classical theists adopt a sort of Platon*ism* without considering the arguments in Plato against seeing any being, even the divine one, as absolute unity. Plato's concept of being has implications for how we should conceive of the greatest conceivable being.

I will start this Platonic analysis with a famous quotation from the *Sophist*:

> I suggest that anything has real being that is so constituted as to possess any sort of power either to affect anything else or to be affected, in however small a degree, by the most insignificant agent, though it be only once. I am proposing as a mark to dis-

> tinguish real things that they are nothing but power. (*Legō dē to kai hopoianoun tina kektēmenon dynamin eit eis to poiein heteron hotioun pephykos eit eis to pathein kai smikrotaton hypo tou phaulotatou, kan ei monon eis hapax, pan touto ontōs einai. Tithemai gar horon horizein ta onta hōs estin ouk allo ti plēn dynamis.*)[8]

Whitehead held in *Adventures of Ideas* that it was in this quotation that "the height of his [Plato's] genius as a metaphysician" was initiated.[9] Quite a claim. When Plato says (through the Eleatic Stranger) that it is the *definition* (*horon*) of being that it exert power or be subjected to the exertion of power, he indicates that the essence of being is to be implicated in causal action on other beings, causal action which constitutes natural law as immanent rather than as externally imposed. I take it that this 'or' (*eite*) does not refer to mutual exclusivity between influence and being influenced. An omnipotent being who is pure cause would be a being with an unintelligible power over the powerless and the un-influence-able. But the import of this passage for philosophy of religion, if I understand it correctly, is that if being *is* power other beings (especially the divine one!) must be affected by the dynamic power of any particular being. Put simply, God cannot be an omnipotent pure cause in the classical theistic sense if being *is* power.

If Plato is defining being in terms of the agency in action *and* of the recipient of action then that which is not acted upon (e.g., the God of classical theism) is a mere "fixture" rather than real being. Action *and* reaction belong to the essence of being, though the mediation of life and mind is required to provide the medium of activity and passivity for the forms. This notion of a medium connecting the eternity of the forms with the fluency of becoming takes many shapes in Plato's dialogues and it is certainly true that there are passages in Plato that are inconsistent with the one under consideration in this section of the chapter. But Plato's genius here lies in his ability to provide a *tertium quid* between the imposition of law on the world found in classical theism, say, and Stoic, pantheistic immanence. That is, according to Whitehead, Plato's definition of being as power in the *Sophist* supplements his efforts in the *Timaeus* to find a moderate view between these (classical theistic and pantheistic) extremes wherein there is both: (i) an active and passive divine creator (who persuades the world and dialogues with it rather than delivers to it authoritarian dictation); and (ii) the action and reaction of the "created" constituents of reality.

A second text where Whitehead treats the concept of being as power is in *Modes of Thought.*[10] Here he emphasizes that "power" is the basis of our notion of "substance" (rather than the other way around) and that in both Plato and Locke one finds a prominent place for power in metaphysics, but neither of these thinkers *fully* developed the concepts of being *as* power and of power *as* the drive of the universe. Whitehead himself tries to develop these concepts fully even though his Platonism is usually associated with eternal objects, an association wherein we abstract from our experience brute particularity here and now; what remains is a residue which *seems* to have no essential reference to the passage of events. That is, Whitehead's appreciation for the concept of being as power led him away from the view of the universe as static, or better, away from the view that all transition was ultimately due to "transition" among individually static forms. Forms, for Whitehead, are explicitly referent to process even if they are only so implicitly in Plato. Life and motion, however, do play a crucial role in Plato's later metaphysics.[11]

The key problem in Whitehead concerns how we should conceive of what Plato calls a complete fact (*pantelōs onti—Sophist* 248E), which Whitehead thinks has seven main factors: the forms, physical elements, *psychē*, *erōs*, harmony, mathematical relations, and the receptacle. In fact, Whitehead thinks that all philosophy is an endeavor to obtain a coherent system out of these diverse factors. It must be admitted that Plato's earlier thought, in which static forms dominate, at times intrudes in his later dialogues.[12] But in the later dialogues, and especially in the *Sophist*, there is a greater sense of the complexity of the world in that being comes to be seen not as static but as individually creative (self-moved, as in the *Phaedrus* and *Laws*) when besouled, and effective in the aesthetic synthesis of others in any event.[13]

I would like to briefly amplify the above points by appeal to *Process and Reality*. Whitehead is clear regarding his "principle of relativity" (or again, his "reformed subjectivist principle") that it belongs to the nature of a being that it is potential for every becoming. In fact, in the "principle of process" itself Whitehead claims that the being of any actual entity is *constituted by* its becoming and its modifying agency; this is his way of putting Plato's very point that being is power. The stubborn facts of this world have power in Whitehead, as they do in Plato and Locke, specifically the power to have the constitutions of other particulars conditioned *and* the power to be conditioned by these other particulars. Once again, the theological implications of these two sorts of power have not been sufficiently digested by classical theists. As before, one of these implications is that God cannot be an immutable, omnipotent, pure cause.

Perhaps the most penetrating look at the Platonic passage in question from a process point of view comes in some neglected studies by the late Leonard Eslick. He (1955, 45) noticed the following:

> The definition of being as power (*dynamis*) in the *Sophist* is often considered as an anomaly not to be explained in Plato's thought. Or else it is simply passed by in silence by commentators rapt in the vision of immobile absolute forms, and unable to see any Plato except the mythical Plato of histories of philosophy. But it is *not* an anomaly or a passing fancy. It is simply an extension of the principles of the dialectical revolution which the *Parmenides* celebrates.

The revolution in the *Parmenides* to which Eslick refers centers around a consideration of the eight hypotheses in that dialogue. It is often noted that two very different kinds of unity are investigated in these hypotheses: the one-in-itself (*to hen haplōs*)—which is the subject of the first, fourth, sixth, and eighth hypotheses—and the one-as-being (*to hen on*)—which is the subject of the second, third, fifth, and seventh hypotheses. The one-in-itself, through Aristotle and the "Neoplatonists," became the basis for the God of classical theism in Philo, St. Augustine, and others. But it becomes apparent that the one-in-itself, a simply one *and nothing else*, cannot mingle and cannot even exist or participate in being, for this would make it not simply one but two in that the concepts "unity" and "being" are different. Further (and this is the point that may be of interest to analytic theists), nothing can be predicated of sheer unity in that it would then be a one among other ones that can have existence or anything else predicated of them, that is, it would then be a multiplicity.

The paradox regarding the one-in-itself of the *Parmenides* is that the famous Platonic *chōrismos* or separation seems to be both necessary to, yet fatal to, discourse and understanding in metaphysics. The resolution of this paradox is the work of the *Sophist*. The criticisms leveled against the one-in-itself are catastrophic for Eleatic metaphysics; for what Aristotle calls Plato's "original" theory of Forms, a theory in need of revision; and for classical theism. The Forms found in Plato's *Republic*, say, are now viewed as surds, just like the letters in Socrates' dream in the *Theaetetus*, of which nothing can be significantly affirmed or denied. Or as Plato says in the *Philebus* (63B), "For any class to be alone, solitary, and unalloyed is not altogether possible."

But if we take a one-as-being (as power) then a one can have relations (indeed it must have relations!) because it is not an absolute unity, rather it is a unity somehow connected to other unities; it is a one and a one among many; a same in relation to others; it is simultaneously being and (relative) nonbeing or otherness. These consequences follow for Plato not by eristic manipulation and equivocation but by real necessity. Plato admits the existence of both corporeal and incorporeal things, of both subjects and predicates. Being as power is claimed to be that which is inherent in both of these pairs, and it is the one-as-being (as power) that is the basis of neoclassical theism through Whitehead's and Hartshorne's critique and retrieval of Plato. It must be admitted that both Plato and Hartshorne could be wrong in theology, but by exploring Whitehead's and Hartshorne's retrieval of Plato's dynamism we might be less likely to (perhaps unwittingly) buy into the classical theistic appropriation of the static view of God also started by the Greeks.

Knowing and being known are *each* active and passive conditions. Being as known, insofar as it is known, is moved since it is acted upon. For something to be known by mind, it must be seen in a context of changing relationships which are other than itself. It is no longer completely at rest but partially "moved" relative to other real things. In other words, if there is no motion, if the forms do not mingle, there is no mind. On the other hand, if *all* things are in flux, mind is also destroyed. In the language of the *Cratylus* (440), to believe in universal flux is "to believe that all things leak like a pot, or imagine that the world is a man who has a running at the nose." If reality were universal change, knowledge would be impossible because every term would resolve into its relations. Being (with God as supreme being) is therefore, once again, between the Scylla and Charybdis of universal rest and universal motion, between Parmenides and Heraclitus (the two hiding places for the sophist). Like a crying child one must plead for both the immovable and the movable (*Sophist* 249c–d). Being is a third, in addition to motion and rest. If God is or has being, then these criticisms of completely unified or absolute being-in-itself cannot be ignored by theists who claim that God is absolute but not relative, permanent but not changing, unified with no multiplicity of parts, and so on.

Our discourse, when seen as a power, is derived from the interweaving of forms,[14] but this does not mean that Plato has completely abandoned the doctrine of *chōrismos*. Being participates in *both* the form "in relation" and the form "in itself." As Plato puts the point in the *Seventh Letter* (343b–c): "there are two separate things, the real essence and the quality, and the soul seeks to know not the quality but the essence." He goes on to say that knowledge is defective *in the sense that* we can never get to the essence, to the one-in-itself, only to the (relative) nonbeing that the essence has in a context of relations with others. As Eslick (1955, 49) puts the point:

> Predicates in Platonic dialectic are always and only masks worn by subjects which never appear in discourse. . . . Platonic dialectic is the theatre in which all actors, like those in Greek tragedy, wear masks.[15]

If being is conceived in a univocal, Parmenidean way such that it cannot admit of intrinsic difference, then all being is one. By way of contrast, Plato's view by the time of the *Sophist* seems to have been that being is dyadic: it is *both* indivisible, static unity and a divisible, dynamic whole of parts; it is *both* in itself and in relation. Once again, this mature Platonic, dipolar conception of being has implications for how we should conceive the greatest conceivable being. Because no being, not even God, can be wholly self-enclosed and separated in complete isolation, it must have some power to affect and be affected by others. Every thing that exists is, in a way, a one-in-itself, yet although each is *a* one none is *the* one in that each one is reflected in the Platonic material principle of relative nonbeing or otherness. As Eslick puts the point, "The Spinozist maxim that all determination is negation is a supreme principle of Platonic dialectic."[16]

Plato was far and away Whitehead's favorite philosopher and Whitehead believed his own metaphysics to be a systematic development of Plato's general point of view.[17] The same is true for Hartshorne. It is in the passage under consideration in the present section of the chapter, however, that we can appreciate why it is good Platonism to believe, as Whitehead and Hartshorne do, that there is nothing in the real world which is merely an inert fact, and that there is an interpenetration of "being" and "becoming." Process Platonism in general seeks permanence in the facts of becoming. But Eslick's interpretation of the passage in question also emphasizes a strong analogy between each being's (including God's) absoluteness or one-in-itself and the *Ding-an-sich* in Kant. Both Plato and Kant wanted to save the knowledge they held to be certain by appeal to, *but only by critical appeal to*, the one-in-itself or the *Ding-an-sich* (to the extent that there is an analogy between these two). As before, being has both an in-itself and an in-relation character.

If the term "metaphysics" refers, as Hartshorne thinks it does, to the non-contingent features of reality, such that any experience confirms these features but none falsifies them, then "being is power" is a metaphysical claim. Its scope is as wide as reality itself, from the least significant creature to God. But if it is true that being is power, then it is not only the concept of being that is Platonic but also the concept of God (see MV and PC).

In their ultimate individuality beings, if they are instances of dynamic power, can be influenced by God, but they cannot be sheerly coerced. As Hartshorne puts the point, "power is influence, perfect power is perfect influence." Or again, to have perfect power over all individuals is not to have all power. The greatest possible power (i.e., perfect power) over individuals cannot leave them powerless if being *is* power, hence even perfect power must leave something for others to decide. In a way even passivity is a type of activity, as we have seen; it is that sort of activity that takes account of, and renders itself appropriate to, the activities of others. Hence we can understand why Hartshorne claims that:

> power must be exercised upon something, at least if by power we mean influence, control; but the something controlled cannot be absolutely inert, since the merely passive, that which has no active tendency of its own, is nothing; yet if the something acted upon is itself partly active, then there must be some resistance, however slight, to the "absolute" power, and how can power which is resisted be absolute? (MV, 89; also xvi, 14)

If being is power then any relation in which one of the related things was wholly powerless would be a relation in which "the thing" was absolutely nothing: an impossibility. No matter how lowly a thing may be, if it is a real individual it reacts upon things; cells, molecules, and electrons do not provide exceptions to the view of being as power (MV, 198–99).

Hartshorne agrees that God has universal relevance, and this largely due to divine omnibenevolence, hence there is nothing completely uninfluenced or completely outside of divine influence or love. But this Platonic view of a God who benevolently creates *ex hyle* (from beings already in existence) is a far cry from the view of God who omnipotently creates things *ex nihilo*, a view held by most analytic theists. We can utter the words "God is omnipotent" or "God has all power" but we cannot really conceive what these words mean if there are other beings in existence, as Hartshorne eloquently argues:

> That God cannot "make us do" certain things does not "limit" his power, for there is no such thing as power to make nonsense true, and "power over us" would not be power over *us* if our natures and actions counted for nothing. No conceivable being

> could do more with us than God can . . . and so by definition his power is perfect, unsurpassable. But it is a power unique in its ability to adjust to others. (MV, 294; also 205, 232, 244)

In short, if God is the greatest conceivable being then it makes sense to attribute to God all greatnesses, both those associated with absoluteness and relativity, and both those associated with activity and passivity. It is really Gunton and others who lean in the direction of classical theism who are open to the charge of polar inequality. By *absolutizing God* as a *purely active* being who has omnipotent power, classical theists once again run into the following problem: if it is the case that being *is* power then *omni*potent power would be an unintelligible power over the powerless and the un-influence-able (IO, 367; also see OO).

A recent exchange between Stephen Davis and David Ray Griffin illustrates well what is at stake here. According to Davis' non-Platonic stance, the process God must be weak enough to be incapable of unilaterally preventing evil from existing, but the question emerges as to whether a being this impotent is a being worthy of worship. Rather, for Davis, this is a being who should be pitied. (Hartshorne's way of putting the point is to say, along with Nicholas Berdyaev, that God is tragic.) Griffin's Hartshornian/Platonic response to Davis is in the following terms:

> The suggestion of process theology is that this experienced fact about our world [that all actualities seem to have self-determining power which cannot be totally overridden] be assumed to be a metaphysical or necessary fact, one that would hold in any world God could create. This is of course an unprovable speculative hypothesis. But the contrary idea that there could be a world with creatures totally devoid of self-determining power is at least equally speculative. In fact—and this is the main point—it is even more speculative, since it is devoid of any experiential grounding. We have no experience of a world totally devoid of freedom or self-determining power. . . . Should there not be a presumption in favour of the less speculative hypothesis?[18]

Further, regarding Davis' criticism of Hartshornian/Platonic theodicy, Griffin (1989) says the following, and in a nonhistrionic way, I think:

> "There is no good news in the news that God is trying very hard and just might succeed." But Davis is by implication saying: "It is better news that the universe is under the control of a being who could have prevented Hiroshima and Auschwitz, but chose not to; who could have prevented the suffering of starving children throughout the world, but chose not to; who could have prevented the extermination of Native Americans, and the enslavement of Blacks in America and South Africa, but chose not to; who could have prevented the occurrence of such diseases as cancer, AIDS, and mental retardation, but chose not to. Your life is in the control of such a being. Rejoice!" In comparison with such a "gospel," is it such bad news to hear that the creator of our universe, who had the power to bring creatures such as us out of nucleons and electrons, is totally *for* us, constantly seeking our wholeness, but that whether we realize that wholeness is finally up to the way we respond?

It should now be clear that there is a strong connection between dipolar theism and divine power. The sort of divine power defended by analytic, classical theists tends to be what can be called linear or unilateral power, where God influences others, but God cannot be influenced. That is, the aim of this power is to create the largest possible effect while being minimally (if at all) influenced by others. To be influenced by someone else is, on this view, a sign of weakness. By way of contrast, the neoclassical view is that the "size" (to use Bernard Loomer's word) of God is diminished as long as power is associated exclusively with initiative and aggressiveness and with a largely nonrelational view. Further, the unilateral view of power, which has unfortunately dominated political and economic thought as well as theological thought, is antithetical to many of the deeper dimensions of the religious life.

Relational power is not antithetical to these deeper dimensions, however, in that one's size and strength (again to use Loomer's words) are enhanced to the degree that one can be influenced by another without losing one's own sense of independence. "The stature of the individual who can let another exist in his or her own creative freedom is larger than the size of the individual who insists that others must conform to his own purposes and understandings"

(Loomer 1976, 18). (As Casey Stengel said after the team he managed won the World Series, "I could hardly have done it without the players.") It is crucial for Christians, in particular, to note that Jesus stands at the bottom of unilateral power, but at the apex of relational power. From what has been argued above it is clear that just as being is an abstract aspect of becoming, so also unilateral power is a special case arising out of the more pervasive relational power of God (see Mesle 1983).

CHAPTER THREE

Divine Embodiment

A. INTRODUCTION

Monopolar, classical theists tend to exaggerate the importance not only of divine immutability and absoluteness, but also of divine nonmateriality. It will be the purpose of this chapter to examine the nonmateriality-materiality contrast.

It is not surprising that Alston is one of the few analytic philosophers who have directly challenged Hartshorne's concept of God. Alston was a student of Hartshorne's at the University of Chicago and has shown published evidence (Alston 1951, 1952) of knowing Whitehead's work well. Further, Alston has twice published in edited volumes dedicated to Hartshorne's thought, (1964-b 1984). The 1984 essay is also a chapter in Alston's 1989 book, *Divine Nature and Human Language*. In this chapter I will look carefully at the former article regarding Alston's indication of the need for divine embodiment, albeit without a commitment on Alston's part to the concept of divine embodiment. Then I will consider Swinburne's slightly more favorable view of divine embodiment from a Hartshornian point of view. In a later chapter I will treat the second article by Alston, in which he makes more concessions to Hartshorne than any other analytic theist, and this perhaps because he has read large parts of—but not all of, as we will see—Hartshorne's work. However, Alston also has many criticisms of Hartshorne's thought, as we will see in the later chapter. His criticisms are based on his own Thomistic-Whiteheadian view, strange as that sounds.

In the present chapter I will treat Alston and Swinburne, but then I will treat the history of philosophy/ideas so as to indicate the problems involved in assuming, as most analytic theists do, that God is purely immaterial. Jürgen Moltmann will be favorably considered regarding the primitive belief in divine embodiment; Richard Mohr will also be considered, but not so favorably as Moltmann, regarding divine embodiment in Plato; Friedrich Solmsen, I will allege, is, like Moltmann, a better source to consider in the effort to get analytic theists to take divine embodiment seriously. The chapter will conclude with a treatment of Plotinus and Origen on the World-Soul so as to ease the transition from the ancient view of divine embodiment to a Chrisian defense of that concept.

B. THE ELUCIDATION OF RELIGIOUS STATEMENTS

In Alston's widely read book *Philosophy of Language* (1964a, xi, 7), he makes it clear that the central problem in philosophy of language concerns the question, "What is it for a linguistic expression to have a certain meaning?" In philosophy of religion Alston is likewise concerned with what it means to say "God is X." (Much depends on what "X" refers to.) And in Alston's essay with the title to this section of the chapter, he makes it clear that it is essential for any view of religion that God make effective contact with God's worshippers *and vice versa*. This claim pushes one immediately into a consideration of divine attributes in a neoclassical way, as does Alston's view that divine attribute statements depend on action statements for their meaning, for example, to call God merciful is to imply that God can perform acts of forgiveness. The task of elucidation of religious statements falls into two parts, according to Alston, corresponding to subject and predicate. But the problem of explaining the subject term is not to be distinguished from the problem of explaining the meaning of certain key predicate terms. This view is at least compatible with, and actually shows a great deal of similarity to, the process view that being can be described only in terms of becoming (1964a, 429–30).

Further, Hartshorne's ideas that God be the prime exemplification of, not an exception to, metaphysical principles, and that our language about God not stretch analogy to the breaking point, are at least compatible with, and in many ways very similar to, Alston's views. The latter contends (in this early book, at least) that the objective reference of God-sentences is borrowed from the prior application of their predicate terms to human beings. For example, to explain "God forgives our sins," it is understandable that we begin with human beings forgiving each other. We have public tests regarding the truth or falsity of the claim that "Jones has forgiven me." Once we have mastered the latter sort of sentence, we can make sense of "God has forgiven me" even in the absence of such tests. Hartshorne would agree here as well, but he would be sceptical of the position that some would take at this point to the effect that it is our experience of, or language about, contingent events that justifies a belief in a God whose existence is necessary (Alston 1964a, 430–32).

The connection between Alston's philosophy of language and his view of divine embodiment can be seen as follows. When one says "My mother forgave me," one implies that she performed some appropriate action essentially connected with bodily activity (speaking, writing, smiling, caressing, etc.). But when a predicate like "forgives" is applied to an immaterial God, no such implication holds. If God is pure spirit, as classical theists hold, then these questions must be answered: In what sense is the term "forgives" being used when applied to God? In what way is the theological use of terms different from anthropological use? Alston's initial response to these questions is to treat three ways to explain to a puzzled listener what is meant by a phrase like "He blew his top." The first is to provide a literal way of saying the same thing that is said nonliterally. For example, if a person did not know what it meant to say "He blew his top," one might say to him instead "He suddenly became very angry." In the second instance, one could describe a situation where a term could theoretically be used in a derivative sense and instruct the pupil to find certain common features, as when sensitive readers grasp fresh metaphors in poetry (1964a, 432–34). The problem with the first approach in religion, according to at least the early Alston, is that there can be no literal way of talking about God. We can introduce new terms (e.g., "divine" or "holy") which are not derivative from nontheological use, but like "God" their use has to be explained in some way by bringing in words whose primary use is elsewhere. And the second approach is defective in religion because there are no reliable ways of showing someone a case of God forgiving or commanding or making. We can describe such a case, but that involves using words in the way we are trying to explicate.

In the third approach one would make explicit the features common to two things already known, say to a top blowing off a boiler and a person becoming violently angry. But when we try to isolate the common features of a human being forgiving another and God forgiving another we are left with a difficult task if, in God's case, we remove all bodily activity involved in forgiving, commanding, or making. Because of Gilbert Ryle and others, Alston refuses to appeal to a ghostly double of overt, bodily action to resolve the issue. But Alston is quick to point out that in the "flush of victory" over the "hoary prejudices" associated with dualism we should not lose sight of the fact that there commonly are private mental states accompanying overt, bodily actions and sometimes an action is preceded by an unobservable decision. That is, even though Alston does not want to be thought of as a cosmic dualist, with the "other" world a ghostly double of "this" one, he is nonetheless tempted to retreat to a region of private accompaniments to explain divine forgiving, and the like. He admits that "pure thought thinking itself" is of no use to religion, but he thinks that one *might* sometimes avoid difficulties by using the "whittle-down method" whereby we asymptotically approach a purely immaterial God who privately rehearses acts of forgiveness (1964a, 434–37).

Alston is clear, however, that this approach is fundamentally flawed as well. Believing in a whittled-down God does not help us to know if and when God really forgives us, nor does it help us know how to address God (437–40):

> The basic trouble is that in removing overt behavior from forgiving, commanding, etc. (and even more if we remove temporal sequence too) we have taken these terms out of the language

> game in which they primarily function without replacing it by another. In etherealizing these action concepts we snip off the rules which normally govern their use—rules which stipulate what is relevant evidence for an application of the term, what constitutes believing that the term applies in a certain case, in what contexts it is appropriate to use the term, to what attitudes, if any, an application of the term commits one, etc. So long as we merely explain God's forgiveness, as being like human forgiveness except that there is no bodily activity, we have taken away an essential condition of the literal use of "forgives" without indicating what is to be put in its place. At this point we have but a fragment of a meaning. (440–41)

Despite the fact that there are other ranges of discourse in which similar problems arise (e.g., scientific explanations couched in terms of unobservable entities conceived by analogy with observable ones), there seems to be something especially problematic with religious discourse *if* one assumes that God is purely immaterial:

> when we go from an observable human being to a non-observable sub-system of the psyche, or from an embodied action to an action of a purely immaterial being, the usual sort of rules is no longer applicable, and we are forced to put something in their place explicitly. An immaterial person isn't simply another kind of person in the way a disagreeable or a talented person is. (442)

Clarification of talk about God, Alston thinks, awaits progress on this task of learning how to deal with the need for divine embodiment.

C. SWINBURNE ON LIMITED DIVINE EMBODIMENT

Several steps toward the clarification of the divine immateriality/materiality issue that Alston desires, can be taken by comparing Swinburne and Hartshorne on the question, "Does God have a body?" Swinburne gives two different responses to this question, responses which appear, at times, in conflict. The purpose of this section of the chapter is to defend one of these responses at the expense of the other. That is, I will defend, and expand on, Swinburne's notion of a limited divine embodiment. In this effort I will be borrowing loosely from Hartshorne, who also defends the idea of a divine body. As Hartshorne puts the issue: In a way, all talk about God short of strict univocity contains *some* negativity, in that God does not exist, know, love, etc., *exactly* as we do. With regard to the divine body, however, most theists—not Swinburne—have allowed this negativity to run wild.[1]

The initial response Swinburne gives to the question, Does God have a body?, can be found at several points throughout his trilogy (1977, 1979, 1981). This response suggests that God is a person without a body; God is a spirit. "That God is a person," he claims (1977, 1, 2, 51, 99), "yet one without a body, seems the most elementary claim of theism." What partly makes the claim elementary is the fact that most Western theists have held it, but Swinburne also holds this position for at least seven other reasons. First, the term "body" has an ordinary and nonambiguous use outside of theology, such that if this term is used analogously in too loose a way in theology one runs the risk of making difficult any proofs for the coherence of theism (1977, 50, 61). Second, the claim "God is not embodied" is a denial that there is any *limited* volume of matter such that God can control only it, and knows goings-on elsewhere only by their effects on it (as we will see, Swinburne leaves open the possibility here for a different sort of divine embodiment) (1979, 90–91).

Third, because personal identity (even in human beings) is not due to bodily continuity, and is unanalyzable into conjunctions or disjunctions of other observable properties, God's personal identity does not require a body (1977, 113, 119). Fourth, God does not need sense organs to see things, as Newton suggested in saying that space was God's sensorium.[2] Whereas human beings see directly images conveyed by sensory nerves and only see external objects indirectly through these images, God "sees" objects themselves directly (1977, 166–67). Fifth, to be embodied is to be limited to parts of the world through which intentions are executed and knowledge acquired. Hence a body is a (mere) instrument, such that an embodied agent is one whose conscious processes interact with instrumental, bodily processes (1979, 160).

Sixth, God's control of the world is immediate, hence God is non-embodied. It is for this reason that Swinburne would reject Hume's suggestion that, on the evidence of the argument from design, we postulate an embodied God. For Swinburne (1979, 149), dissimilarities between effects lead to the postulation of dissimilarities between causes. That is, the evidence of order in nature is too vast and complex to infer a giant, embodied man, as it were, as cause of this order. And seventh, if God's knowledge depended on the proper functioning of intermediaries (e.g., eyes and ears), divine omniscience might be compromised if God did not correct these malfunctioning intermediaries (1977, 222–23).

The issue of divine embodiment is complicated somewhat, however, in some key texts (1977, 102–4, 106–7; 1979, 48–50) where Swinburne gives an apparently different response to the question, Does God have a body? For Swinburne, there are five things being said when one claims that "this is my body":

1. Disturbances in it cause me pain, whereas disturbances in a table are unfelt by me.
2. I feel the inside of this body, as in the emptiness of this stomach.
3. I can move directly many parts of this body, whereas I can only move other things indirectly through this body.
4. I look out on the world from where this body is.
5. My thoughts and feelings are affected by goings-on in this body, as when I drink too many beers.[3]

Swinburne states without argument that God is not embodied in senses 1 and 5. The tradition of classical theism apparently makes argument unnecessary, for Swinburne, on these two points. (In fact, in *The Existence of God*, as opposed to *The Coherence of Theism*, Swinburne either omits 1 altogether or includes it in 5.) He takes an agnostic stance regarding 2 in that we do not know if God "feels" anything in any sense of the term close to our usual understanding of what feeling is. And he is sceptical regarding 4. Although God knows without inference about any state of the world, there is no one place from which God looks out on the world. But Swinburne is more than willing to admit that God is embodied in sense 3. In that God is supposed to be able to move any part of the universe directly, God can make any part move as a basic action.[4]

Herein lies God's limited embodiment, as well as a clue as to how to respond to Alston's challenge, and regarding how we can perhaps render consistent Swinburne's different responses to the question, Does God have a body? The initial response is not to be taken as a denial of divine embodiment altogether, but rather as a denial of:

> more substantial embodiment, and above all the denial that God controls and knows about the material universe by controlling and getting information from one part directly, and controlling and getting information from other parts only by their being in causal interaction with the former part. (1977, 103–4)

Swinburne thinks that this notion of limited divine embodiment may well be compatible with classical theism, even if classical theism often seems to agree only with what I have called Swinburne's initial response. For example, although St. Thomas never alleges that God is in any way embodied, he does equivalently talk about divine omnipresence, and this because he believes that God controls *all* things and knows about *all* things. As Swinburne notes, the medievals were careful to rebut the suggestion that God had in any literal sense a dwelling in "heaven."[5] Nonetheless, Swinburne is aware of the fact that classical theists have tended to overemphasize the extent of God's nonembodiment, an overemphasis which conflicts with some of traditional theism's other claims, for instance, that God acts in the world and keeps it in some sort of order. Swinburne (1977, 107) believes that "in many ways God is not related to a material object as a person is to his body, but in other ways he is so related." That is:

> God is embodied in the very limited respect that he can move and has knowledge of all parts of the material universe. But the claim that God has no body is the denial of more substantial embodiment, and above all, the denial that God controls and knows about the material universe by controlling and getting information from one part directly and other parts indirectly. So when the theist claims that he is arguing to a non-embodied agent, we must bear in mind that it would be perhaps less mis-

> leading to say that he is arguing to the existence of a rational agent who is far less embodied (tied down to matter) than we are, but one embodied to the extent and in the ways which I have just described. (1979, 49–50)

One wonders, however, if Swinburne's notion of limited divine embodiment is sufficient to avoid some of the perennial problems found in classical theism. Obviously Swinburne is correct in not using "M-predicates" (those applicable to material bodies) like "weighs ten pounds" when speaking of God. Instead, he refers to God by way of "P-predicates" (those applicable to persons). But when one looks at Swinburne's *own* examples of P-predicates it seems doubtful that they can be applied to God without a stronger notion of divine embodiment than Swinburne is willing to defend; for instance, "is in pain" (1977, 100, 106). (In the human case, even psychological pain depends on the existence of a functioning central nervous system.) Swinburne sidesteps the problem of how a God who is only embodied in a limited sense can also feel pain by denying that God suffers or experiences pain, à la classical theism. This denial is made in spite of the fact that God cares for suffering creatures, a care which itself leads to a vicarious sort of suffering, unless, of course, "care" is used in a too loosely analogous or equivocal fashion (a situation Swinburne would otherwise want to avoid).

D. HARTSHORNE'S STRONGER VIEW

Hartshorne's stronger defense of divine embodiment would enhance many of Swinburne's best insights, I think, and it would help respond to Alston's challenge regarding the need for clarity on the issue of divine embodiment. (However, Hartshorne would not, because of his denial of the substantial self, refer to his stronger sense of divine embodiment as a defense of a more "substantial" divine embodiment.) Consider that because embodied animal individuals like human beings must, to maintain their integrity, adapt to their environment, mortality is implied. But if we imagine an omnibenevolent and omnipresent God (or what Plato and Hartshorne would call the World-Soul), we must not consider an environment external to deity, but an internal one: the world-body of the world-mind. This cosmic, divine "animal" has such an intimate relation to its body that it must also have ideal ways of perceiving and remembering its body such that it can identify the microindividuals it includes.

We can only tell when cells in our finger have been burned by the fire; we cannot identify the microindividuals as such. Hartshorne notes that in the *Republic* (462c–d) Plato makes it clear that if there is pain in one's finger (note, not the whole hand) the entire community (*pasa hē koinōnia*) of bodily connections is hurt; the organized unity of the individual is such that when one part is hurt there is feeling of pain in the man as a whole (*holē*) who has pain in his finger. Plato shares with Hartshorne the following analogy[6]

S1 : S2 : : S2 : S3 **(SCHEMA 8)**

where S1 stands for microscopic or cellular sentiency, S2 for sentiency per se or sentiency in an embodied individual, and S3 for divine sentiency or feeling or caring. The *uni*verse is a society or an organism (a Platonic World-Soul) of which one member (the Platonic Demiurge) is preeminent, just as human beings or other embodied animals are societies of cells, of which the mental part is preeminent. In effect, it makes sense to say both that the cosmos is ensouled and that God is embodied.

Hartshorne has taken the World-Soul as a clue for present philosophizing about the divine body. For example, if God is omnibenevolent then God cares for the world, hence each new divine state harmonizes itself both with its predecessor and with the previous state of the cosmos. This is analogous to a human being or an animal harmonizing itself with its previous experience and bodily state, but with a decisive difference. The human being must hope that its internal and external environment will continue to make it possible for it to survive, whereas God has no such problem in that there is no external environment for God, as Swinburne would admit. But the differences between God and human beings–animals (e.g., God knows the microindividuals included in the divine life and God has no external environment) should not cloud the important similarities (e.g., the facts that self-change is integral to soul at all levels and that the soul-body or organic analogies used to understand God do not preclude the person-person analogy, which allows a link between human beings and the divine person, a link integral to Swinburne's thought).

The most important similarity lies in the fact that one's bodily cells are associated, at a given moment, with one as a conscious, supercellular singular, just as all lesser beings are associated with the society of singulars called God. In the case of the divine individual, where all entities are ideally experienced, there can be no envy of others or conflict with them in that they are integral to the divine goodness. Less completely are an animal's cells internal to the individual in that neither we nor other animals are aware of individual cells as such. Yet bone cells in a finger are less internal and less fully possessed by an individual than are the brain cells in that the latter unlike the former last throughout life. These considerations regarding divine inclusiveness also explain why the cosmos could not be held together and ordered by a malevolent God or by a plurality of gods, as in Hume, in that these deities are always partly divided within or among themselves, and are incapable of an objective grasp of truth. The cosmos, if in fact it is a cosmos or a *uni*verse, can be held together only by an all-sympathetic coordinator. That is, God is the individual and organic (hence embodied) integrity of the world, which is otherwise a concatenation of myriad parts or a mere machine in need of a machine-maker, as Swinburne would seem to admit.

Belief in a World-Soul (God) is connected with a belief in a world-body, which is superior to our bodies because—assuming that God exists necessarily—there is nothing internal to it (e.g., cancer cells) which could threaten its continued existence, even if the divine body is spatially finite. Further, our bodies are fragmentary, as in a human infant's coming into the world as a secondary lifestyle expressing its feelings upon a mother's system, which already had a basic order among its cells; whereas the divine body does not begin to exist on a foundation previously established. When an animal body dies, its individual lifestyle no longer controls its members, yet the result is not chaos, but simply a return to the more pervasive types of order expressive of the cosmic mind-body. The World-Soul is aware of the divine body, and can vicariously suffer with its suffering members, but it cannot suffer in the sense of ceasing to exist due to an alien force. An individual can influence it (how else can we understand divine love and goodness?), but none can threaten it.

Not even brain death can threaten the divine body because the soul-body analogy cannot be pushed to the point where a divine brain is posited. The contrast between the brain and a less essential bodily part only makes sense because an animal has an external environment. Consider that the divine body does not need limbs to move about, for it is its own place, space merely being the order among its parts, as Swinburne might agree, in his favorable use of Newton. The divine body does not need a digestive system or lungs to take in food or air from without in that there is no "without." So it is with all organs outside the central nervous system, which, as we know but Plato did not, is the organ that adapts internal activities to external stimuli, a function which is not needed in the inclusive organism. Swinburne is close to Hartshorne here when he suggests that God's power is not dependent on having a brain as opposed to having some other (instrumental) organ.[7]

The only function of the divine body is to furnish the World-Soul with awareness of, and influence on, its bodily members. In Hartshorne's refined use of the animal/body analogy, although there is no special part of the cosmos recognizable as a nervous system as opposed to some other bodily part, every creaturely individual becomes, *as it were*, not so much a finger or some other bodily part, but a brain cell *directly* related to the World-Soul.

I emphasize the word 'directly' so as to show once again the similarity between Swinburne and Hartshorne, even though there is at least one major point that divides them. For Swinburne there is no overriding reason for God to make a universe. That is, there is no overriding reason for God to have even a limited embodiment. But this would imply that there is no overriding reason for God to be omniscient or omnibenevolent. Without a world there would be nothing for God to know except divine thoughts and nothing for God to love except divinity, whatever this means. (One might mention the Trinity in this regard, but the second and perhaps the third person of the Trinity can be understood only by reference to the world.) The gap between Swinburne and Hartshorne on this point is partially bridged by Swinburne's admission that, even though there are no overriding reasons for God to have a world (i.e., have a limited embodiment), there are nonetheless good reasons for having a world. For Swinburne (1979, 130–31, 147), if God has a body it must be beautiful and orderly, allowing some ugliness so as to teach human beings the aesthetic merits of different states of affairs.

In sum, I agree with Swinburne that divine embodiment includes sense 3 (see p. 83), and that embodiment in senses 2 and 4 should not be predicated of God. However, much more coherence can be given to the notions of omnipresence and omnibenevolence, and to theism in general, if we also claim that God is embodied in senses 1 and 5. My disagreement with Swinburne is largely due to the fact that I take Plato's theism seriously, whereas he largely (and perhaps unwittingly, like many other classical theists) follows Aristotle.

As we saw earlier, it is strange that although Plato developed a dipolar categorial scheme (where form is contrasted to matter, etc.), his cosmology is ultimately a psychical monism, where the World-Soul holds the cosmos together as a *uni*verse. Aristotle, however, developed a single categorial scheme of embodied form. Paradoxically, from this emphasis on embodied form, Aristotle ultimately constructed a more vicious dualism than any ever envisaged by Plato, in that Aristotle's divinities are *completely* self-sufficient entities, unmoved, and separated from all change, multiplicity, and embodiment. The influence of Aristotle's nonembodied gods, I allege, extends long after St. Thomas, and even touches Swinburne, as in his reluctance to admit anything other than a limited divine embodiment.

E. SOME COMMENTATORS

As we saw in chapters 1 and 2, most analytic theists have ignored Hartshorne's thought regarding the issue of divine immutability. The same is true regarding the issue of divine immateriality. Alston at least raises the question as to whether it is possible to consistently defend the view that God is pure spirit, but he does not answer this question. Swinburne does in fact respond to the question, Does God have a body?, but his reply consists in only a limited notion of divine embodiment, as we have seen. Once again, the monopolar prejudice has a deleterious effect on classical theists when they deal with the issue of divine immateriality/materiality. As a supplement to schema 2 (p. 20), I would illustrate the divine immateriality/materiality correlatives as in schema 9:

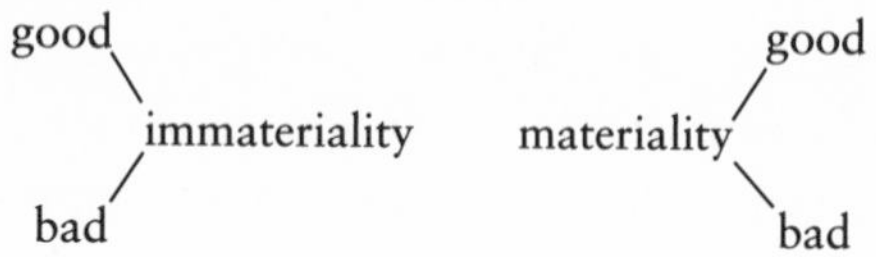

```
good                                    good
    \                                  /
     immateriality        materiality
    /                                  \
bad                                     bad    (SCHEMA 9)
```

By way of contrast, classical theists see the issue in much simpler (less enumerative) terms:

immateriality   materiality   (SCHEMA 10)

with divine immateriality being largely good and divine embodiment being largely bad. As before, all talk about God short of strict univocity involves *some* negativity, in that God does not know, love, and so forth, *exactly* as we do, but there is no need to allow this negativity to run wild when the issue is divine embodiment.

Keith Ward helps matters a bit when he wonders whether there *has to be* a huge distinction between cosmic monism and a belief in God's distinctness from the world. For example, those monists who hold that particular things in the universe are appearances of the Real nonetheless *distinguish* between illusion and the Real, in which there is no illusion. And Christians who say that the world exists gratuitously through a free act of the divine will nonetheless admit that the world exists in *some* sort of relation to God. The way cosmic monists state their case, if they are also pantheists, usually does conflict with the view of those who defend God's distinctness from the world, if they are classical theists. But there is no necessary conflict between cosmic monism and God's distinctness from the world (see Ward 1974, 174–75).

Another way to put the issue is to say, along with Robert Oakes (1987, 58–60) at one stage in his career, that there is strong or sufficient, if not conclusive, reason for holding that theism is compatible with the view that contingent things are aspects or modifications of God. Theism is also compatible with the view that God is in some way distinct from the cosmos; in fact, this distinctness is essential to theism. That is, Oakes sees as the task for theism to find some sort of synthesis of Hartshorne's notion of God as an all-inclusive reality with the notion of God as in some way distinct from the body of the world. It is questionable whether Oakes is correct in claiming that a strong notion of divine embodiment entails pantheism, and it is even more questionable whether 'pantheism' is compatible with 'traditional theism,' as he alleges. But he is correct, along with Ward, in avoiding the false dichotomy between pantheism and classical theism. As we have seen, in that both of these views share the monopolar prejudice they do not really exhaust the theistic alternatives.

William Wainwright (1987, 72–87) is another analytic theist who takes the possibility of divine embodiment seriously, but he, unlike Alston, Swinburne, Ward, and Oakes, tries to trace the notion of *pure* divine immateriality back to its origins to see why the hyperbole started. He is alone among analytic theists in claiming that the Platonic model enables us to speak of the God-world relation as a relation between soul and body without sacrificing what is best in classical theism. (However, despite the fact that he discusses Hartshorne's view, he does not see the similarities between it and Plato's view.) Opposed to this Platonic model is the Aristotelian-Thomistic one. The problem is not so much with Aristotle's and Thomas' hylomorphism, but with their own abandonment of hylomorphism when it comes to God. There are *metaphysical* reasons why the divine soul (the World-Soul) needs the body of the world, the same sort of reasons Aristotle and Thomas themselves use against free-floating Platonic Forms or souls. Wainwright is correct that the issue is not merely the trivial one associated with our inability to imagine God without using corporeal images, as Thomas alleges.[8] A more significant problem that analytic Thomists might raise at this point has to do with divine perfection. If God is perfect one might suppose that God's body is also perfect. The world, however, appears to be infected with various evils and imperfections, therefore some might conclude that the world cannot be God's body. But this view hinges on a belief in divine omnipotence and on a belief in God having absolute control over the world, which in turn hinges on the monopolar prejudice that I have been criticizing throughout this book.

F. MOLTMANN'S VIEW

If belief in (or better, the assumption of) God as purely immaterial is as much based on the weight of the tradition of monopolarity as on rational argument, then examining the history of belief in divine embodiment, and of disbelief in that concept, may be useful. The purpose of this history is to show that it is not necessary that theism be identified with belief in a purely immaterial God, that there are good reasons for defending belief in divine embodiment, and that contemporary defenders of divine immateriality are often the unwitting inheritors of an indefensible version of Platonism (not necessarily held by Plato)/Aristotelianism. By returning to Plato we can get clues as to where classical theism went wrong.

The earliest testimonies of religion suggest the belief in a World Mother, in the notion of the world as a great living being. Stripped of its mythical description, and bolstered by theological and philosophical arguments, it is precisely this view of the world that Hartshorne and others, including Jürgen Moltmann (1985), refer to as panentheism. A decisive move occurred in primitive religion when the World Mother was replaced by Mother Earth, who was only one constituent in a dualistic view of religion. The other constituent was her superior, Father Heaven. The transcendent God of classical theism grew out of the Father Heaven symbolism, such that when the mechanization of the earthly world through seventeenth-century science occurred, which extinguished any semblance of divine immanence, deism and then agnosticism and atheism were logical results. That is, any effort to restore theism to health must be concomitant with the effort to develop a sexually egalitarian theology and philosophy of God so as to avoid the denigration of embodiment (traditionally associated with Mother Earth, who was subjugated by Father Heaven).

One of the difficulties connected with this latter effort is that ever since Spinoza it has been assumed by most that the only alternative to a transcendent, classical theistic God as father was the indifferent, purely immanent deity of pantheism. Hence the importance of the *tertium quid* provided by panentheism, whereby the natural world is included in God through divine knowledge and sympathy, but the natural world does not exhaust God. (Classical theists have always *said* that God included the world through knowledge and sympathy, but it is not clear that they could say so consistently if God is strictly immutable and immaterial.) And on Moltmann's (partially Hartshornian) view panentheism is more compatible with trinitarian theology and with scriptural descriptions of God than is classical theism (see Bracken 1991; Ford 1978). Like his Catholic counterpart David Tracy, the Lutheran Moltmann looks to Whitehead and other process philosophers (like Hartshorne) to provide the philosophical underpinnings for a theocentric panentheism. Specifically what is needed is a metaphysical doctrine of relations whereby the really significant difference in the universe is not that between a human being and a nonhuman animal, but that between creatures (who must share the earth together) and God. Philosophers of religion can learn much from Moltmann, not least of which is the fact that the present ecological crisis of domination of nature is due in part to an unreflective acceptance of theological and philosophical theories which act as ruses for Father Heaven, who is not only sexist but is also (as an omnipotent yet super-natural being) permissive of the destruction of the natural environment.

G. MOHR AND PLATO

Nonetheless, it will be difficult to get contemporary analytic philosophers to take the World-Soul (which animates the body of the world) seriously. Richard Mohr, the most recent in-depth commentator among analytic philosophers on Plato's cosmology, is probably not alone in his claim that Plato's World-Soul is the oddest of many odd components in Plato's cosmology in that it is highly counterintuitive.[9] Most of the world, according to Mohr in *The Platonic Cosmology*, "just does not feel like an animal. Most of it is clearly inert" (175—*Is* this clear?). Further, the World-Soul is either redundant (if the World-Soul is merely one more autokinetic soul then it has no special function in Plato's cosmology) or useless (if the World-Soul crafts external objects then it becomes indistinguishable from the Demiurge).

Mohr realizes that the World-Soul is an important doctrine for Plato, as is evidenced by the fact that it appears in four of the later dialogues (171–77). But if the body of the whole universe is alive and possesses a single World-Soul, it is an "odd-sounding creature" in need of contemporary explication. The purpose of this chapter is to offer such an explication, and to make the World-Soul not only an intelligible concept but also to *defend* belief in the World-Soul such that one need not exhibit Mohr-like or Alston-like reluctance to take Plato's World-Soul seriously. Mohr's response to the supposed oddness of the World-Soul consists in an attenuated version of the concept whereby the World-Soul is disassociated from the autokinesis of soul found in the *Phaedrus* and *Laws* X and from any cosmological function other than the mere maintenance of an already established order.

Mohr notes that in the *Statesman* (269d) the universe is described by the Eleatic Stranger (and, presumably, by Plato) as a living creature (*zōon*) endowed with reason (*phronēsin*). But he is premature in divorcing the World-Soul from self-motion. When the Stranger says that we must not claim that the universe moves itself (269d), he seems to be denying that it could go anywhere in that the World-Soul animates the whole body of the world, as Hartshorne also claims; there is no place for it to go. Later in the same speech (270a), however, the Stranger makes it clear that when the Demiurge withdraws from the world the soul of the world must "move" by its own innate force. That is, the World-Soul must take control of the affairs of the universe when Cronus or the Demiurge "withdraws" (274a). As we will see, there are problems created if one claims, as Mohr does, that the "separation" of the Demiurge from the World-Soul is more than a literary device. Further, Mohr ignores altogether the comparison made by the Stranger between the universe as a whole and the individual human being (274d). Because there is no denial of autokinesis to the World-Soul, the definition of soul as self-motion in the *Phaedrus* and *Laws* X would seem to apply to the World-Soul as well as to other souls.

The comparison between a human being and the World-Soul is *noticed* by Mohr in his treatment of the World-Soul in the *Philebus* (30a–b), but it is not used, as it is in Hartshorne, to make intelligible to modern readers why Plato believes in the World-Soul, why Plato sees the World-Soul as a cause, and why the besouled (*empsychon*) body of the world is fairer (*kalliona*) than our bodies. Despite numerous clues in the *Timaeus* as to how to ameliorate the oddness of the World-Soul, Mohr concentrates on the "parallel structures and synchronized motions" between the World-Soul and the world body. That is, he does not seem to see them as integrally connected in such a way that the World-Soul animates the body of the world. Timaeus (and, presumably, Plato) makes it clear (30a) that God desired that all things should be good, to the extent that this is possible (*boulētheis gar ho theos agatha men panta, phlauron de mēden einai kata dynamin*) by intelligently creating order out of disorder (*eis taxin auto ēgagen ek tēs ataxias*). But divine intelligence, it is equally clear (30b), *presupposes* soul. Mohr does not emphasize this. In fact, the world "came into being" when God put intelligence into the soul of the bodily world—a living creature (*ton kosmon zōon empsychon ennoun tē te alētheia dia tēn tou theou genesthai pronoian*).

The world is made in the likeness of an animal (*zōon*), or better, the individual animals in the world are parts of the whole animal; that is, the World-Soul is the original animal (30c). The need for the World-Soul becomes apparent when Plato comes to the realization that there is only one world (31a), literally a uni-verse. If there were two worlds there would be a need for a more comprehensive being to include both. The fact that the World-Soul is called the solitary, perfect animal (*monōsin homoion ē tō pantelei zōōi*) is an invitation, refused by Mohr, to think through what Hartshorne has called the logic of perfection.

Because divine intelligence presupposes the World-Soul (30b), and because divine intelligence is eternal, it should not surprise us that the world is not liable to old age or disease (33a) in that it must be eternal, too. (Or better, as Hartshorne puts the point, it must be everlasting or sempiternal.) Further (33c), there is no need to push the animal body comparison so far as to claim that the world has eyes because there is nothing outside of itself to be seen; nor is there any need for ears to hear any being external to it. The excellence of the World-Soul/world body complex consists largely, but not exclusively, as we will see, in its self-sufficiency (33d—*autarkes*). The absence of external enemies eliminates the need for hands for defense (34a) and, as we have seen, there is no possibility for the world to move to another place because it is its own place. There may well be other sorts of motion, however, contra Mohr, of which the World-Soul is capable.

Three significant points are made in the *Timaeus* (34b) which militate against Mohr's trucated version of the World-Soul:

1. The World-Soul is diffused throughout the body of the world (*psychēn de eis to meson autou theis dia pantos te eteinen kai eti exōthen to sōma autē periekalypsen*), and hence does not have a mere parallel or epiphenomenal structure with relation to the body of the world, as Mohr alleges.
2. The World-Soul is not to be divorced from God in that it is itself "generated" by the Demiurge as a blessed God (*dia panta dē tauta eudaimona theon auton egennēsato*).[10] In order to understand the World-Soul one must therefore determine *how* the Demiurge and the World-Soul are both divine, as Hartshorne tries to show.
3. Timaeus makes it clear that the soul was not made after the body; in fact, because the universe is eternal (37d), and because the body of the world cannot antedate the World-Soul, the World-Soul must also be eternal such that the independence of the Demiurge from the World-Soul cannot be literally construed as temporal priority.

Mohr does not treat Plato's use of the World-Soul in the *Laws* (177), perhaps because of his belief that the World-Soul does not possess self-motion and the *Laws* is the prime text when self-motion is treated. The Athenian (presumably, Plato) makes it clear that self-movement is the *definition* of soul (896a—*tēn dynamenēn autēn hautēn kinean kinēsin*), which implies that *all* soul possesses this property or it would not be soul.

What does it mean to explain the world? At the very least it means to elucidate the unitary principle behind the apparent duality of mind and matter. Plato wavers, for Hartshorne, between seeing this principle in the Forms and seeing it in soul (*psychē*). Hartshorne emphasizes the difficulty in offering an explanation through a Form that is not really an explanation through soul. The Neoplatonists were justified in interpreting the Forms as divine ideas, inseparable from intelligence (*nous*); and Plato gives some warrant for this interpretation when he makes the Demiurge ideally aware of the highest Form, that of the good. That is, the Forms are items internal to psychical process, as we saw in chapter 1 in the section on Plato.[11]

Cosmological speculation must, for Hartshorne, be in terms of: (*a*) soul, including the World-Soul and Platonic forms; (*b*) matter; or (*c*) both soul and matter. Did Plato make his way to the first, panpsychist option? Not quite, although he came rather close on Hartshorne's view. That is, because the second option would have been anathema to Plato, he was left with a version of dualism which Hartshorne thinks is confused. (Consider the evidence of the *Epinomis* 983d, where there is no *tertium quid* common to both soul and body, yet soul is the universal cause of body.)

The question for Hartshorne is, How close did Plato come to panpsychism? His view seems to have been, at first glance at the *Phaedrus* (245e) and the *Laws* (896a), that souls initiate change and transmit it to others; whereas bodies merely receive and transmit change. But what does it mean to be self-moved? If the theory of Forms is stressed, it might mean that bodies can only be moved by other moved things, whereas soul can also be moved by the motionless Forms. Yet if the Forms are items in (divine) psychical process, then soul in some sense is fundamental for cosmological speculation, and hence Plato comes quite close to panpsychism. For cosmological purposes the word *psychē* is used by Plato to refer to experiencing, thinking, remembering, feeling,and so on, and only for ethical or religious purposes does he use the term to refer to an entity behind these processes (IO, 24, 364).

A defect in Plato's treatment of these psychical processes would occur if he assumed that they are only examples of self-motion and not also examples of being moved (AW, 29). Indeed in the *Sophist* (248–49) Plato indicates that he thinks of knowing in these terms, that is, it is active whereas being known is passive. The problem here is that to think of soul as influencing others without being influenced is, as Hartshorne emphasizes, to reduce soul to an object (think of the damage a rock can do while remaining unmoved by the event). But surely Plato does not always exhibit this tendency. For example, in the *Republic* the degree of adequacy in the mind of the knower is due to the adequacy of influence it receives from the object known.

Hartshorne thinks that Plato hints at the panpsychist position (in which only concrete singulars feel, and in which the abstract is real only in the concrete, thus soul is the inclusive form of reality) when Plato indicates that soul is coincident with every action and passion. But no Greek was in a position to fully understand the difference between singulars and aggregates in the smaller parts of nature. That is, there is a vast difference between soul as such or soul as a generic principle, on the one hand, and animal soul (including human soul or the World-Soul), on the other. Hartshorne's "(revised) Platonism" holds that it is the lack of self-motion in macroscopic inanimate things that has caused materialists or dualists to suppose that the microscopic parts of these things also lack self-motion. It should be remembered that in Plato's dialogues we learn that soul is the universal cause (*aitias tou holou—Epinomis* 988d), that it is (metaphysically) prior to body (*presbyteras e sōmatos—Laws* 892a), that bodies are derived from soul (*sōma de deuteron te kai hysteron—Laws* 896c), that we receive our being from soul (*Laws* 959a), and that soul is the primary source of all things (*psychēn genesin hapantōn einai prōtēn—Laws* 899c). So although Plato could not fully understand the cosmological significance of panpsychism, it would be a mistake to think that he was totally ignorant of such significance, either by returning to primitive animism (all things are full of gods) or by defending (cosmic) dualism *simpliciter.* Aristotle, however, *does* end up with a cosmic dualism in describing his gods, a dualism which is largely the source of the analytic, classical theist's assumption that God is purely immaterial.

The meaning usually assigned to Plato's theory of Forms was really born in the first book of Aristotle's *Metaphysics*, according to Hartshorne. Hence it is implausible to think, according to Hartshorne, that the greatest problem in Plato's cosmology is this theory of Form, but rather it is that of sufficiently grasping the functions of soul as both creative and receptive, and the related problems of understanding internal and external relations and how the soul interacts with body (IO, 27–28; CA, 208–9). Plato's analysis of becoming remains incomplete (see the *Sophist* 248–49) because if knowing something is to change that something, as Plato sometimes indicates, then past events go on changing when we think about them. Plato probably flirted with this idea (that knowing something changes it) as a reaction against the opposite view that the past completely determines the present in souls as in bodies. The self-motion of soul must mean that soul originates change, which is at least compatible with the view that necessary, although not sufficient, causal conditions are inherited from the past. Soul does not merely transmit tendencies from the past, nor just receive them, as in bodies. It is no stretch of the imagination to say that Plato anticipated the process transcendental "creativity" (IO, 32–33).

It is an error to assume that Plato's only alternative to being determined by the past is to be determined by an ideal, for no ideal can be applied without *creative* particularization (IO, 34). An understanding of soul as self-creative sheds light on at least three additional areas:

1. Plato had at least an inkling of the truth that "the creative, temporal character of experiencing yields all the light upon modality as ontological that we are going to get" in that "particular and actual are essentially one, and so are universal and potential" (CS, 225).

2. The lack of complete order in the world is at least partly explained by there being many souls. These many self-active agents imply indefinitely great if not complete disorder unless there is a "supreme soul to 'persuade' the many lesser souls to conform to a cosmic plan. They cannot completely fit such a plan for then they would not be self-determined" (WV, 23). That is, Hartshorne's theodicy is essentially Platonic because the divine plan cannot be completely definite and detailed.
3. The phrase "God has power over us" has a meaning only if we return to Plato's notion of a self-moved mover of others who is partially moved by these other self-movers. God can "rule the world" by setting optimal limits for free action. The divine can control the changes in us by inspiring us with novel ideas; by molding *itself* God presents at each moment a partly new ideal (DR, 139, 142).

Dipolarity is manifest in all reality, supremely so in God (PS, 2, 5). Each category and its contrast—for instance, being and becoming, unity and diversity, and so on—admits of a supreme case or a super-case. This is true whether we speak univocally or analogically about God. Therefore we are left with either two supreme beings or one supreme being with two really distinct aspects. Only a superficial interpretation of the *Timaeus* would allege that Plato took the first option. Relying on Cornford, Hartshorne holds that Plato took the second option, albeit vividly presented in myth as if the first option were chosen.[12]

For the sake of argument, Hartshorne would drop his thesis regarding *phases* of Platonic development, but he refuses to give up the thesis that there are two *facets* in Plato's thought (PS, 39–40, 43). The first is a diaeresis of existence into the quantitative and the qualitative, the mutable and the immutable, or better the material and the formal (or ideational). Both soul and God are put in the latter (immobile) pole of these pairs. However, in the second facet (or phase) of Plato's thought, motion is granted to both soul and God. The real opposition here is between dependent and independent mobility, that is, between body (taken as an insentient aggregate of sentient constituents) and soul (including the World-Soul). *Within* the World-

Soul there is a principle of immutability, a principle which characterizes soul per se in the first facet (or phase). This complex of opposed concepts cannot be simplified by reducing God to the idea of the good. Not even in the first facet (or phase) did Plato ever make this equation. Rather, the good, although it is not God, is nonetheless compatible with the rule of a supreme, conscious being. In short, the conflict of opposing categories must be viewed as inherent in the Platonic framework. Reality, including divine reality, is one but this unity can only be discursively or metaphysically revealed as two, like centripetal and centrifugal forces in equilibrium. Hartshorne claims that the two poles of Plato's theism are brought together with almost equal weight in the *Timaeus*. But the word "together" is problematic in that Plato mythically fixes the correlative categories in different beings, the Demiurge and the World-Soul, with the latter seemingly providing an answer to the criticism in the *Parmenides* that an absolute God could not know or be related to the world.

The path of much later philosophy was to seek "consistency" and sacrifice one of these poles, and this path was in some ways encouraged by Plato himself in that the two poles cannot be related if both are considered concrete divine natures. This is why Hartshorne sees the Demiurge, which mythically makes the World-Soul, as eternal and the World-Soul as everlasting (PS, 54–57). And this is what he thinks Plato could or should have done, for if Platonism means anything it is that there are distinct levels of ontological abstractness. Relying on Wolfson, Hartshorne thinks of eternity as the absence of temporal relations, hence God's eternal aspect cannot be concrete; yet the World-Soul is obviously concrete or is related to the concrete.[13]

Hartshorne is confident that his treatment of the Demiurge and the World-Soul follows from basic Platonic distinctions, and that it continues the direction of Plato's logic in the *Timaeus*, which attempts to render consistent the inconsistent positions on God of the *Phaedo* and *Republic*, on the one hand, and the *Phaedrus*, on the other. This is not to suggest that all of the threads in Plato's view of God have been picked up. For example, Plato sometimes multiplies gods into a pantheon of astral spirits, but these are mythical expressions which have never detained philosophers.

But even a multiplication of astral spirits is not incompatible with a monotheistic intent, for to call these "deities" or "gods" in a loose way is a concession to ordinary language where precision is not sought. Monotheism is close to the surface of Plato's approach, according to Hartshorne, in that God is not posited by Plato as a mere fact to explain some other observed facts; rather God must comprehend the *entire* realm of Forms, for God is the very principle of order in the world, the means by which the totality of things is one cosmos, a *uni*verse. Our task now is to zero in on Plato's notion of perfection so as to understand why both the Demiurge and World-Soul are needed.

God's immutability is inferred from God's perfection in the *Republic.* This ascendency of the principle of fixity has been taken by most historians of philosophy (including analytic historians) to be the Platonic view of God *simpliciter.* Although it would be *hubris* to think that one could easily replace this view, Hartshorne thinks that another interpretation may be a bit more plausible. It is helpful to notice that the World-Soul is the supreme example of soul but it is not perfect *if* perfection entails immutability. Or, mythically expressed, the World-Soul is merely the most perfect of created things. Absoluteness (or perfection, as traditionally conceived) only belongs to an abstract, eternal aspect of God, that is, to God's essence rather than to God's concrete actuality. Hence, Hartshorne finds no fault with the view of perfection in the *Republic*, but he tries to place it within a more inclusive view of God (PS, 31, 56; AW, 4–5, 30). If Plato is to be faulted it is because his spokesman in the *Republic* misleadingly talks of a being—instead of a mere abstract aspect of a being—so "perfect" that it could not change for the better or worse. That Hartshorne is not imposing his dipolar view on Plato is supported by the following consideration. If God were an *ens realissimum*, a most real being that could not change, either by improvement or by influence from others, God would come dangerously close to violating the definition of being as dynamic power in the *Sophist* (CS, 69, 229). "The absolutely insensitive is the absolutely dead, not the supremely alive. The Platonists [including classical theists], perhaps not Plato, are blind to this truth" (AD, 232—my insert).

The two "gods" of the *Timaeus* (the creator God and the created God—the Demiurge and the World-Soul, respectively) are aspects of one and the same deity. The uni-verse as an animate and rational effect is superior to all other effects "as the whole or inclusive effect is superior to parts or included effects" (DR, 79–80).[14] But as in the *Republic* (381b), God is in every way the best possible (*ta tou theou pantei arista echei*). It is for this reason that Plato does not think that certain things are shameful in God merely because they are shameful in human beings; rather, anything less than the best possible is shameful in God because it is incompatible with the logic of perfection and with the divine nature itself. And "best possible" has implications not only for ethical issues, but also for God's knowledge of the Forms.

Hartshorne has spent a good deal of his career criticizing the Neoplatonic and medieval worship of being as opposed to becoming—"a doctrine riddled with antinomies"—a worship largely due to the influence of Parmenides on Plato, and on the assumption that such influence constitutes Plato's entire philosophy. Hartshorne criticizes most interpreters of Plato in assuming that Plato's last word on God was that in the *Republic* to the effect that God, being perfect, cannot change. To a lesser extent he also criticizes Plato for going so far down this road before realizing that "an absolute maximum of value *in every conceivable respect*, does not make sense or is contradictory" (WP, 167; OO, 2–3). Like the "greatest possible number" the words "absolute maximum value" can be uttered, but they do not say anything if finite beings contribute something to the greatness of God, as they do to the supreme memory of the World-Soul.

One of the reasons Hartshorne thinks of Plato as among the "wisest and best" of theologians is that he thinks Plato may have realized that the Demiurge *is* the World-Soul in abstraction, that is, is that part of the World-Soul considered as having an eternal ideal which it is forever engaged in realizing. (It must be admitted, however, that here more than elsewhere Hartshorne is interpreting Plato rather loosely for the purpose of present philosophizing. The connection he draws between the Demiurge and the World-Soul is much closer than anything stated explicitly in the *Timaeus*.) This process of realization is what Plato meant in the *Timaeus* by the "moving image of eternity." Hartshorne's tempting way of reading Plato alleges that God, utilizing partly self-created creatures, "creates its own forever unfinished actualization." Thus, God is aware of both us and other noncosmic animals and the lesser souls, on the one hand, and eternal ideals, on the other. Even though God is the "individual integrity" of the world, which is otherwise a concatenation of myriad parts, Hartshorne's view is easily made compatible with the claim that God does not survey all events in the future with strict omniscience (OO, 52–53, 59, 94).

These thoughts on the divine body are not just consequences of Hartshorne's use of the soul-body analogy to understand God; they are also logically entailed in his metaphysics. Hartshorne has often claimed (contra Kant, et al.) that there are necessary truths concerning existence, for example, "Something exists." The absurdity of claiming that "there might have been (absolutely) nothing" is derived from Plato himself, who, when he commits parricide on father Parmenides in the *Sophist* (241–42), only admits the existence of relative nonbeing or otherness, not the existence of absolutely nothing, which would be a logical contradiction in that *it* would then be something (IO, x–xi). Hartshorne agrees with Plato that all determination is negation, but this inescapable element of negation is precisely Plato's form of otherness or relative nonbeing. The statement "Nothing exists" could not conceivably be verified, that is, a completely restrictive or wholely negative statement is not a conceivable yet unrealized fact, but an impossibility (CS, 22, 159). Particular bodies can pass out of existence (or better, pass into an other sort of existence), but the divine body of the universe has no alternative but to exist.

That is, Plato's treatment of the World-Soul is not unrelated to his anticipation of the ontological argument (see Johnson 1963; Esser 1910; and AD). God's bare *existence* is quite abstract, about as noncompetitive as "reality as such." It has an infinite range of variations and flexibility. But God is not characterless or "flabby" because of

God's *actuality* in some embodied state (AD, 57–59). And Hartshorne notes that there were atheists in Plato's day, and even before that (*Laws* 887c), so that Plato's argument from order—blended with the cosmological argument—starts the important tradition of knowing how to rationally answer the nonbelievers. Plato's use of this argument in book ten of the *Laws* shows both the importance of the World-Soul and that Plato was "one of the most penetrating of all intelligences," a mind with "imaginative subtlety" which dwarfs his most famous followers (NT, 125; PS, 25). Further, the proof is intended as a series of hints, to be filled in by the reader's meditations, which Hartshorne is obviously willing to do. But even though the proof is really an outline, it furnishes the material for an argument that is quite strong.

The outline looks something like this: (1) Psychical process or soul is the only self-explanatory process, the only self-determining type of change. (2) Order among souls, and hence in reality generally, can be explained only through a supremely good soul, which persuades the others to conform to its decisions. (3) Disorder and evil are not due to the supreme soul's decisions (as they are, directly or indirectly, in classical theism), but to the conflicting decisions of other souls. Although Plato came too close to identifying disorder and evil (for Hartshorne partial disorder is needed to balance order so as to produce beauty—sheer order is not beautiful but monotonous), his wisdom is seen when Hume and Kant suggest that the disorder in the world might be explained polytheistically. This is an extreme and inadequate way to put Plato's very point, if by "gods" is meant souls. And we have already seen why order cannot be explained by a divine committee. One further reason for this claim needs to be stated here: Because the higher the consciousness the more "widely and abruptly" it can disagree with other consciousnesses which are its peers, a pantheon of gods would be even more in need of a single superior to understand the world as a cosmos than a plurality of earthly animals.

Hartshorne agrees with Burnet that Plato's greatest discovery regarding God does not concern the Forms, but rather concerns soul or psychical process. This discovery allows us: to understand the primordial and everlasting ideal for the cosmos—the Good—in the supreme soul; to realize that "creativity" is the true transcendental, which applies to creator and creature alike; to claim that cosmic order requires one soul to order the others, yet disorder does not require one soul (e.g., Satan), only a multiplicity of agents able to get in each other's way; and to urge that the traditional theistic "problem of evil" could not arise in Plato's thought because God is not totally responsible for the world (IO, 36–38). (Although Plato does waver between attributing evil to "matter" and to the freedom of souls—OO, 53.) Nor does Hartshorne think that it would be a good thing for God to be so responsible: beauty requires partial disorder and cosmic creativity per se is a good thing. This is no trivial attempt at theodicy on Hartshorne's part in that there are metaphysical reasons for these claims. From Plato Hartshorne has learned that every negation (relative nonbeing or otherness) implies an affirmation, that is, there are no merely negative truths. To say that "divinity does not exist" is to say something positive about the reality whose existence is incompatible with God. Usually it is the positive existence of evil in the world which is assumed to be incompatible with (an omnipotent) God, but if there is no such incompatibility, then Plato's argument from order stands, as does the tragic view of life, because there are pervasive elements of chance, partial disorder, and frustration in reality.

For both Plato (perhaps not Platon*ism*) and Aristotle the abstract must somehow be embodied in concrete actuality. This embodiment is in God, for Plato. For Aristotle is is either *in re* (embodied in a material thing) or *post rem* (abstracted in the mind of the knower). So for Plato and Aristotle no particular concrete reality is required by the abstract entity. A "necessarily instantiated attribute could be clearly nonidentical with its instances, and yet in its very being, as an attribute, instantiated somehow" (AD, 289). But there is a difference of emphasis in the two thinkers, with Aristotle developing a single categorical scheme of substance instead of Plato's dipolarity. Paradoxically, however, as we have seen, from this emphasis on substance Aristotle ultimately constructs a more vicious dualism than any ever envisaged by Plato, in that Aristotle's divinity is a *completely* self-sufficient entity separated from all change and multiplicity. Painting with a rather wide brush, the Hartshornian view seems to be that Plato's cosmology of psychical monism can only be understood and explained through a dipolar categorical scheme, as seen above, whereas Aristotle's troublesome cosmological dualism (which historically gave rise to all of the—seemingly insoluble—problems of classical theism) is elaborated through a monopolar scheme favoring eternality.[15]

H. SOLMSEN AND PLATO'S THEOLOGY

Hartshorne's favorable treatment of the World-Soul is both an attempt to make intelligible to modern readers some rather difficult texts in Plato on the World-Soul *and* an attempt (largely successful, I think) to suggest why belief in a World-Soul is superior to either disbelief in God or belief in pantheism or belief in God as a strictly transcendent, supernatural, purely eternal, unmoved mover (this last belief typical in some way or other of most analytic theists). Solmsen's project, which supplements Hartshorne's, is to concentrate on Plato, to locate the World-Soul within the context of Plato's theology as it developed throughout his career (Solmsen 1942). I would like to show why Solmsen's work is one of the best on Plato's thoughts on God to date; that is, Solmsen is able to show *why* the World-Soul is a central element in Plato's theology, an ability not indicated by most subsequent commentators on Plato.

Solmsen makes it clear (1942, 8) that the background to Plato's theology is provided by a traditional view of civic religion whereby piety of a nonpolitical sort or a purely secular patriotism would have been a contradiction in terms. The destruction of the old religion had both a positive and a negative effect: it both made it possible for a more sophisticated, intellectual conception of God and it opened the door to atheism.[16] Plato meant both to close this door and to elevate religious discourse. This elevation would, given Plato's lifelong interest in politics, have to be able to establish some sort of rapprochement with civic religion even if the primitive identification of the interests of the polis with a particular deity would have to be dropped. Further, this elevation would have to continue the pioneering work of the presocratics, whose objective was to connect the deity (or deities) to cosmic processes in nature (1942, 40), a connection which very often led to belief in the World-Soul.[17] In fact, according to Plutarch, *all* of the ancient philosophers, except Aristotle and the atomists, believed that the world was informed with an animal soul!,[18] a claim which, even if an exaggeration, nonetheless shows how comfortable the ancients were with the World-Soul, a comfort matched by the contemporary discomfort of most analytic theists.[19]

Plato's attempt to reform religion is initially seen in the effort to define piety (*eusebia*) in the *Euthyphro*, a reform which is intensified in the *Republic* (Solmsen 1942, 63–64). One practical result of this reform was a confrontation with the theodicy problem, which, as we have seen in Hartshorne's interpretation of Plato, is resolved in Plato by noticing the limits of divine power (limits which are perfect in their own way in that they allow creatures self-motion) and the purity of divine goodness (Solmsen 1942, 68–69). Nonetheless, in the *Republic* the gods (Plato often wavers between the singular and the plural) occupy a plane below the highest; like poetry, religion has a wider appeal than philosophy. The gods are not inconsistent with the Forms in the *Republic*, but their relation is not made clear in this work. Solmsen's tempting way of putting the problem is in the following Aristotelian terms: the Forms provide, of course, the formal cause of goodness in the world, yet goodness will never be concretely produced in the world unless there is an efficient (divine) cause, an efficient cause made explicit in later dialogues (1942, 72–73) in divine dipolarity (World-Soul/Demiurge).

As before, the *Sophist* exhibits a theory of Forms where the stiffness and isolation of the Forms is abandoned in favor of dynamic power (Solmsen 1942, 77). The preparation for this dynamism is found in the *Phaedrus*' principle of *psychē* as self-motion, a principle which makes it possible for the World-Soul to be an *organic* whole, such that neither materialism nor the theory of Forms contains the full truth about reality.[20] However, Plato is quite willing, as we have seen, to "materialize" the whole by admitting divine embodiment, an embodiment also defended by Hartshorne (Solmsen 1942, 78–80).

While the first part of the *Theaetetus* makes us aware of the dangers of absolutizing movement, these dangers are not necessary if one keeps *dynamis* regulated by form, and if one realizes that the dynamic whole is an orderly one, a cosmos. What is to be noted is that almost every one of the late dialogues makes some contribution to the theory of movement, not least of which is the *Timaeus*, where the World-Soul is seen as the source of movement,[21] and the *Laws*, where there is an elaborate classification of movements (Solmsen 1942, 84–85).

Mind (*nous*) thinks about the Forms, which are, "in themselves," eternal and immutable abstractions. Hence mind (i.e., the Demiurge) "by itself" lacks the right kind of contact to link up with life and flux. Only soul can do that because soul both animates what would otherwise be the dead body of the world and has, through its mental component, communion with the Forms (89). Perhaps the most insightful commentator on the amphibious nature of soul is J. N. Findlay (1974). The World-Soul has its "feet" in both the eidetic and the instantial camps; it is not merely a "link" between these regions, it is a living channel. The eidetic mind works only by way of the World-Soul in which it is instantiated. The timeless mind is an "elder" God, in a way, but for Findlay the World-Soul fulfills all of the tasks that could be demanded of God, as detailed by Hartshorne in his many writings.

At once Plato's concept of soul preserves the best in the Orphic, Pythagorean, and mystery religion traditions regarding soul; it makes soul the locus of political virtue; it allows soul to be used to explain the cosmos in religious terms (Solmsen 1942, 90–91); and, in fact, as we have seen, it even makes mind the auxiliary of soul (92–94). According to Solmsen and Hartshorne, the supreme soul, the World-Soul, is Plato's attempt to connect the world of flux with that of sameness into an integrated theory of reality (98). Hence the function of God in the *Timaeus* is not so much to impart life to the universe as to make its life as excellent as possible (Solmsen 1942, 102). The philosophical consideration of the beauty of the universe (through astronomy and music, where apparently discordant elements are brought into harmony) makes the human soul at least akin to, if not homogeneous with, the Soul of the Cosmos (107).[22]

God (the supreme *psychē* with supreme *nous*) confronts the elements of the world which remain discordant with persuasion (*peithō*), not force (*bia*). But God still has power (*kratos*), specifically the immense power to persuade the world by offering it a model of perfection. Although Solmsen (unlike Hartshorne) is hesitant to literally *identify* the Demiurge with the World-Soul on the evidence of the *Timaeus*, he is willing to see the two as aspects of one God which deal with separate functions: the World-Soul with movement and life and the Demiurge with order, design, and rationality. In the *Laws*, however, such an identification is legitimate (Solmsen 1942, 112–13). As we have seen, in the *Laws* mind *presupposes* a living soul, even if mind itself is eternal (and even if the Demiurge is mythically depicted as prior to the World-Soul in the *Timaeus*—114–17).

Solmsen reinforces Hartshorne's notion of a personal deity: once Plato's doctrine of a cosmic soul had taken shape it not only succeeded in "respiritualizing" nature,[23] it also transformed the indirect kinship relation between the individual and God into a direct, and hence personal relationship. The ardor which this relationship fosters constitutes Platonic piety, which, as at the end of the *Euthyphro*, is a type of service (Hartshorne would say contribution) to God (125–26).

It should not surprise us that in the *Laws* (book ten) the argument against atheism is described as a prelude (*prooimion*) for the whole body of laws; religion is the basis of Plato's city here and plays a much more significant role than it did in the *Republic*. It was actually his aim to refute three types of atheism: the denial of God altogether; the belief that divinity does not care for us; and the claim that God can be bought off with sacrifices, and so on (132–34). Plato's refutation is in terms of his own theological tenets, including belief in the divine animal, a belief that is almost entirely foreign to analytic theists.[24] The World-Soul in the *Laws* often surfaces not as an individual entity (as in the *Timaeus*) but as a generic principle, as the texts treated above indicate. Soul does not, however, manifest itself with equal distinctness in every phase of the cosmos; it is in some way intensified in animals, especially in human animals and in the divine animal (138–40).

As before, the Aristotelian conception of a self-sufficient God who thinks about only itself is as alien to Plato as it is to Hartshorne. God's *telos*, if there is such, is the best possible harmony for the sum of things; the parts are for the whole, but the whole only flourishes with healthy parts, as Hartshorne also agrues. God is like the good physician who does not give his attention to a single, isolated organ, but rather to the body of the world as a whole (152–54).[25] Although it would be rash to suggest that Plato felt himself in his later years more at home in the cosmos than in the polis, it must be admitted that he prepared the way for the Hellenistic escape from politics into the life of the cosmos, say by his flirtation with panpsychistic beliefs (156).

Solmsen is quite explicit that "The concept of a divine World-Soul as the fountain of movements and as the intelligent power controlling the world of Becoming is the cornerstone of the whole new system," a theological system based on physics (162). Before individual or political experience can be understood, the validity of religion itself has to be understood on cosmic grounds. This understanding makes it possible to consider oneself more of a "citizen of the Universe" than a citizen of any mere political community, a view which has influenced Hartshorne's own political philosophy. Law in a polis is indeed important, but only if it is seen against a larger background, specifically the theological background of the *Timaeus*[26] and *Laws*, which were attempts to stem the process of disintegration in Greek culture which had been in existence for almost a century (Solmsen 1942, 168–69).

Plato never abandoned his theory of Forms, but the World-Soul takes over functions previously fulfilled by the Forms, for example, knowledge (*epistēmē*) and craftsmanship (*technē*) are elevated to positions of great dignity because they either have affinity to soul or are skills which soul itself can attain. God extends control over the region of becoming due to the fact that reason, regularity, order, and form are not limited to the sphere of being (*ta onta*), but can be used by God as values in the (Whiteheadian?) harmonization of the world (Solmsen 1942, 172).

The sadness is that Plato's thoughts on God have been obscured in the history of Platon*ism*. He was the last Greek to discuss God in a context of a political system, and after his death ancient theistic philosophers went in one of two directions: Aristotle moved toward a conception of divinity as transcendent and the Stoics moved toward pantheism, leaving no one, as it were, to guard the Platonic fort (Solmsen 1942, 177–95). Solmsen seems to agree with Hartshorne that classical theism, including analytic classical theism, has largely followed the Aristotelian move, albeit designated at times as "Platonic."

It must be admitted that Solmsen and Hartshorne, despite the fact that they mutually reinforce each other, engage in two quite different types of scholarship. Solmsen is much more interested than Hartshorne in justifying his claims on the basis of evidence from the Platonic texts themselves, but this should not lead us to assume that he was a naive positivist in that he certainly brings his own theoretical baggage to those texts. And Hartshorne is much more interested than Solmsen in doing intellectual work with Plato in the effort to respond to issues in contemporary philosophy of religion, but this should not lead us to assume that Hartshorne is indifferent to the integrity of Plato's texts. Nor is Hartshorne's approach imperialistic in the sense of his wishing to crowd out other interpretations of Plato. Rather, it is *because* he has in fact read Plato carefully that he thinks it is appropriate for other scholars, including analytic theists, to at least take the World-Soul seriously as an intellectually respectable position rather than as a piece of antiquarian lore.

My hope is that by taking the World-Soul seriously we might: (1) eliminate the oddness of this doctrine as it is conceived by many, analytic theists and Mohr among them; (2) make better sense than most commentators have (Solmsen excluded) of the movement of Plato's theology in the later dialogues; and (3) learn how to use Plato to respond to several important issues in contemporary philosophy of religion. That is, paradoxical as it may sound, Plato's theology is at once archaic (in that it is an attempt to preserve the best in civic religion, the Great Mother tradition, the mystery cults, and pre-Socratic religiosity) and future-oriented (Solmsen 1942, 170). It is future-oriented both because it points toward Hellenistic, cosmic religion, and because it provides important clues to show us how to: (*a*) solve some of the unnecessary problems regarding theodicy which have plagued classical theism for centuries; and (*b*) bridge contemporary philosophical concern for ecology with philosophy of religion, but without an appeal to pantheism. Hartshorne's philosophy, as opposed to the philosophies of most analytic theists, I allege, delivers on these promissory notes largely because he has been influenced by Plato's World-Soul.

I. THE TRANSITION TO CHRISTIANITY

Some analytic theists will at this point perhaps object that even if there are very good reasons in favor of divine embodiment, in favor of God as the World-Soul for the body of the world, the World-Soul is just not a Christian doctrine, and that Christian philosophers must maintain a belief in pure divine immateriality, no matter what the philosophical price, in order to remain true to the tradition. I will respond to this objection by looking at two crucial figures, Plotinus and Origen, who rubbed elbows together, as it were, as fellow students of Ammonius Saccas. Plotinus, as is well known, was the last great philosopher in antiquity, and Origen was one of the first great Christian thinkers. Considering these two figures will help us locate belief in divine embodiment not only philosophically but also theologically in a Christian context.

Plotinus is quite explicit at one point (IV.4.32) that the universe is all bound together in shared experience and is one living creature (*sympathes dē pan touto to hen, kai hōs zōon hen*) such that even parts of the universe that seem far away are felt by the whole, as a finger (*daktylos*) is part of the shared experience of a living being. Plotinus is well aware of the fact (IV.3.3) that if individual souls are parts of the whole—as a toe or a finger is part of the living being—then there is a risk that there is no soul outside of body. But this is not a dangerous risk in that if the material world, the Platonic forms, and God have always existed, as Plotinus (and Hartshorne) thinks, then

God has no alternative but to bring the world together as a besouled individual.[27]

Support for the claim that Plotinus has relied on Plato (again, *Republic* 462c–d) can be found when he makes the exact Platonic point regarding pain. Pain in the toe is indeed localized in the toe, but also the pain is in the region of the ruling principle (*peri to hēgemonoun*). Although Plotinus is unclear as to how this happens (IV.7.7), he is clear that in fact it happens that pain can occur in one's finger and as a consequence the individual as a whole can feel miserable. The best Plotinian (and Hartshornian) efforts to explain how individual soul as part and individual soul as whole (World-Soul) relate occur when he uses the organic metaphor of a living animal body, an effort which is buttressed by Plotinus's awareness, however dim, of nerves (IV.3.23—*neurois*), which are found in the organs of touch, like the fingers, despite the fact that they begin in the brain (*archomenōn de apo engkephalou*). Hence, if a finger is cut off an individual's soul is not cut off (IV.3.8), just as the World-Soul would survive the death of any individual body. Or more precisely, because the soul is everywhere in the living body, it perceives affections in the body; but sometimes localized pain does not much affect the soul of the individual (IV.4.19), say in the case of a minor scratch. In that the soul is everywhere (*pantachou*), however, it can easily turn out not only that the finger has pain but also that the man has pain because of *his* finger.

Within the metaphor of the living body Plotinus inscribes another metaphor of a living body in dance (IV.4.33–35). Just as a slight movement in the hand affects the whole dance, so is the All at least partially constituted by the arrangements among the parts. That is (IV.5.2), sympathy depends on there being one living thing (*sympathes tō hen zōon einai*), even if the head is ranked higher than a foot, or, presumably, a finger (IV.4.45), and even if an eye is more noble than a finger (VI.7.10). But although there is a hierarchy of bodily parts, and although one hand may not know what the other is doing (IV.9.2), the parts are nonetheless for each other in that they all have their *telos* in the flourishing of the whole (VI.8.14). If Plotinus was using a political metaphor here he would appear totalitarian because we would be led to infer that one could lose one's individuality while being swallowed up by the whole. But his point seems to be that each individual contributes what it can to the whole, *including* the value of its present well-being (indeed Hartshorne calls his view "contributionism"), just as pleasant sensations in one's finger contribute to the well-being of an individual, even an individual with a headache (VI.4.6).

Although the relationship between soul and body in Plotinus is obviously a difficult topic, it is clear that soul is not in body the way wine is in a jar, nor is it in body the way a steersman is in a ship (IV.3.20–21). Rather, it seems more accurate to say that *body is in soul*, and in every soul there is a mental pole, where the soul leans in the direction of intellect (*anō pros noun*), and a physical pole, where the soul leans in the direction of body (IV.8.8—*katō pros sōma*), a view that is not unlike Whitehead's and Hartshorne's. The point I would like to emphasize is that despite these two tendencies there is a unity in every animate soul, the fact of sympathy, which is a community of feeling possessed by the World-Soul as well as by individual human and animal souls (IV.3.8). The belief that the body is in soul is a crucial one, I allege, in the effort to combat the objection that divine embodiment is anti-Christian.

One perceives so well what happens in one's finger because it is a part of the same living thing as the one perceiving. From this Plotinus suggests that perceived objects (*aisthēta*) can be perceived by perceiving subjects (*aisthanomena*) only because both are part of the same living thing: the world body of the World-Soul, which provides the sympathetic connection (*to sympathes*) necessary for perception to occur (IV.5.8). And there is an infinity of perceptions, not only by the World-Soul, but by any soul, in that each part has perceptions (IV.7.6). That Plotinus is serious in his notion of an infinity of perceptions can be seen when he says that it is impossible (*adynaton*) for minds to come from mindless things (*noun gennan ta anoēta*—IV.7.2). According to Plotinus, if someone says that:

> atoms or things without parts make the soul when they come together by unity and community of feeling, he could be refuted by their (mere) juxtaposition, and that not a complete one, since

> nothing which is one and united with itself in community of feeling can come from bodies which are without feeling and unable to be united. (IV.7.3)

Plotinus, like Hartshorne, is not opposed to atoms but to lifeless, insentient atoms.

There is nothing foolish about Plotinus's or Hartshorne's panpsychism, however. Plotinus is aware of the fact that the existence of soul as a single nature (*mia physis*) comprising a plurality does not preclude the existence of bodies (e.g., a table or a wall) which are mere composites of manifold, diversified parts (VI.2.4–5). Panpsychism only appears foolish if one assumes that rocks and walls are the primary realities; but these masses and magnitudes, which have a certain thickness (*pachea*), are derived from something more simple (V.1.5). That is, to understand the World-Soul as an animate unity it is important to distinguish it from other sorts of unity or pseudo-unity: The unity found in composites such as an army or a chorus, although not a fiction, is only a unity in an equivocal sense because there is no real community of feeling (VI.2.10; VI.6.13); although a house apparently has more unity than an army or a chorus, it does not really bring its manifold parts together for a common purpose, as does soul, especially intellectual soul (VI.2.11); even a well-organized army has more in common with a crowd or a festival than with a soul (VI.6.12); and groups of things or loose aggregates like "two men" or "a man and a dog" are not real unities, or at least are not as real as besouled unities (VI.6.16; VI.9.1).

In sum, despite the fact that Plotinus often falls victim to the monopolar prejudice, he is instructive both for the way in which he defends the view that body is ultimately in soul and for the way in which he illustrates the intellectual milieu in which Origen flourished. Origen also held a version of the Platonic or Neoplatonic World-Soul in his *On First Principles*.[28]

Solmsen is premature in suggesting that Origen, despite his attraction to the doctrine of the World-Soul, did not need it if he really learned that God cared for individual souls. But how, Origen seems to be asking, *could* God care for individual souls if God is *super*natural? How could such care possibly take place if God is immutable?

And how does God make the universe literally a uni-verse, an orderly cosmos where the diverse parts of the world are brought together into a providential harmony? It is in response to these questions that we can see not only why Origen was attracted to the belief in a World-Soul, but also why he really needed such a doctrine so as to achieve the synthesis he desired of ancient and Christian wisdom. Whereas many Catholic thinkers have emphasized the mystical aspect of the mystical body of Christ, Origen also emphasizes the bodily aspect of that doctrine.

Origen's debt to Plato can be seen when Origen refers to the universe as the divine animal, a comparison made by Plato in the *Timaeus*, as we have seen, when he refers to the World-Soul as a *zōon*. Origen is unique, however, in that he tries to cite biblical support for this comparison, as when he cites a question from Jeremiah (23:24): "Do not I fill heaven and earth, says the Lord?"; and a passage from Isaiah to the effect that the earth is the footstool at God's feet (66:1), a passage to which Jesus alluded (Matthew 5:34). Further, there is the famous passage from St. Paul, devoid of any primitive anthropomorphism, especially because it is part of his oration to the Athenians, which suggests that "*in* Him we live and move and have our being" (Acts 17:28—my emphasis), a divine inclusiveness which makes perfect sense if one believes in a divine, animate, soul for the world, but which makes little or no sense otherwise. (Once again, classical theists have *said* that God is omnipresent, but how can a strictly immutable and immaterial being really be present in a changing and material world?) It will be remembered that Plotinus also thought that body existed in divinity and not the other way around. Origen also could have cited another of Paul's claims often used in support of the mystical *body* of Christ, that "We are members one of another," or the remarkable thought that "The body is one and has many members, but all the members, many though they are, are one body, and so it is with Christ" (1 Cor. 12:12).

Christ is identified by Origen with an omnipresent *logos*, with the *agapē* which binds all things together, with the soul for the body of the world. Origen, following Plato (*Timaeus* 33c), realizes that the soul-body analogy used to describe God cannot be pushed to the point where, say, a divine mouth is posited, as it is in biblical anthropomorphism, because there is no need for God to have a mouth to bring in food from the outside in that there is no outside to an omniscient, all-inclusive being. For Origen, bodily expressions when applied to God, such as fingers or eyes, are meant to indicate divine powers, powers which are so extensive in comparison to our limited ability to unify our puny, degenerative bodies that Origen has no trouble preserving the mysterious grandeur of God (17, II.8.5). Divine unification of the world is seen by Origen not only in cosmological terms, so as to insure that the universe remains a uni-verse, a cosmos, but also in moral and aesthetic terms, so as to insure that the seemingly chaotic diversity of free, rational wills is actually arranged according to merit so as to preserve the notions of a just desert and a harmonious beauty, albeit produced by diverse vessels of "gold and silver, but also of wood and earth" (2 Tim. 2:20) [17, II.9.6].

Thus far I have argued that Origen is instructive regarding the difficulty in reconciling divine omniscience and omnibenevolence, on the one hand, with God as supernatural, on the other; and he is instructive regarding how God as the soul of the world, as the individual integrity of the world, allows us to see God as personal, contra pantheism. Origen is clear that our one body (*corpus nostrum unum*) is composed of many members (*multis membris*), which are held together by one soul (*una anima*). Likewise, the universe is an immense animal of many members, which are held together by God (*ita et universum mundum velut animal quoddam immensum atque immane opinandum puto, quod quasi ab una anima virtute Dei*). It is not immediately clear why Butterworth translates Rufinus' Latin version of Origen's Greek as "monstrous." *Immensum* entails something so vast, perhaps, that Butterworth may be thinking of *immensum* as boundless or as a translation of the Greek *apeiron*, which would, in fact, be "frightful" for any Greek. But Origen's point is that God brings the world together within the boundaries of the divine body (17, II.1.3).

In this chapter I have moved from Alston's queries regarding the possibility of divine embodiment, to Swinburne's defense of a limited form of divine embodiment, to Hartshorne's defense of a much stronger version of this view. I have also considered the work of several other scholars in order to argue in favor of a tradition that spans both ancient philosophy (Plato and Plotinus, in particular) and Christianity regarding the need for divine embodiment in some form other than a minimalist version of this concept.

If we start with the microcosm, we can then easily understand how cells are brought within the order of our "mesocosmic" bodies. But such an understanding was not always easy; it was not until the early nineteenth century that cell theory took coherent form in the work of Bichat, Muller, Schleiden, Schwann, and Pasteur, work which still has not been assimilated into philosophical or theological discourse. The purpose of this chapter has been to show that it is at least plausible to move to the other side of the mesocosm, where we can see ourselves as parts of a macrocosmic whole. Plato, Plotinus, and Hartshorne have indicated the need for such a move in philosophy. And Origen and Hartshorne have indicated the theological reasons for such a move within Christianity.

CHAPTER FOUR

ALSTON AND MORRIS ON THE CONCEPT OF GOD

A. INTRODUCTION

It is crucial in Hartshorne's way of thinking to avoid both classical theism and pantheism. Hartshorne is obviously not a classical theist, but some (e.g., Gunton) may wonder whether he is closer to pantheism than he is to classical theism. The purpose of this chapter is twofold: (1) to briefly indicate why a critique of classical theism and a defense of divine embodiment, as detailed in the previous chapter, do not entail pantheism; and (2) to use Hartshornian panentheism to respond to two analytic theists: William Alston, in his second essay devoted to Hartshorne's concept of God, and Thomas Morris, in two recent books.

B. PANENTHEISM, NOT PANTHEISM

Thomas McFarland (1969, 127) is correct in noting that "pantheism" like "Platonism" are vast, general words thrown about by almost anyone able to string sentences together:

> It is almost as though . . . commentators have entered a kind of silent conspiracy never to challenge one another as to the exact meaning of these ideas, or as to the appropriateness of their

> invocation. Indeed, it sometimes seems as though complete understandings of "pantheism," of "Platonism" . . . are, like freedom of speech and the franchise, the born rights of every citizen in a democracy . . . they should no more be sprinkled, undefined and unexamined, through . . . history and commentary, than should formulas from quantum mechanics.

To avoid McFarland's criticism one can begin, as we did in chapter 1, by noting that pantheism, as opposed to panentheism, is a type of monopolar theism wherein the contrast between permanence and change is an invidious one when applied to God. In pantheism reality is permanent or necessary and change or contingency are illusory. Hence pantheism is also often associated with a denial of human freedom.

Yet all of the significant criticisms a classical theist can make of pantheism can also be made by a panentheist, but more consistently, and without the defects of classical theism. Hartshorne has a certain admiration for Spinoza in that he delivered the first significant wound to classical theism, from which it has not recovered, and indeed from which it cannot recover. But panentheism or neoclassical theism is just as far from Spinoza as it is from classical theism. Spinoza was unusually skillful at concealing the paradoxes in his thought. For example, if *all* things are contained in God as *necessary* qualifications of deity, then there is no contrasting term to "necessity," and not only "contingency" loses meaning, but also "necessity" itself. Hence Spinoza's mistake was largely grammatical, as is Quine's when he says that nothing is necessary. To say that every "possible" entity is "necessary" is to destroy the meanings of both terms. So also, if *all* things follow from God's essence, then "metaphysical" has no distinctive meaning.

In pantheism the modifications of deity can be either contingent or necessary; Spinoza denies the former. But what *is* a necessary modification or a necessary qualification of deity if not the divine essence all over again? If the modification is necessary it does not really modify, and the most trivial thing in the world is as valuable as deity. Hartshorne agrees with some of Spinoza's critics that there is a strong case for either viewing Spinoza as "God-intoxicated" or as an atheist. In order to make sense of divine modes Spinoza would have to avail himself of the contingent pole he denies. When principles of contrast are violated, when instances of becoming cannot be distinguished, then all true propositions become equivalent and mutually implicative. The point to notice is that Spinoza's inadequacies as a monopolar thinker cannot be remedied by another form of monopolarity. In fact, it is the pure actuality of the God of the classical theists—who can only inconsistently be said to love—which leads to Spinoza's denial of God's freedom and love. On this point Spinoza is more consistent than the classical theist in that his God is *really* a pure act, without even the pretense of divine love. Spinoza's famous saying that "If we love God, we cannot desire him to return our love, for then he would lose his perfection of becoming passively affected by our joys and sorrows," shows his monopolarity. Of these three views—classical theism, pantheism, and panentheism—it is only panentheism which can *consistently* defend the belief in God as a person (or, if one prefers, as three persons).

There are at least three logically distinct views regarding God:

1. God is merely the cosmos, in all aspects inseparable from the sum or system of dependent things or effects (pantheism).
2. God is both this system and in some way independent of it (panentheism).
3. God is not the system, but is in all aspects independent (classical theism).

(1) and (3) are simple views, (2) is complex. (1) and (2) refer to God as "the inclusive reality," but, as we have seen, much depends on what one means by this phrase. That (1) and (2) are not identical can be seen by the fact that for *both* (2) and (3) the error of pantheism is to deny the externality of concrete existence to the essence of deity. Note that "God is all things" (1) is not equivalent to "God includes all things" (2)—for instance, through divine omniscience or love. The differences among these three views can also be seen in their relation to the ontological argument. Spinoza, Hartshorne, and many classical theists have assented to this argument, but with different results. Spinoza confuses the necessary *existence* of God (i.e., the

fact *that* God must exist) with the concrete *actuality* of God (i.e., *how* God exists), hence he believes that everything relating to God is necessary. Panentheists need not deduce the "necessity" of the totality of things from an abstract definition, even if they do accept the ontological argument. God, for panentheists, is necessary or absolute or self-sufficient only in bare essence or existence, but is contingent in actuality in that *how* God exists at least partially depends on the other things that exist, which enrich the divine life. The actual state of the deity is partly determined by creatures as a consequence of the social character of the divine self-decision.

It is no wonder that theologians were shocked by Spinoza's views, and that the principle of divine inclusiveness was easily mistaken for its Spinozistic, necessitarian form, such that certain Christian thinkers felt compelled to retreat back into classical theism, even if they knew there were defects in that position. But it is too wide a use of "pantheism" to have the term cover all varieties of divine inclusiveness. The distinction between pantheism and panentheism is certainly no literary flourish; it is due to logical differences. Hartshorne holds that Spinoza missed the truth yet had great genius. Part of his genius was in not finding either his view *or* those of his classical theistic critics in scripture. Spinoza was the first to expose the skeleton in the classical theistic closet: an *exclusively* absolute and eternal God cannot be related to a contingent world. Hence an individual is to be identified with its career in that contingent predicates must be denied of substance, so as to preserve the absoluteness of deity; the essence of the substance, on this reasoning, determines its entire career. As before, the defects in Spinoza's position stem from the monopolar reasoning he inherited from classical theism; his God is an unmoved mover knowing an unmoved (or better, noncontingent) world. Nor do his geometrical analogies help him here—in geometry necessary properties are not modifications, but intrinsic properties.

In short, in panentheism, as opposed to pantheism or classical theism, one can articulate how God can be influenced by embodied creatures, how God can act in the world, and how God can be omnipresent. All of these abilities are best understood on the analogy of our own ability to be influenced by our cells, even though we can also exert an influence over our bodily parts, in that we are "omnipresent" in each part of our bodies. Care for members of the same natural organism does not make sense if God is, as in classical theism, super-natural, or if God lacks, as in pantheism, *any* distinction from nature. The divine soul is not in the body of the world the way a bean is in a box any more than the human *psychē* is in the body in such fashion. Rather, it is in *psychē* that a bodily cell lives and moves and has its being, just as Paul suggests that we, as members one of another, are in the mystical body of Christ.

C. ALSTON'S FIRST GROUP OF ATTRIBUTES

As was mentioned in chapter 3, Alston is not scandalized by Hartshorne's panentheism or neoclassical theism; in fact, he accepts much of what Hartshorne says about the concept of God. But even Alston eventually parts ways with Hartshorne's view. Alston's basic criticism is that the contrast Hartshorne draws between his own neoclassical, panentheistic view and that of, say, Thomas' classical theism is too sharp. That is, he thinks that Hartshorne presents neoclassical theism and classical theism as complete packages whereas it would be better to be able to pick and choose among individual items within these packages. Alston, like Creel, seeks some sort of rapprochement between Thomism and neoclassical theism, a rapprochement which Hartshorne himself would like to bring about to the extent that he is a neo*classical* thinker, but which is difficult to accomplish to the extent that he is *neo*classical.

Consider the first group of attributes treated by Alston (see schema 11) in his second article on Hartshorne (1984).

SCHEMA 11 (79)

Classical Attributes	Neoclassical Attributes
1. Absoluteness (absence of internal relatedness)	Relativity (God is internally related to creatures by way of His knowledge of them and His actions toward them)
2. Pure actuality (there is no potentiality in God for anything He is not)	Potentiality (God does not actualize everything that is possible for Him)

3. Total necessity (every truth about God *is* necessarily true)	Necessity *and* contingency (God *exists* necessarily, but various things are true of God—e.g., His knowledge of what is contingent—that are contingently true of Him)
4. Absolute simplicity	Complexity

Regarding absoluteness or lack of internal relations in religion, which Alston sees as the key contrast, two lines of argument are distinguished. Alston thinks that only one of these is successful. A relation is internal to a term (Hartshorne would say, to a concrete individual) if that term would not be exactly as it is if it were not in that relationship.

Hartshorne's first line of argument, on Alston's interpretation, is to say that if the relation of the absolute to the world really fell outside the absolute, then this relation would necessarily fall within some further and genuinely single entity which embraced both the absolute and the world and the relations between them. Thus we must hold, according to Hartshorne, that the God-creature relation is internal to God; otherwise we will have to admit that there is something greater or more inclusive than God. Alston does not find this argument impressive because it includes the claim that God "contains" the world due to the internal relations God has with the world (1984, 82). Alston's view is that the entity to which a relation is internal contains the terms only in the sense that those terms enter into a description of that entity, but it does not follow from this that those terms are contained in that entity as marbles are in a box.

But this is surely to misunderstand Hartshorne's panentheism and his theory of divine embodiment. Divine inclusiveness, for Hartshorne, is sometimes like the inclusion of thoughts in a mind, but usually it is described as being like the inclusion of cells within a living body. It is never like the inclusion of marbles in a box, in that the inorganic and insentient character of a box is completely inadequate as a model for divinity, and never like the inclusion of theorems in a set of axioms, as it might be for certain idealists, contra Alston's interpretation (UB, 13). Divine inclusiveness in Hartshorne is *organic* inclusiveness, a point which Hartshorne has been defending ever since his 1923 doctoral dissertation at Harvard:

> The entire history of philosophy indicates that it is only mind or spirit that unifies; and that history also provides . . . strong evidence for the conception of the unifying principle as not simply mind as bare thought or awareness (no such entity may exist) but as that identification of self with another in terms of value, which is suggested by such terms as sympathy, love, fellowship, or any term signifying a unity in respect of *purpose* and valuation. . . . One can only say that no one ever imagined that the terms God, or The Supreme Being, or the Absolute Mind, have been used to denote all individuals as instances of the class or kind of Divinity, or of Absoluteness. The One is not a class of members, but a Reality with contents or included elements . . . the contents of the One *Life*. (UB, 26, 49)

The second argument noticed by Alston in Hartshorne's defense of dipolarity with respect to absoluteness-relativity fares much better (according to Alston). Alston agrees with Hartshorne's stance regarding the cognitive relation God has with the world: in any case of knowledge, the knowledge relation is internal to the subject, external to the object. When a human being knows something, the fact that she knows it is part of what makes her the concrete being that she is. If she recognizes a certain tree she is different from who she might have been if she had not recognized the tree; but the tree is unaffected by her either way. Likewise, according to Alston, one cannot maintain that God has perfect knowledge of everything knowable and still hold that God is not qualified to any degree by relations with other beings. The classical theist's response to Hartshorne and Alston on this point would be that since creatures depend for their existence on God their relations to God affect *them* but not God. But even if beings other than God depend for their existence on God, it still remains true that if God had created a different world from the one that exists at present then God would be somewhat different from the way God is at present: God's knowledge would have been of *that* world and not this one.

Alston's concessions to Hartshorne's concept of God extend to contrasts 2–4 in schema 11. The above argument for the internal relatedness of God as cognitive subject presupposes that there are alternative possibilities for God, and if there are alternative possibilities for divine knowledge then this implies that there are unrealized potentialities for God. *Pure* actuality and *total* necessity cannot be defended as divine attributes. Alston's version of Hartshorne's argument goes as follows (1984, 84):

1. (A) "God knows that W exists" entails (B) "W exists."
2. If (A) were necessary, (B) would be necessary.
3. But (B) is contingent.
4. Hence (A) is contingent.

We can totally exclude contingency from God only by denying God any knowledge of anything contingent, a step that not even classical theists wish to take.

The final contrast in schema 11 must also be treated in a dipolar way in that the main support for a doctrine of pure divine simplicity (à la Mann) was the absence of any unrealized potentialities in God. In sum, the only problem with Alston's treatment of divine attributes in schema 11 is his partial critique of divine inclusiveness, a critique that mentions several different sorts of inclusiveness, but not the organic sort defended by Hartshorne.

D. ALSTON'S SECOND GROUP OF ATTRIBUTES

Regarding a second group of attributes, however, Alston diverges from Hartshorne rather significantly (80):

SCHEMA 12

Classical Attributes	Neoclassical Attributes
5. Creation *ex nihilo* by a free act of will. God could have refrained from creating anything. It is a contingent fact that anything exists other than God.	Both God and the world of creatures exist necessarily, though the details are contingent.
6. Omnipotence. God has the	God has all the power

power to do anything (logically consistent) He wills to do.	any one agent could have, but there are metaphysical limitations on this.
7. Incorporeality.	Corporeality. The world is the body of God.
8. Nontemporality. God does not live through a series of temporal moments.	Temporality. God lives through temporal succession, but everlastingly.
9. Immutability. This follows from 8. God cannot change since there is no temporal succession in His being.	Mutability. God is continually attaining richer syntheses of experience.
10. Absolute perfection. God is, eternally, that than which no more perfect can be conceived.	Relative perfection. At any moment God is more perfect than any other individual, but He is surpassable by Himself at a later stage of development.

Concerning contrast 5, Alston takes creation *ex nihilo* to be fundamental to theism because it has "deep roots in religious experience" (1984, 84). What it means to *experience* creation out of absolutely nothing we are not told. Alston's overall point regarding creation *ex nihilo*, however, is that to say that God has unrealized potentialities and contingent properties (which Alston would grant) is not to say that God *must* be in relation with some world of entities other than God. Alston admits that Hartshorne legitimately points out some of the internal contradictions contained in the classical theistic version of creation *ex nihilo*, but he claims that there is no connection drawn by Hartshorne between divine creation and metaphysical principles regarding relativity, contingency, and potentiality. (Alston's belief now is that those who accept creation *ex nihilo* are not saying that there is absolutely nothing at any stage: there is God! Rather, creation *ex nihilo* only means that there is nothing out of which God creates the universe. On this interpretation, however, it might be more accurate to talk of creation *ex deo* rather than creation *ex nihilo*.)

But Alston's stance here is problematic for two reasons. First, although it is not the job of this chapter to trace the history of creation *ex nihilo* or to determine when it became the orthodox view, it is clear that it is not the sort of creation described in Genesis, in that when the Bible starts with the statement that the spirit of God hovered above the waters, one gets the impression that both God and the aqueous muck had been around forever. If one believes in creation *ex nihilo*, however, as Alston does, one might nonetheless claim that creation *ex nihilo* does not necessarily mean a temporal beginning to the act of creation. But even on this hypothesis there are problems, and this is my second point. As I argued in chapter 2, if Plato and Hartshorne are correct that being *is* power then the sort of unlimited power implied by creation *ex nihilo* is impossible. That is, Alston is incorrect in claiming that Hartshorne has not even tried to connect his belief in creation *ex hyle* (as opposed to creation *ex nihilo*) with his basic metaphysical principles. Creation *ex nihilo*, a convenient fiction invented in the first centuries B.C.E. and C.E. in order to exalt divine power, is not the only sort of creation that religious believers have defended, nor is it defensible if being *is* power.

Concerning contrast 6, Alston claims that belief in creation *ex nihilo* and belief in divine omnipotence are separate beliefs such that to argue against the former is not necessarily to argue against the latter. Hartshorne tries to do too much, he thinks, with the claim that being is power when he uses this claim to argue against divine omnipotence. According to Alston, God can have *unlimited* power, power to do anything God wills to do, without having *all* power in that, if being is power, the creatures also have some power.

But this strategy plays right into Hartshorne's hands. God can have unlimited power but not all power on Alston's view because God *delegates* some power to others. That is, although God does not have all power, on Alston's view God *could* have all power. In effect what Alston has done is reduce his stance regarding divine omnipotence to that regarding creation *ex nihilo* in that the claim that God *could* have *all* power is due to the prior belief that God brings everything into existence out of absolutely nothing, a belief that Alston assumes, at least in the article under consideration here, has to be the traditional one and in point of fact is intelligible. It is not quite clear to me, however, that it is unquestionably the traditional one; and it is most definitely not clear to me that we can develop an intelligible concept of "absolutely nothing." At the very least Alston and other analytic theists who believe in creation *ex nihilo* need to explain what they mean by "absolutely nothing." For example, Bergson (1911, 1977 [1932]) has painstakingly developed (Platonic) reasons in his version of process metaphysics against creation *ex nihilo*, yet analytic theists have largely avoided these reasons.

Bergson's argument regarding the unintelligibility of "absolutely nothing" is a complicated one, but, in simplified form, it looks something like this: one can in fact imagine the nonexistence of this or that, or even of this or that class of things, a fact which gives some the confidence to (erroneously) think that this process could go on infinitely such that one could imagine a state in which there was "absolutely nothing." However, not every verbally possible statement is made conceptually cogent by even the most generous notion of "conceptual." At the specific, ordinary, empirical level negative instances are possible, but at the generic, metaphysical level only positive instances are possible: the sheer absence of reality cannot conceivably be experienced, for if it were experienced an existing experiencer would be presupposed. "Exist" and "exist contingently" do not, as defenders of creation *ex nihilo* like Alston imply, say the same thing (CS, 21, 57, 245, 283).[1] Or again, one cannot predicate "being" of a thing, even if one can predicate "necessary being" of a thing, for unless one has already in thinking the thing, unless one has thought its being, one has thought nothing (UB, 115).

Contrast 7 was treated in detail in chapter 3, but one additional comment is needed here regarding the connection between divine embodiment and Hartshorne's critique of divine omnipotence. In "Hartshorne and Aquinas" (as opposed to "The Elucidation of Religious Statements"), Alston is willing to grant (1984, 87) that God is embodied in two senses: (1) God is aware, with maximal immediacy, of what goes on in the world; and (2) God can directly affect what happens in the world. That is, in this later article Alston defends a limited version of divine embodiment similar to that defended by Swinburne. However, Alston is still sceptical regarding a stronger version of divine embodiment wherein the world exists by metaphysical necessity such that God *must* animate it. Alston is willing to accept the idea that God has a body but *only if* having such a body is on God's terms. It is correct to claim, as Alston does, that this weaker version of divine embodiment defended by Alston himself and Swinburne, as opposed to Hartshorne's stronger version wherein there is essential corporeality in God, stands or falls with the defense of creation *ex nihilo*. In fact, despite Alston's desire to examine each contrast individually, as opposed to Hartshorne's stark contrast between classical theistic attributes (all ten of them) and neoclassical attributes (all ten of them), he ends up linking his criticisms of Hartshorne regarding contrasts 5–7, at the very least. All three of these classical theistic attributes stand together only with a defensible version of creation *ex nihilo*, a version not supplied by Alston. (In fairness to Alston it should be noticed, however, that it is possible to hold that there are some connections among these attributes without thinking that the connections are as tight as Hartshorne suggests.)

In chapter 1 I treated contrasts 8–9, but a new wrinkle is added by Alston to issues surrounding divine nontemporality and immutability. Once again, there is an understandable linkage on Alston's part between divine temporality and mutability, despite his promise to examine each attribute individually without Hartshornian linkage among them. And Alston concedes that *if* God is temporal, Hartshorne has offered us the best version to date of what divine temporality and divine mutability would be like. Alston dismisses as idle the view that God could remain completely unchanged through a succession of temporal moments, but this admission still leaves us, he thinks, with the following conditional statement: "God undergoes change if he is in time" (1984, 88). Alston (1984, 89) reports on Hartshorne's view in the following way:

> If God is what He is partly because of the way He is related to the world, and if the world is in different states at different times, thereby entering into different relations with God at different times, it follows that God must be in different states at different times. For at one time God will have one set of relations to the world; at another time another set. Hence, if these relations are internal to God, the total concrete nature of God at the one time will be partly constituted by the relations He has to the

> world at that time; and so on with another time. Since these relations will be different at the two times, the total concrete nature of God will be correspondingly different.

Alston's critique of this view consists in a refusal to grant that contingency and temporality are coextensive in the way mutability and temporality are. Alston believes, contra Hartshorne, that God can be in some way contingent (that any relation in which God stands to the world might have been otherwise) and still be nontemporal.

Alston knows that the notion of a nontemporal God who is qualified by its relations to temporal beings will strike Hartshorne as unintelligible (1984, 90). His attempt to make his position intelligible rests on his own Thomistic-Whiteheadian stance, or better, on his Thomistic or Boethian interpretation of Whitehead. We should not think of God as involved in process or becoming of any sort. The best temporal analogy, he thinks, for this conception is an unextended instant or an "eternal now." For Alston this does not commit one, however, as Hartshorne would allege, to a static deity frozen in immobility. On the contrary, according to Alston, God is eternally active in ways that do not require temporal succession. God's acts can be complete in an instant. Alston explicitly includes here (1984, 90) God's acts of knowledge, a stance which seems to conflict with one of the concessions he made to Hartshorne regarding the first group of attributes (82–84).

Alston returns to the Boethian-Thomistic notion of the specious present for God on the analogue of a human being's perceiving some temporally extended stretch of a process in one temporally indivisible act. For example, one can perceive the flight of a bee "all at once" without first perceiving the first half of the stretch of flight and then perceiving the second. One's perception can be without temporal succession even if the object of one's perception is in fact temporally successive. All we have to do, on Alston's view, is expand our specious present to cover all of time and we have a model for God's awareness of the world (1984, 91). This is a much more difficult project for me to imagine than it is for Alston. Apparently he thinks it is easy to conceptualize God "seeing" Neanderthal man, Moses, Cleopatra, Jesus, Leonardo da Vinci, Rasputin, Dorothy Day, and

Ted Bundy all at once. But even if it were possible to have nonsuccessive *awareness* of a vast succession, which I deny, it is even more implausible to claim, as does Alston, that God could have nonsuccessive *responses* to stages of that succession. As we saw Creel argue in chapter 1, it would make more sense for Alston to say "indesponses" or "presponses" rather than "responses."

It has not escaped Alston's notice that his classical theistic notion of the specious present will be too much for some to swallow, hence he (if the mixed metaphor is permitted) refuses to slug it out on this notion and instead is willing to give ground and confront Hartshorne with what he takes to be Whitehead's concept of a nontemporal deity:

> This decision is prompted not only by cowardice, but also by the conviction that the Thomistic conception, excluding any sort of divine process or becoming, does run into trouble with divine-human *interaction*. It is surely central to the religious life to enter into commerce with God, to speak to Him and be answered, to have God respond to one's situation, to have God act on and in us at certain crucial moments. These back-and-forth transactions are not felicitously represented in the classical scheme. (Alston 1984, 91)

Relying on an article by Lewis Ford,[2] Alston defends the view that for Whitehead God unifies a set of initial prehensions into a more or less satisfying experiential whole without temporal succession: all the parts of God as an actual entity are present to each other in a felt immediacy. God undergoes the process of divine development nonsuccessively, he thinks (1984, 93). Although it is not *entirely* clear to Alston that we can form an intelligible conception of divine process without temporal succession, it is this view that he thinks is the best one and as a consequence he defends it.

God is, in Alston's view (and in Whitehead's view, on Alston's interpretation of Whitehead), a single actual entity, albeit an infinite one. God is not a (Hartshornian) society of temporally successive actual entities the way a human being is. That is, God is subject only to the kind of process involved in "concresence" (a growing together of components in a nontemporal way), not to the kind of process involved in "transition" (a successive process from one actual entity to its successors). Alston admits that his interpretation of Whitehead is controversial even though Whitehead repeatedly refers to God as *an* actual entity. Divine concresence is so radically different from human concresence because the divine sort takes its start not from *many physical* prehensions of other actual entities but from a *singular conceptual* prehension of abstract, eternal objects. (A prehension, for Whitehead, is the operation by which an actual entity "grasps" some other entity.) There is a strong affinity between Whitehead's view of God as infinite concresence, according to Alston, and that of God as eternal in Boethius. In fact, Whitehead is to be commended, he thinks, for doing a better job of describing the classical theistic God than either Thomas or Boethius. Once again, Alston stops just short of wholly embracing the Thomistic (or Thomistic-Whiteheadian) God, but he does indicate rather forcefully that he is closer to this view than he is to Hartshorne's regarding the latter's claim that divine contingency necessarily carries with it divine temporality (Alston 1984, 94).

What are we to make of this view? A good place to begin a critique is with an article by Rem Edwards (1981) that treats Elizabeth Kraus' (1979) Boethian interpretation of Whitehead, an interpretation that is very similar to Alston's. Both Kraus and Alston in effect turn time into space from the divine perspective in that all "times" are co-present to God. No doubt there are some passages in *Process and Reality*, and these are largely associated with the *primordial* nature of God (with what Hartshorne would refer to as God's being in the midst of becoming), that support Kraus' and Alston's view. But there are also many passages in *Process and Reality* which conflict with Kraus' and Alston's view, passages which deal either with the *consequent* nature of God (with what Hartshorne would refer to as God's becoming) or with the relationship between the consequent nature and the primordial nature. For example, in *Process and Reality* (1978 [1929], 19) Whitehead says that God's consequent nature "evolves in its relationship to the evolving world without derogation to the eternal completion of its primordial conceptual nature," and is "always immediate, always many, always one, always with novel advance, moving onward and never perishing" (1978, 525). Whitehead insists that God "is ever enlarging itself" (530), and that "the actuality of God must also be understood as a multiplicity of actual components in process of creation" (531); "in every respect God and the World move conversely to each other in respect to their process" (529).

It is obviously not the purpose of this section of the chapter to do detailed Whitehead scholarship, but I would at least like to indicate, on the evidence of the above texts: (1) that it is no easy matter to defend a Boethian-Thomistic interpretation of Whitehead; and (2) that by attempting to modernize classical theism by associating it with Whitehead, Alston does not significantly alter the classical theistic position (hence the traditional problems associated with classical theism remain). Alston is correct in noting that there is no loss in God, but this is not incompatible with God's temporality. There can be succession in God without there being loss or perishing, as Whitehead indicates in *Process and Reality* (1978 [1929], 531), due to the fact that God's inheritance of what happens in the world and God's memory are ideal. And Whitehead and Hartshorne agree that the future is incomplete and indeterminate for God as well as from our limited perspective; this is precisely what is meant when Whitehead says that God is fluent (528). Alston, by way of contrast, wants to defend a God who is not strictly necessary in actuality but is contingent *despite the fact* that God does not undergo temporal change, nor is God fluent. Edwards' (1981, 34) snappy way of putting this view in its place goes as follows: "One of the greatest virtues of process theology has been its intense effort to eliminate such blatant self-contradiction in theology, and it is much less than helpful to start playing the same old fun and games all over again." There is something worthwhile in what Edwards says here even if his point could be put more charitably.

Alston's treatment of contrast 10 in schema 12 follows from what he has said regarding contrasts 8–9. Relative perfection in God, as opposed to absolute perfection, has a point only for a temporal being, hence God is absolutely perfect, according to Alston (1984, 94–95). A being that does not successively assume different states could not possibly surpass itself. Here, once again, Alston engages in linkage, thereby, at the very least, confirming Hartshorne's belief that we need both to consider the divine attributes together and to determine whether the classical theist's linkage or the neoclassical theist's linkage is more defensible. For the most part, Alston opts for classical theism. Or more precisely, he thinks that the strongest concept of God is acquired when we take a modified version of the neoclassical attributes in schema 11 and combine them with the classical attributes in schema 12.

But here is where Alston's linkage of attributes *within* the first group and *within* the second group needs to be corrected by Hartshorne's greater concern for reticulating the attributes in groups one and two (i.e., in schemata 11 and 12). Alston gives no explanation regarding how he can be committed to both monopolar and dipolar theism. For example, Alston ends up defending the (inconsistent, I think) view that God is changed by the objects God knows (pace the neoclassical, dipolar attributes), but these are not changes that occur in time (pace the classical, monopolar attributes). It is one thing to say that God exists in a nontemporal specious present, and it is another to say that God is changed by temporal things in a nontemporal specious present. The former view is at least problematic; the latter seems to be part of the same old classical theistic game whereby inconsistency goes in the guise of mystery, to put the point in Edwards' terms.

E. MORRIS AND DIVINE INDEPENDENCE

Like Alston, Thomas Morris thinks that Hartshorne, in particular, and process thinkers, in general, have made a mistake when they claim that in some way or other God needs the world. Such a denial of the possibility that there could have been no created world, Morris rightly argues in *Anselmian Explorations* (1987), involves a related denial of creation *ex nihilo*. Morris asserts without argument, however, that it is "greater not to be dependent on anything else for what one is than to be so dependent." In a way this is correct in that regarding God's *existence* it would be a defect if God depended on some other being. But regarding God's concrete *actuality* Morris is less than helpful. To assert here that God is utterly independent is to call into question divine omnibenevolence. It is not necessarily a limitation on God, indeed it is part of what it means to say that God is perfect, to claim that if God is to love others God needs the others to love. Morris's response to this criticism seems to be connected to his belief in divine immutability: Even though God is described in the Bible as having done different things at different times, these changes, and the dependence on the world exhibited in these changes, are not real but "merely relational." The problem with this response can be seen when Morris's own examples are considered. Merely relational, as opposed to real, change is exhibited when there is a person just now who stands exactly two miles to one's right but one is unaware of this fact; or when Smith thinks of vanilla ice cream and then thinks of chocolate, in which case the flavors remain unaffected by the switch (1987, 127, 130–31).

Morris realizes that the classical theistic approach here is problematic, to say the least. The classical theist says that all change is merely relational in God, never does God really change "in himself." For example, God changelessly and eternally wills to speak *to* (n.b., not *with*) Abraham at time-t, to Moses at time-t + n, and so on. But this makes God very much like the ignorant human being or the chocolate ice cream in the above examples, a fact which leads some classical theists to deny even relational change to God. According to these thinkers, who are at least to be commended for seeing that there are severe problems with the way classical theism is usually defended, there is only the appearance of relational change in God and not the actual occurrence of relational change. In short, Morris admits that the extreme classical theistic view, wherein there is real change in creatures but only the appearance of relational change in an immutable God, is incompatible with the biblical portrayal of God, with the Incarnation, and, if I understand Morris correctly, with religious experience (1987, 132–34).

The key question to ask, I think, is whether Hartshorne's belief in God's immutability of existence, in God's supreme moral dependability, and in the impossibility of God ever losing the defining attributes of divinity, are enough to satisfy Morris. Or, in theological terms, the question is whether the social (trinitarian) view of God, which stretches back at least as far as the Cappadocian fathers, is enough to satisfy Morris; or does he require God to be The (ineffable) One, a view traceable back to Augustine and certain Neoplatonists (1987, 137, 140)? In the essay titled "God and the World: A Look at Process Theology" in *Anselmian Explorations*, Morris surprisingly leaves these questions unanswered in any explicit way, but at several points he, like Alston and Creel, drifts back toward classical theism almost as soon as he admits the legitimacy of certain criticisms Hartshorne has made of that position. In *The Logic of God Incarnate* (1986) Morris explicitly returns to classical theism after a few pats on the back to Hartshorne, and he explicitly refers to process theism as heretical.

In process thought every existent object is viewed as essentially related to other existent objects, hence God is of necessity a Creator, albeit a loving one. As with Alston, Morris wishes to maintain a belief in God's freedom to create or not create a world distinct from God. Hartshorne believes that God is as powerful and as loving as any being can logically be, but it is difficult to see how the classical theist can maintain a belief in both extreme omnipotence (perhaps a redundancy) and omnibenevolence. If God is so powerful that He (again, the masculine pronoun is crucial here) could create a world out of absolutely nothing, as Alston (at least at one stage in his career) and Morris believe, then there is a serious question regarding whether or not omnibenevolence is a fifth wheel, on the assumption that all-lovingness requires others to be loved. That is, if the concept of God in classical theism forces one to choose between divine omnipotence and divine omnibenevolence, as I think it quite unfortunately does, it is clear that Alston and Morris would take the former.

F. DUAL TRANSCENDENCE

It is significant that neither Alston nor Morris examine Hartshorne's magnum opus, *Creative Synthesis and Philosophic Method*, where the strongest versions of his views are found. Here it is clear not only that his theism is dipolar, but also that on the becoming-potentiality-relativity side God is preeminent or "transcendent," hence Hartshorne sometimes refers to his dipolar theism as "dual transcendence." Deity should indeed be thought of as uniquely independent, impassible, and necessary to the extent that, and in the ways that, these are admirable; however, this is only half the story. Alston, and perhaps Morris, wants to separate contingency and temporal change in God, but on this matter one needs to confront not only Hartshorne but also Aristotle. The latter held that accidents do not happen in eternity: "with eternal things to be possible and to be are the same." It follows, Hartshorne thinks, that any contingent aspects of deity must be noneternal:

> For me, Aristotle's dictum, quoted above, is about as intuitively obvious as anything so fundamental can be. I believe that our understanding of contingency is inseparable from our intuition that, whereas past events are settled and definite, future events are not settled or definite. Indeed, as Whitehead says, there are no such entities as future events. There are only the *more or less definite possibilities* or probabilities constituting the future so long as it is future. Futurity and real possibility are one. Here Alston, somewhat to my surprise, argues that it would follow that there could have been no possibility of yesterday having been otherwise than it has been. He seems to forget that yesterday was once tomorrow. To say that yesterday might have been otherwise is to imply that, as things were the day before yesterday, or a year or a century ago, or at the big bang, or . . . , it was not entirely settled what yesterday was to be. (EA, 99)

The biggest flaw in Alston's concept of God is the fact that he accepts both sides of the dependent/independent and contingency/necessity contrasts as applicable to deity, but not changeable/unchangeable, embodied/bodiless (although Alston does make some concessions to Hartshorne here), or self-surpassable/self-unsurpassable. Alston is like Creel and Morris and Karl Barth in the attempt to finesse belief in holy change into a God who ultimately has no potentiality to change. Alston and especially Morris are interested in preserving the best in the biblical view of God. But on Hartshorne's interpretation the best in this tradition is the God of love, and the monotranscendent, monopolar view of classical theism does not really contain the idea of a God who *is* love. Dual transcendence or dipolar theism can achieve, indeed celebrate, such a concept. If God cares for me God will react to, and care for, what happens to me tomorrow, but if what I do tomorrow is not, cannot be, wholly definite now, still less is it definite eternally (EA, 100–102).

In short, neither Alston nor Morris consistently defend dual transcendence or dipolar theism. Despite important concessions made to Hartshorne by Alston, the latter is still committed to creation *ex nihilo* without offering an indication of what it might be like to conceive of absolute nothingness; to divine contingency without divine temporality, whatever that might mean; to monopolar *and* dipolar theism without a clear statement regarding how these two are compatible; and to a divine knowledge of creatures that both affects God and leaves God unaffected. Further, Alston, who almost always reports Hartshorne's views accurately, inaccurately thinks of divine inclusiveness in Hartshorne as physical containment, on the model of marbles in a box, or in idealistic terms wherein theorems are contained in a set of axioms. Morris makes fewer concessions to Hartshorne than does Alston, and he is more securely ensconced within classical theism than is Alston. Morris' monopolarity is seen when he depicts independence as a virtue *simpliciter*; when he attributes only relational change to God, and perhaps only the appearance of this, perhaps leaving him two steps removed from the truth, in my estimation; and when he devalues divine omnibenevolence in the face of divine omnipotence, a devaluing which is largely due to the fact that a God who is only capable of relational change and not real change, and perhaps only of the appearance of relational change, cannot be benevolent in any way analogous to human benevolence.

CHAPTER FIVE

DESCRIBING GOD

A. INTRODUCTION

In this chapter I will examine the work of two more analytic theists who have commented on Hartshorne's concept of God. These thinkers—James Ross and Michael Durrant—have both written major works in analytic theism followed up by articles on Hartshorne. Ross' classic, *Philosophic Theology*, (1969) treats Hartshorne only tangentially, but his more recent article, "An Impasse on Competing Descriptions of God" (1977) deals exclusively with the challenge to classical theism posed by Hartshorne. Durrant's *The Logical Status of "God"* (1973) does not treat Hartshorne explicitly, but his recent article titled "The Meaning of 'God'" (1992) is largely about Hartshorne.

All four of these studies are instructive (intentionally or not) regarding Hartshorne's approach to religious language, which has not received sufficient attention from scholars, and regarding the inadequacies of classical theism when certain issues in philosophy of language are considered. Durrant does not seem to make as many concessions to Hartshorne as do Ross, Alston, Gunton, and Creel. (In fact, Ross pays a greater compliment to Hartshorne's thought than he perhaps realizes.) But Durrant is consistent in his adoption of classical theism's inconsistencies, and he at least makes some sort of effort to argue in favor of his classical theism, rather than assuming it without argument, as in the cases of Robert M. Adams or Robert Audi.

At the end of the chapter I will also treat the connection between mysticism and Hartshorne's concept of God. Specifically I will try to show how the great Christian mystics support Hartshorne's distinctions among the different sorts of religious language: literal-1 and literal-2, analogical, and symbolic.

B. ROSS AND PHANTOM INCONSISTENCY

Ross is like Alston in thinking that God has no accidents, even if some of God's characteristics are logically (not causally or temporally) contingent. This is a belief that some, like Hartshorne, might think is incompatible with the classical theistic commitment to divine simplicity. But, according to Ross, God is an entitatively simple being who possesses a logical plurality of properties; that is, the properties God possesses contingently do not fit into a continuous logical ordering with God's necessary properties. Hartshorne's response to Ross here would, I think, be twofold: (1) The contingent properties of God are, in fact, at odds with the classical theistic claim that God is simple *simpliciter* (not a redundancy: according to Hartshorne, in one aspect of the divine nature God is simple, but in terms of concrete relatedness to creatures God is preeminently complex); and (2) Ross is premature in claiming that we cannot "spell out" the concept of God: according to Hartshorne, some of God's properties *can* be discussed univocally even if some need to be treated analogically, as we will see later in this chapter (see Ross 1969, 63, 95).

It is to Ross' credit that he notices that the sort of rapprochement between neoclassical theism and classical theism attempted at various times and in different ways by Hartshorne himself, Creel, Gunton, Alston, Morris, and others can only accomplish so much. Hartshorne's theism is both neo*classical* and *neo*classical, depending on which aspect of his dipolar theism one chooses to emphasize. When one concentrates on the *neo*classical aspect, as Ross does, one is confronted with a God who is quite different from the one found in classical theism. But there are not two Gods, hence one of these two descriptions must have failed, he thinks.

The point to Ross' article on Hartshorne, "An Impasse on Competing Descriptions of God" (as opposed to an earlier article wherein classical theism was seen as entirely consistent[1]), is that there is an irresolvable impasse between the neoclassical and the classical theistic descriptions of God. Both descriptions arise from the doctrine of *vestigia dei*: In all things, and particularly in the interior life of human beings, there is a representation of God from which our conception of God arises. It is one thing to prove the existence of a being who is God (the existential stage), and it is quite another to show that some being whose existence has been proved *is* God (the identification stage). This distinction follows from the familiar criticism received by classical theists to the effect that their God could not possibly be the God of love found in the tradition. In contemporary philosophy there have arisen two prominent descriptions of God based on the same sorts of existential proofs. This leads Ross to ask the question as to whether one "can justify one characterization of God over another, for Aquinas says God is omnipotent, unchangeable, impassible and the like, while Hartshorne says God is almighty but not omnipotent, eternal but changeable and not impassible" (Ross 1977, 235). This impasse is caused, according to Ross, partly by divergent possible deductions from some initial premises and partly by informal application of certain religiously relevant properties. I have tried to show in chapters 1 through 3 above that the problem is also in part due to undue weight placed in the history of philosophy on being as opposed to becoming; once again, on a Platonism not necessarily held by Plato (Ross 1977, 233–34, 236–37).

Both St. Thomas and Hartshorne use "self-existent and perfect" as a basic property of God, but the former adds "immutable" while the latter adds (contra Ross's less than accurate version of Hartshorne) "immutable in one aspect, reactive to other persons and self-surpassing in another aspect." Ross considers at least three possible ways in which one might select between these competing descriptions.

1. *Linguistic Grounds.* The test question here would be, "Which of the two descriptions more faithfully presents the term 'God' in reli-

gious discourse?" Ross responds to this question by claiming that neither Thomas nor Hartshorne faithfully represent the *whole* of religious discourse, hence there are no linguistic grounds for deciding between the two (1977, 238–39). He leaves unexamined, however, the possibility that one of the two represents a greater portion of religious discourse than the other, for example, divine perfection regarding permanence *as well as* responsive change, unity *as well as* variety, and so on, as opposed to only one element in each of these pairs. It should be clear by this point in the book which of these two descriptions, on my reading, has the advantage in this regard.

2. *Religious Grounds.* Another possibility is that we could decide in favor of that description which best accords with religion or religious experience. Ross sees two limitations to this method. First, choosing on this basis would constitute a *mere* pragmatic justification without *philosophical* authority. By saying this, however, Ross assumes that the contributions of the classical American philosophers are negligible. Hartshorne has a far higher estimation of Peirce (see Vitali 1977), James, and Dewey. We saw in chapter 2 that once position matrices regarding a philosophical problem have been developed, and once inconsistent positions have been eliminated, pragmatic criteria *are* philosophical criteria, they *do* carry philosophical authority, contra Ross. Or, stated negatively, a philosophical position that did not agree with paradigmatic human experience would be, other things equal, a weak philosophical position. When St. Teresa of Avila and St. John of the Cross say, in language reminiscent of the *Song of Songs*, that God (the bridegroom) is *changed* by the love God has for some particular soul (the bride), how are we to respond to the familiar charge made by these mystics and others that the God of "the philosophers" (i.e., of the classical theists) is at odds with the God of religious experience? Are we to assume that philosophical description per se is incompatible with religious experience (pace Ross) or should we, as I would argue, try to develop a philosophical theology that can account for *both* the religious experience of divine constancy and the religious experience of divine mutability?

The second limitation Ross sees in trying to resolve the conflict between the classical theistic description of God and the neoclassical one on the basis of religion or religious experience, is that, if I understand Ross correctly, we may end up being confronted with an impasse not only regarding description of God but regarding religious experience as well. Suppose, for example, we find one sect asserting the superiority of its religious experiences over those in another sect. In this case appeal to religious experience will not help resolve the impasse regarding description of God. Hartshorne, however, seems to think that in Judaism, Christianity, and Islam, at the very least, classical theism is deficient with respect to common features of religious experience in these traditions (e.g., regarding divine love), although there are also, as we will see, some differences. The point here, however, is that the similarities dominate. Ross does notice that Hartshorne's "maximally powerful God" is as compatible as classical theistic "omnipotence" with respect to the experience of God as powerful in Judaism, Christianity, and Islam. This is a significant admission on the part of Ross, an admission not made by the vast majority of analytic theists. (And this seems to conflict with Alston's aforementioned belief that creation *ex nihilo* is deeply rooted in religious experience.) Regarding religious experiences other than those associated with divine power, however, Hartshorne's theism is more religious, not less, than classical theism on the evidence of the great Jewish, Christian, and Muslim mystics themselves, as I will argue. These "experts" with respect to religious experience testify that God is moved by love, that God reacts to human (and other) suffering, that God's responsiveness is dependable, et al. (Ross 1977, 239–41). For Hartshorne, process theism is superior to classical theism *precisely because* it does a better job of handling the religious emotions of love, wonder, awe, and worship, and it does as good a job as classical theism with respect to the religious emotions associated with divine power.

3. *Metaphysical Grounds.* Ross is also sceptical as to whether or not the impasse between neoclassical theism and classical theism regarding the description of God can be resolved on metaphysical grounds, and his criticism here allows us to locate the key problem with his unsuccessful attempt to resolve this "impasse." Ross's view is that differences on basic metaphysical claims cannot be dislodged

if these differences are based on differences regarding normative claims *such that* each side suggests that the other's description of God is internally inconsistent. Hartshorne has spent a career pointing out inconsistencies in the classical theist's concept of a God who loves the creatures but is not changed by them even when they suffer, and so on. But the charge usually made by Hartshorne's critics is that his God violates crucial elements in the tradition (e.g., regarding divine power, a charge that Hartshorne thinks he can rebut—with Ross's help!), *not* that Hartshorne's concept of God is inconsistent. As far as I can tell, Creel, Gunton, Alston, and Morris all think that Hartshorne's concept of God is, for the most part, consistent. In fact, their criticisms of his concept of God often consist in a de-emphasis of his rationalism; that is, they often indicate that Hartshorne's concept of God is *too* consistent. Perhaps what Ross (1977, 242) means by inconsistency in Hartshorne's view is as follows:

> Each accuses the other of providing a description that falls short of some standard of conceptual accuracy and each argues on normative grounds that one metaphysical requirement must give way to the other: "Sociality demands self-surpassibility" (Hartshorne); "Change entails dependence and imperfection" (Aquinas). . . . [T]hough metaphysical preferences may be rational and relevant, such preferences will not justify the selection of one description of God over the other because of the importance of normative differences which precede.

But this classical theistic charge of inconsistency in Hartshorne is only half-hearted. Once the distinction between divine existence and divine actuality is made it is difficult to make the charge stick, as Ross tries to do, that responsive, loving divine change entails imperfection on God's part, or that such change entails divine dependence on creatures for God's very existence (1977, 245).

There is a sceptical consequence to Ross's failure to ameliorate this impasse. In a way this impasse indicates an accomplishment on Hartshorne's part in that his view is put on a par with that of the classical theist; it is seen by Ross as a legitimate candidate for an adequate description of God. However, Ross is equally insistent that there is nothing to be gained by Hartshorne's emphasis of the superiority of neoclassical theism to classical theism. Once again, Ross makes this point on the basis of the alleged or phantom inconsistency in Hartshorne's view between divine change, on the one hand, and divine independence, on the other. It is unfortunate that Ross does not criticize Hartshorne's view as Hartshorne would state it: The fact that God does not owe the divine existence to creatures (i.e., the fact that God's *existence* is independent of creatures) does not contradict the fact that God's *actuality* or God's concrete state at any particular moment is partially dependent on the creatures (Ross 1977, 247–49). That is, it is difficult to assess Ross's claim that there is an irresolvable impasse between neoclassical theism and classical theism regarding the concept of God because Ross does not exactly confront Hartshorne head on as a dipolar theist but rather does so obliquely with monopolar assumptions.

C. DURRANT AND THE LOGICAL STATUS OF "GOD"

Durrant is as sceptical of the logical status of "God" as Ross is regarding description of the concept of God. "God," as an item of Christian language, exhibits the incompatible features of: (1) being a descriptive predicable (Frege's *Begriffswort*); (2) being an abstract term, and (3) being a proper name. No single logical status of "God" can be given because "God" has to play different and incompatible roles in Christian language. Any sentence of the form "God is F" where F is, from the standpoint of grammar, an adjective can have manifold meanings such that there are "fatal difficulties" involved if one claims that "God" has a single status. For example, to say that "God" can stand as a logical subject is not to say that "God" is necessarily a proper name. Or, again, it is not a sufficient condition of an expression being a proper name that the personal pronoun can be used with it. Such personal pronouns can also be used in connection with descriptions. It is crucial to notice, according to Durrant, that in some contexts "God" functions as a proper name and in other contexts it functions as a description (e.g., Lord of all power and might) or as an abstract term (1973, ix-x, 1, 4, 78, 110).

It is clear that although Durrant painstakingly distinguishes among the different logical uses of "God" throughout his book, he assumes without argument that "God," in whatever use we find it in Christianity, is to be thought of in classical theistic terms. For example, when he thinks of "God" being used as a description he assumes that "Lord of *all* power and might" (my emphasis) is a noncontroversial example of such a description. He does notice that tenses can attach to descriptive predicables, but not, as Aristotle also noticed, to names. Yet the self-proclaimed radical distinction he makes between names and descriptions does not lead him to take seriously the neoclassical stance that one way to describe God is in temporal terms. Durrant assumes that God cannot sensibly be spoken of in temporal terms because this would imply, he thinks, that God would then be amenable to coming into existence and passing out of existence, to suffering change *and therefore* decay. As we have seen, however, to be mutable is not necessarily, as Durrant assumes, to be corrruptible if the being in question is eminently mutable. The closest Durrant comes to giving reasons why his analysis of the logic of "God" supports classical theism comes when he notices that when "God" is used as a proper name it can only occur in the subject place of a subject-predicate proposition and never, by itself, in the predicate place (1973, 3, 7, 16, 18, 24).

There are at least two problems here, however. First, even if "God" is being used as a proper name, and even if proper names can only occupy the subject place in a subject-predicate proposition, and even if proper names cannot have tenses attached to them, it does not necessarily follow that classical theism is correct. For example, a proper name may very well be associated with the abstract features that are common to a series of events in a personally ordered sequence. For the process philosopher, "Dan" is the name used to refer to the continuity of experience-found in me from time-1 (at my birthday party when I was five years old) to time-2 (when I turned twenty-one) to time-3 (myself in the present), and so on. Or, in other words, we should not assume, as Durrant does, that proper names that occupy the subject-place in subject-predicate propositions necessarily have the substantive properties alleged by Aristotle. And second, on Durrant's own theory "God" as a proper name is only one of the uses to which the word can be put such that when "God" is used as a description "God" can (again, on Durrant's own criteria) have tenses attached to it. The point to these criticisms is not to denigrate entirely the Aristotelian notion of substance utilized by Durrant. Some of the "living" elements in the Aristotelian view are that: In this view individuality, although not the only concern, is nonetheless a metaphysical concern carefully addressed; in this view the principle of self-determination (or creativity) is rightfully emphasized; and in this view the principle of permanence receives deserved attention. But there are also, from a process point of view, some "dead" elements in the Aristotelian notion of substance utilized by Durrant: In this view there is an emphasis on a vacuous and static substratum for reality, including divine reality, rather than on concrete, experiencing actualities (e.g., when Durrant "attaches" tenses to this static substratum); and on this view there is a tendency to view real things in isolation from their accidents, or better, to view independence as a virtue which crowds out any positive function for dependence—and as a result real relations are hard to find (see Christian 1959, 106–15).

Durrant also shows his classical theism in his utter denial of divine embodiment and indeed his assumption that God must be thought of as pure spirit. He repeatedly asserts, but does not argue for, the view that God is, à la classical theism, outside of both time and space (1973, 27, 33–35, 43–44, 48, 51, 94). Emphasis of this point regarding divine nonconcreteness leads Durrant to suggest that "God" is an abstract term; grammatically speaking, an abstract noun. Common nouns do not take an initial capital letter, and proper names are not translatable between languages. Abstract nouns, by way of contrast, are translatable between languages and they sometimes do occur with an initial capital letter, as in "God" (1973, 42). But although "God" can be used as an abstract term, it cannot be used to refer to the sort of being who is in time because this would mean that we could say that God: (1) still exists; or (2) could go on existing; but also (3) comes into existence; and (4) ceases to exist (1973, 52). It is not the case, however, as Durrant thinks, that if God is in time we are necessarily committed to (3) and (4). Once again, Durrant assumes that if God is changeable God is *therefore* corruptible (1973, 75). In short, in *The Logical Status of "God"* Durrant may have done yeoman's work in showing the strengths and weaknesses of viewing "God" either as a proper name or as some sort of description, but he has made very little progress regarding the concept of God itself.

The classical theistic assumptions made by Durrant in his book are carried over into his article on Hartshorne, "The Meaning of 'God'." Here he defends at least three theses: first, that "God" is not a proper name but a common noun (even in his book his criticisms of "God" as a proper name were harsher than those regarding "God" as an abstract or common noun); second, that "God" can be described; and third, that previous efforts, including those of Hartshorne, to reconcile the description of the God of the philosophers and the description of the God of religion, fail. No harm is done for the sake of argument by agreeing with Durrant on the first two theses, but the third thesis is in need of critique.

Durrant is correct to criticize Janet Martin Soskice (1985), who claims that we may only name God and never describe God. She contends that "God" is, in effect, a (Russerllian) proper name that has reference only. Durrant's criticism goes as follows: "I may only claim that I am pointing towards something in my use of an expression if I can at least offer *some* description of what it is I am pointing towards—otherwise how can I ever claim that I have been or currently am *successful* in my pointing?" (1992, 73). Two people can only refer to the same individual by the alleged proper name "God" if we are able to say that we are both referring to the same F, where F supplies a criterion of identity for the name. What is putatively referred to by the proper name "God" must be describable in *some* way. In short, "God" is grammatically a common noun (1992, 74).[2]

It should be obvious that Durrant's criticism of the conception of God as the wholly other, of God as *totaliter aliter*, of God as a proper name, entails a willingness to come up with a description of God. But his description is the traditional one wherein God is the perfect or greatest conceivable being who is the omnipotent, omniscient, and omnibenevolent creator and sustainer of the world; the ultimate reality responsible for the existence and activity of everything else (1992, 78–79). There are many problems with this description (or better, with these descriptions), at least one of which is of concern to Durrant himself: How can the classical theistic, immutable God *also* have the properties of being personal, merciful, loving, forgiving, and concerned with the welfare of creatures? (1992, 80).

As has been seen throughout this book, I think that the boldest attempts in twentieth century thought to reconcile the God of the philosophers/theologians and the God of religion have been developed by process thinkers like Whitehead and Hartshorne. But Durrant rejects these attempts, as is evidenced in two criticisms he has of Hartshorne's neoclassical theism wherein supposedly divine properties like immutability, omnipotence, and omniscience are called into question or are redefined. To take one example, regarding divine immutability Hartshorne makes a crucial distinction, as we have seen, between divine existence and divine actuality. It is only the former which is, as in Anselm, necessary. But *how* God exists is not necessary; indeed God's actuality or God's *mode* of existence changes as the creatures change. To say that "God loves the suffering creatures" and that "God remains immutably unmoved by the creatures" is, to say the least, to stretch to the breaking point the classical theistic notion that discourse about God must be analogical, a notion with which Hartshorne agrees (with qualifications). It may even be the case that these two statements contradict each other. What sort of love even remotely analogous to human love can we imagine that allows the lover to remain unmoved while the beloved suffers?

Durrant's two criticisms are as follows: (1) "I know of no part of the admittedly complex Christian tradition which actually regards God as an effect or as finite in whatever unique or special sense"; and (2):

> Hartshorne claims that God is cause in a radically unique or "eminent" sense and that he is effect in an equally unique sense. The problem arises as to *what* sense. There can be *no* "radically unique" sense of "cause" which applies and which *can* apply *only* to a single individual however eminent, for this would turn "cause" from being a general term, which in principle has appli-

> cation to more than one thing (though in fact may only apply to one thing), into a sort of proper name, which cannot be said to have application *at all*, but merely stand for an object. Similarly in the case of "effect." Hartshorne is only able to advocate his case at the expense of converting a general term into a sort of proper name; yet he requires "cause," "effect," etc., *not* to be proper names for he has spoken of God as coming under both sides of the basic contraries. For God to come under both sides of the "basic contraries" demands that "cause," "effect," and the rest *remain* general terms for, as Geach has argued, proper names do not come in contradictory pairs and neither do they come in opposite pairs, whereas general terms do. Further, proper names and general terms are absolutely distinct as Frege in his distinction between "object words" and "concept words" makes abundantly clear. (1992, 82)

There are several problems with Durrant's stance that I will be treating in the remainder of this chapter. Among these is his (unexamined) monopolarity. Finitude of existence, say, is a defect, but in order to relate to a particular being who suffers here and now there is a sense in which an omnibenevolent being would have to be finite. Likewise, infinite existence throughout time is a mark of divine perfection, but a being that was infinite in *every* sense would, as the Greeks noticed, be a formless chaos (*apeirōn*), contra Durrant. Or again, biblical theism and mysticism are, if anything, rich testimonies to the belief that God is responsive to us, to the belief that in some sense God *is* supreme effect.

Hartshorne refers to God not as a "special fact" but as a "general principle." Hence Durrant is premature in infering that Hartshorne is more likely to think of "God" as a proper name than as an abstract term. (It is also inaccurate to think that it is more likely that he would think of "God" as an abstract term than as a proper name.) Hartshorne's description of God as "radically unique" is meant not so much to play into the hands of those who hold that God cannot be described but only named, but rather to indicate that God is the only one who can be *described* as offering a maximal response to concrete reality. God is unique in that divinity is the upper limit of the series of causes *and* effects; God's uniqueness follows from rather than contradicts these series. Even Durrant admits that it is possible for a description to apply to only one being. Hartshorne speaks of:

> the gap between abysmal ignorance and omniscience, and between *partial and shifting inhibition* of the interest of others by self-interest, as contrasted to *certain and absolute coincidence* of other-interest and self-interest. . . . Nevertheless, there is even in us a partial coincidence of desire for self and desire for others; and this is the analogical basis for theism. (RS, 141; also 30, 138)

Hence it may be wise on Durrant's urging to drop the adverb "radically" and say instead that "God is unique" both because God alone most penetratingly loves the creatures and because God alone exhibits the abstract character trait of permanence in such love. Hartshorne's neo*classical* theism enables one to say that in describing (not naming) God as the unsurpassable we are bound to claim that God is unique (MV, 9). And his *neo*classical theism enables him to say that God is supreme effect.

D. HARTSHORNE ON GOD AS ABSTRACT-CONCRETE

One of the virtues of Durrant's treatment of the logical status of "God" is that he (unwittingly) supports the case for dipolar theism: "God" can be used as a descriptive predicable or abstract term, on the one hand, or as a proper name of a concrete being, on the other. One of the consequences of the sorts of (at times, confusing) distinctions made by Durrant is that Hartshorne's classification of theistic doctrines found in schema 6 in chapter 2 (p. 51) is in need of refinement. In schema 6 the number of cases of perfection was limited to six plus the purely negative case, making a total of seven. The needed refinement has to do with the distinction between surpassibility by nothing at all and surpassibility by self only. There are two other possibilities: (1) complete passibility by both self and others; and (2) surpassibility by others only and not by self. It is easy to ignore these two possibilities if one assumes that by "God" is meant a concrete being or a proper name, not a description or an abstraction or an abstract noun. It seems that only an abstraction could be unsurpassible by itself and yet surpassible by others, as when politeness is said to be inferior to morality, but politeness cannot improve upon itself: it is always just politeness (MV, 54).

Once we open up the possibility that "God" can be used as a descriptive predicable or as an abstract term *as well as* a proper noun, then we have fifteen possible combinations of the four modes of surpassibility and its negation together with the threefold division of respects of greatness into all, some, or none. The four modes of surpassibility are: (i) surpassibility by *both* self and others: B; (ii) surpassibility by self only: R (i.e., unsurpassibility relative to others); (iii) surpassibility by others *only*: O; and (iv) surpassibility by neither self nor others: A. In schema 6 in chapter 2, (p. 51), B and O were treated indifferently as I. The fifteen combinations are shown in schema 13 (MV, 54):

SCHEMA 13

Group	Case		
I	1 – A		
II	2 – AR	3 – ARO	
	4 – ARB	5 – ARBO	
	6 – AB	7 – ABO	8 – AO
III	9 – R	10 – RO	
	11 – RB	12 – RBO	
	13 – B	14 – BO	15 – O

What progress can be made regarding the concept of God by considering the options made available by B and O? First, it should be noted that the new distinctions leave group I (or A) unchanged. Changes do occur in group II, but options 3, 5, 7, and 8 do not seem to constitute significant conceptions of God because a being which could not itself improve and yet could be surpassed by others would not seem to be the supreme being, the most venerable. This applies *a fortiori* to options 10, 12, 14, and 15. Self-surpassibility does not necessarily imply a defect, as we have seen, and may actually imply a virtue, unless, of course, one begs the question by assuming that God is outside of time and the possibility of growth altogether. But to be surpassed by others "seems a defect pure and simple" (MV, 55). Hence B in all its instances is defective (i.e., cases 4, 5, 6, 7, 11, 12,

13, and 14). And the defects in option 9 have been treated earlier in the book. In short, O and B imply negative properties or deficiencies *simpliciter* whereas A and R contain (between them!) what is positive in the concept of God. As Hartshorne puts the issue:

> It hardly seems reasonable to expect a being which enjoys one or both of the two forms of positive perfection to possess aspects so inferior as to conform to the definitions of O and B. . . . Thus it seems unlikely that the combinations of A and R with B and O represent real (other than purely formal) possibilities. The essential problem is thus, in all probability, to determine the significance of the A and R conceptions, and of their joint denial. . . . The essential questions are: (1) Is there such a thing as absolute or static perfection? (2) Is there such a thing as relative or dynamic perfection? (3) Is there a being possessing either or both of them and in what respects? (MV, 55–56)

The defects in cases 3–15 indicate how close Hartshorne's view (case 2) is in many respects to classical theism (case 1), and how "classical" his neoclassical theism really is. But failure to consider options 3–15 at all indicates a troublesome neglect regarding the possibilities, a neglect evidenced in the common assumption that A just *is* theism.

E. LITERAL, ANALOGICAL, AND SYMBOLIC LANGUAGE

In order to adequately understand philosophical description of God it will be useful to be precise regarding three different uses of language in Hartshorne, all of which have been used either by neoclassical or classical theists in the effort to describe God. In this effort we will see at different points where Ross and Durrant support some of Hartshorne's views and where they diverge from them. What is crucial from a Hartshornian point of view is that two extremes be avoided: that we can capture deity in some verbal formula devoid of any doubt or obscurity, on the one hand, and that we are totally in the dark in the effort to describe God, on the other. The latter extreme leads to atheism, or at least to agnosticism or fideism, whereas the former extreme leads either to intolerance or idolatry (EA, 39).

"Literal" terms applied to God, as Hartshorne uses the word, are not matters of degree but must be matters of all or none. That is, literal terms express a purely *formal* status by classifying propositions as of a certain logical type. For example, the categorical terms "absolute" and "relative" have a literal meaning when applied to God as an individual: Either God is independent of creatures for divine existence or not, and either God is related to creatures in the divine actuality or not. (As we will see, however, when considering the *concrete* way in which God is independent of others, or is related to others, we can say that God is *supremely* absolute and *supremely* relative, hence indicating a matter of degree.)

"Analogical" terms applied to God, as Hartshorne uses the word, by way of contrast admit of matters of degree as they apply to different entities *within* the same logical type. For example, concrete individuals feel in different degrees of intensity and with different levels of adequacy, with God being the supreme example of feeling.

And "symbolic" terms applied to God, as Hartshorne uses the word, are used to apply locally and not cosmically to a particular kind of individual in a particular culture, and so on, with an even greater degree of specificity than analogical terms, as when God is referred to as a shepherd or king.

There is an obvious distinction at work in Hartshorne between formal and material predication. To compare God with a rock, a king, a shepherd, or a parent is a material description that cannot be literal. Formal or nonmaterial predication is illustrated when one refers to God as noncorporeal or nonrelative *or* (and this point is often missed) when one refers to God as corporeal or relative. That is, when the abstraction "concreteness" or "corporeality" is applied to God one is not identifying God with any particular concrete thing but is rather contrasting the abstraction "materiality" with the abstraction "immateriality." Hartshorne emphasizes that the formal (literal) predicates of deity are not exclusively negative. If God's very existence cannot be contingent, the question arises: Is God's necessary existence to be conceived as having the ability to be related to creatures or simply as the absence of relativity? These are two categorically or formally opposite ways of interpreting the necessary truth of the proposition "God exists." On either interpretation something literal is being said of God. In between the formal, literal terms (absolute-relative, being-becoming, etc.) and the most material, particular, symbolic ones (shepherd, monarch, etc.) there are analogical terms (love, personality, etc.). To the extent that analogical terms involve qualitative distinctions of degree they are removed from the all-or-nothing character of literal terms: Who can say literally how divine love differs *qualitatively* from ours? (LP, 134–41).

Neither abstractness nor concreteness have been properly understood by analytic, classical theists, overly influenced as they are by the tradition of negative theology. It is easy enough to say that one is being modest in claiming that human language cannot properly apply to God, hence, as Alston and Ross, among others, allege, we cannot speak literally about God. But, according to Hartshorne, the negative theology of analytic theists itself may be a sort of presumption:

> So it is held to be quite safe to say, without qualification, that he is *not* finite, *not* relative, *not* passible or open to influence. I think, however, that the modesty is only apparent. We dare to forbid God to sustain relations, to accept the definiteness that comes through limits, to respond to the creatures and thus be influenced by them. He may, we conclude, do these things "symbolically," whatever that may mean, but we tell him in no uncertain terms that he must not literally do them! Is this modesty—or is it monstrous presumption? Have we this veto power upon divinity? (CS, 151)

It makes sense to say that God is not literally a shepherd or ruler, but is these things only symbolically, because shepherds and rulers are quite specific sorts of things; to "forbid" God to literally be a shepherd does not really restrict God:

> It is, however, a very different affair when we treat utterly abstract terms like "finite" or "relative" in this same manner. There are not an infinity of miscellaneous possible positive forms of reality alternative to being relative; there is only being non-relative or absolute. If God is not literally finite and rela-

> tive, then he is literally and exclusively infinite and absolute. For there is no third possibility: here the law of excluded middle must, I submit, apply. (CS, 152)

It may well be the case that if God is not a shepherd God could be a super-shepherd, whatever that means, but "super-relative" can only be thought of as an eminent form of relativity if "relative" implies in some way or other being constituted by contingent relations: "either one might, or one might not, have been otherwise. *Tertium non datur*" (CS, 153).

The modesty of negative theology is suspect because it puts a human veto on the wealth of the divine life:

> Traditional theological theory had a headlong tendency, almost wholly ungovernable, and even today in many circles largely uncontrolled, to "plump" for one side—the negative side—of the ultimate polar contraries, in application to God. But this indeed "limits" God—for instance, if we deny him all definiteness, or all responsiveness to the contingent creatures. . . . And we think to honour God by offering him this vacuity as his sole portion! (CS, 153)

All abstractions, even the abstraction "concreteness," are impassible, as Durrant seems to realize. But this does not mean that God is entirely impassible if God is both abstract in one sense and concrete in another, contra negative theology.

Hartshorne's view is that regarding abstractions we can speak literally about God, contra Alston and Ross; and regarding the most specific, concrete predicates we can speak (indeed we must only speak) symbolically. But in between there are psychical terms like "knowledge," "will," and "love." These denote states or functions like the human ones, but, as is well known, there is a central philosophical issue regarding how far psychical terms can be broadened beyond the human application. Hartshorne's response to this problem is to suggest the broadest possible meaning of *psychē*-terms, a meaning which is applicable to all concrete singulars, from atoms to God. This meaning is so broad that psychic terms are almost categorical, like absoluteness or relativity:

> There is, however, a difference. For only individuals, not abstractions, can feel or think or remember, whereas both individuals and abstractions (other than those of uttermost generality) can have aspects of relativity, can depend in some way and degree upon contingent relations. . . . [T]heir meaning does not vary from one level to another in the scale of beings. (CS, 154)

In some abstract way God's knowledge is like human knowledge in that merely absolute, wholly nonrelative "knowledge" is an impossibility for anyone. In fact, Hartshorne goes so far as to claim that "the veto upon literal relatedness (a veto which must itself be literal or else merely misleading) is in my view unwitting blasphemy" (CS, 155).

But to say that God is literally relative because God knows, as Hartshorne consistently admits and as Alston sometimes does, is not to deny that we should be sensitive regarding the *levels* of knowledge and relativity that different beings possess. That is, in one *abstract* aspect of the divine nature God is relative and this can be stated literally, but regarding what it is like to be *concretely* related to the entire world through knowledge, as God is, can only be talked about in outline, or analogically, with the full details of concrete occurrences left out of the picture (OO, 11). We cannot speak literally about what it is like to *be* God. At times Hartshorne confuses matters by saying that the concrete complexity of divine knowledge can only be talked about symbolically rather than analogically (EA, 41), but his overall point here remains that we can only speak of God in literal terms if we do so abstractly; we can only talk about what it is like to *be* God concretely in, at best, analogical terms. But if there is no sense whatsoever in which univocal meaning or literal terms (roughly equivalent in Hartshorne) can be used regarding the concept of God, then talk about the concept of God is not of much use. Maximal conceptual flexibility is perhaps needed regarding analogical and especially symbolic terms, but there is a real impediment to progress in philosophy of religion when vague or flabby analogies or symbols are used regarding philosophical abstractions (MV, 194, 221).

Before leaving the issue of literal terms or univocal meaning connected with the concept of God, it is necessary that we treat a second sense of the term "literal" in addition to the sense in which Hartshorne usually uses the term, that is, to refer to those abstract terms which can be used to describe God as exhibiting a certain logical type or not. Confusing as it sounds, the second sense of the term (hereafter: literal-2) refers to a certain distinction within the use of analogical terms. It is a commonplace in philosophy of religion (pace St. Thomas, Alston, Ross, and Hartshorne) that we start with human experience or human *psychē* and then analogize regarding God. In learning the meaning of words we necessarily follow the us-to-God path, but once we reach some understanding of the concept of God the reverse path is also crucial. As Hartshorne puts the issue:

> I have . . . sometimes argued that, unless we have in our own natures instantiation of concepts (say that of decision-making) which we use to conceive God, we could not have these concepts. But I have also sometimes argued that we can conceive our own form of knowing, say, by introducing qualifications into what we know of divine cognition. God knows—period; we—partially, uncertainly, vaguely; and much of what we can hardly avoid taking as knowledge is erroneous belief. The appearance of contradiction here has sometimes occurred to me. (EA, 38)

As Feuerbach and others have (over)emphasized, God has always somewhat resembled human beings, but theists have also always been convinced that there is something deimorphic about human beings.

There is a sense in which analogical terms apply literally-2 to God and only analogically to us. We are said to "know" certain things, but we are always liable to make mistakes. Our having "knowledge" means that we have evidence, which falls short of indubitable proof, that certain beliefs are true. The indefiniteness of our "knowing" is in contrast to the divine case. God, as infallible, has conclusive evidence regarding all truths: "God simply knows—period" (LP, 141). God literally-2 knows. In effect, what Hartshorne is doing is issuing a call not so much for the old negative theology as for a new negative anthropology. And he has the same view of love as he does of knowledge in that human love is intermittent and mixed with apathy, vanity, and fear. Human love enables us to analogize so as to talk about divine love, but once one has experienced divine love one realizes that "God appreciates the qualities of all things—period" (LP, 142), whereas we love in a bastardized way. If we allocate to ourselves properties like knowing or loving in a literal way, there is little left to characterize deity. This is precisely the monumental error made by negative theologians, including many analytic theists overly influenced by classical negative theology. Consider the issue of memory. We remember only tiny scraps of the past and these indistinctly. By way of contrast, God remembers literally-2; God remembers—period.

It is both true that we form the idea of divine knowledge, love, and so on, by analogical extension of our own knowledge and love *and* that we know what knowledge and love are partly by knowing God: "To 'know' *ought* to mean, having conclusive evidence, such as God has; but to apply this idea to man we must tone it down drastically indeed" (CS, 155). It is precisely the amphibious nature of analogical terms that makes them so problematic. Analogical terms are problematic for Hartshorne, however, for a different reason from that which makes them problematic for classical theists. Hartshorne denies that human knowledge is a mere symbol for an otherwise inaccessible divine reality (the classical theistic view) at the very least because human "knowledge" is, in a sense, derivative. What Hartshorne has accomplished through his treatment of literal-2 terms (he refers to them simply as "literal" terms, thereby creating confusion for some interpreters—see Ogden 1984) is a way of understanding the importance of mysticism in the religious life. Those who have, to use Alston's phrase, "perceived" God's knowledge and love (or who have, to use Hartshorne's phrase, "intuited" these) make it possible for us to use literal-2 terms regarding God, terms which push our analogical terms closer to literal-1 terms than to symbolic ones, as Hartshorne emphasizes:

> The real trouble is less in the exaggeration of literalness than in the idolatry of infinity, being, cause, and absoluteness, accepted as substitutes for the divine unity of the contraries, finite-infinite, being-creativity, cause-effect, absolute-relational. . . . [M]any theological terms are more or less symbolic; others may

> be now symbolic (here better termed analogical), now literal, depending upon the availability of religious intuition; but the most completely abstract general terms applicable to deity are quite literal. (CS, 157)

God is the literal-2 instance of analogical terms because God is the preeminent instance of them. It is by self-flattery that we think of ourselves as loving beings when we notice the limitations of our social awareness. This is in contrast to God, as the Soul of the World, who is socially aware—period. The heavy influence of the *via negativa* on classical theism, including analytic, classical theism, has created the illusion of safety in what is not said regarding description of God. But negative theologians have typically atoned for their paucity of discourse by an orgy of metaphors. Hartshorne is not opposed to metaphor; in fact, he thinks religious metaphor has a crucial role to play in moving the emotions toward God. But description must be based on *some* literal terms (whether literal-1—those of the metaphysicians—or literal-2—those of the mystics) "or it is a scandal" (DR, 37). Analogy itself, as a comparison between things that are somewhat similar and somewhat different, ultimately rests on there being *some* univocity of discourse so as to secure the similarities. It is true, however, that the contingent or the concrete (as opposed to the abstraction "contingency" or the abstraction "concreteness") transcend reason in the sense that these realities must ultimately be felt as sheer facts. Regarding God as contingent or as concrete we can talk analogically or symbolically, but when God is symbolized as judge or monarch there is always the danger of distorting what the best available arguments indicate is the case metaphysically:

> It is one thing to know an individual as distinguished from all others. It is another to know that same individual in its actual "state." . . . To know the actuality of deity, as relative to the present and past actual universe, would be to know that universe as God knows it. (DR, 40)

F. MYSTICISM

David Tracy is correct in noting that Hartshorne spends a great deal of time urging classical theists to eliminate talk of divine mystery when that talk really is a cover for incoherence or contradiction or confusion. But Tracy (1985) also wishes that Hartshorne would spend more time trying to retrieve the real divine mystery worthy of worship. Hartshorne is not opposed to Tracy's desire here, as we have seen above regarding the need for authentic religious experience so as to decipher how to use literal-2 terms concerning God.[3] But Hartshorne insists, as Tracy also notices, that any worship worth the effort must be coherently conceived in philosophy. (In this regard Hartshorne is very Catholic and very Thomistic.)

The issue is complex, however. Coherent thinking should shape our emotions and our perceptions, but, as Peirce among others has shown, we should also be open to experiencing surprising facts that will alter how we think. In this final section of the chapter I would like to support the case for at least the *partial* autonomy of mystical experiences against the possible hegemony of the intellect; in fact, I will argue that the experiences of the mystics should help to shape how we think. The possible hegemony of the intellect I will be criticizing comes from two different directions. First I will consider the thought-provoking view of Steven Katz (1978, 1983) that the phenomenological content of all experience, including mystical experience, is shaped by (indeed, it is in part caused by) a complex, culturally acquired, sociopsychological mold consisting of concepts and beliefs that the experiencing subject brings to the mystical experience. I will attempt to limit this hegemony of intellect in Katz, as well as a different sort of hegemony of intellect, through a consideration of one particular concept and its correlative (divine immutability/divine mutability) as it is found in mystical literature, in general, and in John of the Cross's, in particular. I will also rely heavily and in a positive way on a recent work by Nelson Pike (1992).

Katz's view is that there are no purely immediate experiences, that experience is always preformed or preconditioned. Hence mystical experiences largely have the content they have because mystics come to their experiences with traditional religious concepts as a background. Hindus have experiences which phenomenologically are of Brahman and Christians have experiences which phenomenologically are of Christ. In fact, there are as many kinds of mystical experience as there are significant religious contexts. Katz's "forms of intuition" theory is explicitly Kantian, or better, it is a sociopsychological version of Kant's mind-construction theory of human experience applied to the special case of mystical experience.

The strongest case made by Katz is when he talks about Jewish mysticism, wherein the conceptual background of a God who is ontologically distinct from humans defines in advance what the experience is that the Jewish mystic wants to have. The ultimate goal of Jewish mystics is *devekuth*, a loving intimacy with God, but not identity with God or absorption into God. By way of contrast, in Christian mysticism there are reported experiences of both a nonabsorptive type, which are reminiscent of *devekuth*, and of an absorptive or unitive type in which the self is absorbed in God in an all-embracing unity. The latter, Katz seems to say, are due to Christianity's incarnational theology wherein it is more difficult than in Judaism to think of God as *totaliter aliter.*

I would like to make it clear that in criticizing Katz one does not have to move to the other extreme, say to the position of Walter Stace (1960a, 1960b), where something like a presuppositionless experience occurs which is later interpreted and described and expanded in terms of a subject-object structure and in terms of the traditional attributes given to God by Christian thinkers. That is, a Kantian approach to the problem may in fact be the best one *if* what it means to be a Kantian is to insist that in any experience something is contributed by the experiencing subject and something is contributed by something or someone outside the subject. The problem with Katz's Kantianism lies in his overemphasis of the subject's contribution to the mystical experience. The inadequacy of Katz's account, however, does not justify Stace's claim that the Christian mystic does not really experience a personal God in that this descriptive content (of God as personal) of the experience is added at a later interpretive moment. Stace's view, which is not supported by an analysis of the writings of John of the Cross and other famous Christian mystics, is that Christian mystics would, if left to their own spontaneous inclinations, affirm a metaphysical identity between themselves and God (and hence deny orthodox theism). Under the threat of punishment as heretics, however, most Christian mystics, according to Stace, interpret their experiences in orthodox terms.

On Stace's view the theistic interpretation of mystical experience as union with *God* is like J. S. Mill's example of someone seeing a colored surface of a certain shape and concluding that he was seeing his brother. Regarding the question as to how we can determine where the report of the mystic is accurate and where it includes a later interpretive element, Ninian Smart (1965) offers the following (Stacean) response: A mystic's writing is interpretive rather than descriptive to the extent that it contains doctrinal ramifications or propositions that are presupposed as true by the description in question. In sum, Katz is on the right track in his Kantianism until he overemphasizes the role of the experiencing subject; and Stace and Smart (and Zaehner 1961) are on the right track in claiming that we should not accept at face value the *ex post facto* interpretations mystics give of their experiences, but there are good reasons, as we will see, not to go so far as to rule out, as Stace does, the possibility that mystics experience a personal, loving God.

Pike emphasizes a part of the conceptual inheritance of orthodox Christianity which is alleged to either precondition mystical experience (Katz) or be read into mystical experience after the fact (Stace): the belief that God is immutable. But if the soul of the mystic were to become one with God, then something would have been added to God (Pike 1992, 34). Even if mystical union refers to a phenomenological reality rather than a metaphysical one, as Pike wishes to argue, it is nonetheless undeniable that the pervasive use of the bridegroom metaphor in the literature of Christian mysticism, and especially its use in John of the Cross, indicates that in mystical union God is the receiver of a definite benefit. Relying on stanzas 30–35 of John of the Cross's *The Spiritual Canticle*, Pike says the following:

> God is also the receiver of a definite benefit. He, too, is embraced and loved by his submissive and adoring Bride (the soul). God benefits too!? Of course . . . John says, God too is "wounded" and "captivated"—that is, made "prisoner"—by the love received from the soul. Appropriately enough, God also gives thanks to the soul for the gift he receives. . . . [T]he mutual

> embrace of union is, indeed, *mutual* embrace and . . . the bridal metaphor carries the pictorial implication of *equal* partners sharing *equally* the benefits of the love embrace. . . . Not surprisingly, John covers the seemingly inappropriate overtones of this analysis by insisting that it is God who is ultimately responsible for the fact that the soul is his equal. . . . [A] symmetrical exchange of delights. (81–82)

Of course, there are other metaphors used to describe God in mystical literature, say the view of God as parent or sustainer, in which the relationship between God and creatures is an asymmetrical one. But to the extent that the bridegroom metaphor is to be taken seriously we must also take divine mutability seriously (Pike 1992, 82–83).

Both sorts of metaphor—those that indicate an asymmetrical relationship between God and the mystic and those that indicate a symmetrical relationship—are essential parts of the literature of Christian mysticism. Pike's key contribution to the topic of the present section of the chapter consists in the way he alerts us to the fact that symmetrical metaphors, and the partial divine mutability which is their implication (the *constancy* of divine love indicates that divine mutability is only part of the story), conflict in important ways with traditional theological expectations (1992, 85–86). Sanjuanistic mysticism in particular provides a locus for both divine steadfastness and constancy of love, on the one hand, and passionate-sensuous mutability, on the other. God is unique in being *always* mutable, whereas we mortal beings can be changed by those whom we love for only a short while. Further, as we have seen, on the evidence of divine mutability provided by the mystics we can say with confidence that God is literally related to us.

Pike rightly remains unconvinced by Stace's claim that pressure from ecclesial authorities is a major factor in determining what the mystic eventually says about the mystical experience itself (1992, 111). If Stace were correct, then we would not find as many symmetrical metaphors as we do (metaphors which only make sense against the background of abstract divine relativity taken literally), wherein divine mutability is a prime component of the mystic's experience and of the mystic's description of the experience. As before, Katz and

Stace are each somewhat correct in their interpretations of mystical experience, even if they are also somewhat hyperbolic. For example, Stace is correct that when interpreting their experiences Christian mystics sometimes refer to God as "immutable," and this perhaps due to the weight of theological (not biblical) tradition and perhaps due to the fear that a partially mutable God could be misinterpreted as a fickle God. And Katz is correct that what is "given" in mystical perception is difficult to separate from the preconditions which make the given possible.

But Pike is more instructive than Katz because of a distinction he makes that Katz does not make between two sorts of givenness. The *theoretical* given is what is taken for granted in a theory and hence functions as an epistemological category only indirectly applicable to mystical experience, whereas the *discernable* given is that which can be discerned in an act of reflection as having been given not in a theory but in some particular perception or experience. For example, if one sees a white patch outside one's house on a dark night it could be variously interpreted as a ghost, a sheet, or as a painted rock. But on a clear morning when one sees a white teapot in the kitchen, the fact is that "it's a teapot" expresses a presentational element of consciousness that is part of the discernable given (Pike 1992, 142–43). Or again, when a mystic experiences a loving relation with God the fact that God is changed by the loving embrace is part of the discernable given, it just *is* what is experienced and hence is reported by the mystic even if the mystic's preconditioning and *ex post facto* interpretation both militate against the existence of divine mutability.

The doctrine of divine immutability has been taken as the orthodox standard when determining theological or metaphysical truth, but not when determining the phenomenological truth in mystical experience. Some thinkers may, even after considering the evidence of Christian mystics like John of the Cross, continue to insist on divine immutability when the metaphysical status of mystical experience is *assessed* (but even here, as we have seen, there are problems), but one cannot insist on divine immutability when the phenomenological content of the experience is being *described* (Pike 1992, 156–57). It is true that phenomenological *context* in part determines phenomenological *content*, as when the silence before the last measure of the Hallelujah Chorus is part of the auditory experience, or as when Teresa of Avila compares Christ as present near her to the awareness one might have of someone present in the dark when one cannot see (Pike 1992, 135, 165). But even if context in part determines content, there is an insistency to the phenomenological content of mystical experience which neither Katz's Promethean forethought nor Stace's Epimethean hindsight can explain away.

Even given the possible differences noted by Katz between Jewish and Christian mysticism, we should not on Katzian (or Stacean) grounds expect to find Christian mystics sometimes using symmetrical metaphors and indicating that God literally changes in mystical union. But we do find them sometimes (or better, often) using such metaphors and talking about literal divine change. Neoclassical theists like Hartshorne have been saying for years that on independent metaphysical grounds there are good reasons for believing that there are problems with seeing divine permanence and divine change as opposites. Rather, as before, they are mutually reinforcing correlatives. God is immutably mutable, the being who is *always* affected by the creatures loved. The mystics come to know this.

My point throughout this section of the chapter has been to suggest that we cannot explain away (in a Katzian or Stacean way) the mystic's experience of divine mutability. And my proposal here at the end of the chapter is to have us take seriously the mystic's experience of divine mutability such that divine mutability might gain intellectual respectability as a metaphysical, not just phenomenological, reality. In guarding against the hegemony of intellect I am obviously not necessarily committed to the hegemony of religious experience. Rather, religious truth is developed when *both* our attentiveness to experience and our intellectual operations are at their highest pitch of discipline. Religions die when they find their inspiration in their dogmas, say in the dogma regarding divine immutability. The bases of religious belief lie in the experiences of *and* in the thoughts of the finest types of religious lives. These bases are always growing, even though some highly admirable expressions lie in the past.[4] Records of these sources are not formulae, but spurs to elicit in us affective and intellectual responses that pierce beyond dogma, in this case the dogma that God is immutable.[5]

Further, in addition to showing the connection between the evidence provided by the great mystics and a defense of neoclassical theism, in this chapter I have shown that Ross, in particular, is an analytic theist who has engaged neoclassical theism in a constructive way. It is perhaps not an exaggeration to say that Ross's efforts a generation ago to keep philosophical theism alive among analytic thinkers were heroic. It is true that he (along with Anscombe and Geach, also analytic theists who are Catholic) remains a classical theist, but he makes three points that are crucial from a neoclassical point of view. First, Ross's distinction between the existential stage, where rational argument is used to establish the existence of God, and the identification stage, where an effort is made to see if the being whose existence is proved is in fact God, is in many respects similar to Hartshorne's distinction between divine existence and divine actuality. Second, he argues that Hartshorne's "maximally powerful God" is as compatible as the omnipotent God of classical theism with the experience of God as powerful in Judaism, Christianity, and Islam. This argument is significant in that many criticisms of Hartshorne by classical theists start from the assumption that Hartshorne's God is too weak in this regard. And third, Ross argues that the neoclassical concept of God, which admittedly he does not adopt, is nonetheless as plausible a candidate as the classical theistic one in the effort to explain the experience of God in the aforementioned Abrahamic religions. Once again, this is quite an admission.

CHAPTER SIX

The Concept of God and the Moral Life

A. INTRODUCTION

In the previous chapter one of the key points discussed was that Perfect Love is in fact love; or better, it is "no more than love without any contrary tendencies or qualifications of apathy or hostility" (UB, 281). Throughout Hartshorne's work one gets the impression that his metaphysics and philosophy of religion are based on certain aesthetic principles or tendencies that have an impact on how we should think about the moral life. The purpose of this, the final chapter in the book, is to make some of these implications explicit. That is, the two concepts of God treated throughout this book—the classical one used by most analytic theists and the neoclassical one—will be brought to bear on the moral life.

In the Introduction I had occasion to point out George Lucas' book *The Rehabilitation of Whitehead*, where the author correctly points out the parallel paths that process philosophers and analytic philosophers have tred since Whitehead and Russell apparently parted ways early in this century. Lucas is also correct to emphasize that these two paths are in fact often parallel to each other rather than widely divergent. The upshot of Lucas' book is that process and analytic thinkers should make up for lost time by comparing notes, a comparison which, he alleges, will be of benefit to both (see Clarke 1987).

The purpose of the following sections of the chapter is to continue Lucas' work by looking at the analytic philosophy of Thomas Nagel from the perspective of process thinkers like Whitehead and Hartshorne. I will concentrate on Nagel's 1979 work, *Mortal Questions* (1991 [1979]), which has all of the signs of becoming a contemporary classic: it has been reprinted eleven times, it has been translated into foreign languages, and it has recently been published in a new edition. It will become clear in the following sections of the chapter that Nagel covers much the same ground as Whitehead and Hartshorne, but not under their influence. Rather, he takes his cues from some of the major figures in analytic philosophy. I will claim that in three key areas—death and the absurdity of life, the concept of freedom, and the mind-body problem—Nagel is paradoxically both very close to, yet far from Whitehead's and Hartshorne's treatments of these areas. I will argue that even where he is close to process philosophy he is instructive regarding how the tools of analytic philosophy can further illuminate territory already familiar to process thinkers; and that where he reaches conclusions different from those of Whitehead and Hartshorne he is nonetheless helpful in locating exactly where process philosophers and analysts need to work together. Nagel himself, although he does not mention process philosophy in particular, indicates his willingness to explore regions outside of traditional analytic concerns so long as the analytic philosopher's typical fear of nonsense is kept alive (1991 [1979], ix). Process thinkers, too, I would claim, have more of this kind of fear than many analytic thinkers would realize. In the following sections of the chapter we will see the parallels between Nagel's philosophy and process thought; the reasons why Nagel should, on his own principles, take Whitehead and Hartshorne seriously; and the reasons why the "inevitable" clashes in Nagel's thought are avoidable.

Throughout this chapter I will be showing some of the problems created by a view of things *sub specie aeternitatis*, a view made famous by classical theists. I will also argue that taking polytheism seriously, even though polytheism must ultimately be rejected, acts as a corrective to classical theism's emphasis on the view of things *sub specie aeternitatis*. Eventually I will deal with some practical, contemporary applications of the classical and neoclassical concepts of God, most notably the impact these two concepts have on the abortion debate. As before, the pragmatic dimension of Hartshorne's method will receive its due.

B. DEATH AND THE ABSURD

If a process philosopher were asked to state the thesis of Nagel's famous essay titled "Death," he would say that Nagel had explored death in light of the aysmmetrical theory of time wherein at a given moment one is internally related to one's past but externally related to the future; what has happened is settled but there is always a certain degree of indeterminacy—and sometimes a great deal of it—with respect to the future. In Nagel's own terms, death is an evil because it deprives us of something (1991, 1):

> There are elements which, if added to one's experience, make life better; there are other elements which, if added to one's experience, make life worse. But what remains when these are set aside is not merely *neutral*: it is emphatically positive. Therefore life is worth living even when the bad elements of experience are plentiful. (1991, 2)

It is *being* alive and *doing* certain things that is good. That is, it is not the static state of death which is evil, but the loss of the process of living (3).

Nor is death evil merely because it implies one's nonexistence. The asymmetricality of time is most apparent in the fact that we do not regret the period before birth even if we are bothered by the period after death (3–4). Obviously, there are evils besides death, but to know these as evil also very often requires a knowledge of the asymmetrical history of the person in question, a knowledge of what has occurred thus far and what the possibilities or probabilities are for the future. It is very often not the categorical or the temporally isolated state one occupies in the present which determines evil: we do not mind that an infant drools like an idiot, indeed at times it is cute that it does so, but we do mind a great deal that an intelligent woman with brain damage from a car wreck drools like an idiot. In the latter case our concern is due to our knowledge of the person she was as opposed to the person she is now. "Success" or "failure" in general are process or relational terms (Nagel 1991, 5–6). Obviously a corpse is not to be pitied, but a person who seems most likely to become one soon perhaps is (5–7).[1]

Process thinkers would agree with Nagel's claim that Lucretius misunderstood temporal asymmetry: We should not mind, Lucretius thought, posthumous nonexistence any more than prenatal nonexistence. But in between these two existences, as Nagel notes, is life itself and awareness and hope. Nagel puts his view as follows (1991, 7):

> The direction of time is crucial in assigning possibilities to people or other individuals. Distinct possible lives of a single person can diverge from a common beginning, but they cannot converge to a common conclusion from diverse beginnings. (The latter would represent not a set of different possible lives of one individual, but a set of distinct possible individuals, whose lives have identical conclusions.) (1991, 8)

The key question regarding the degree to which death is an evil is, *How* possible are our possibilities? The death of Keats at twenty-four is a monumental loss, but the death of Tolstoy at eighty-two is still a loss. Blindness is not a nightmare for a mole because it is not the sort of being one would ever expect to have vision, but:

> The trouble is that life familiarizes us with the goods of which death deprives us. We are already able to appreciate them, as a mole is not able to appreciate vision. . . . [O]bserved from without, human beings obviously have a natural lifespan. . . . A man's sense of his own experience, on the other hand, does not embody this idea of a natural limit. His existence defines for him an essentially open-ended possible future, containing the usual mixture of goods and evils that he has found so tolerable in the past. Having been gratuitously introduced to the world by a collection of natural, historical, and social accidents, he finds himself the subject of a *life*, with an indeterminate and not essentially limited future. Viewed in this way, death, no matter

> how inevitable, is an abrupt cancellation of indefinitely extensive possible goods. (9–10)

Some, including some process thinkers like Hartshorne, might object that the *inevitability* of death should make it tolerable, otherwise we simply fail to understand ourselves as biological animals. Nagel's view of this particular point, by way of contrast, seems to be an improvement over Hartshorne's. Nagel argues as follows:

> Suppose that we were all inevitably going to die in *agony*. . . . Would inevitability make *that* prospect any less unpleasant? . . . If the normal lifespan were a thousand years, death at 80 would be a tragedy. As things are, it may just be a more widespread tragedy. If there is no limit to the amount of life that it would be good to have, then it may be that a bad end is in store for us all. (10)

It should be emphasized that Nagel is dealing here with the topic of death by itself apart from considerations of immortality, considerations which make a difference to theists like Hartshorne, who believes in "objective" if not subjective immortality (LP, 245–62). The key difference regarding death between Nagel, on the one hand, and Hartshorne, on the other, however, lies not so much in the question of an afterlife as in Nagel's belief that death provides the background against which we can come to see our lives as absurd while we are still alive. One can legitimately wonder if our lives are leading nowhere in that we die and in that those that we have an effect on die as well. Perhaps we can contribute something to God (Hartshorne's objective immortality), Nagel admits, but we can always doubt that this is the case (1991 [1979], 12, 16).

But on Nagel's view a consideration of death only starts us on our way to a coming to grips with the absurd. Even if we lived forever our lives might be "absurd" if the term refers to:

> a conspicuous discrepancy between pretension or aspiration and reality: someone gives a complicated speech in support of a motion that has already been passed . . . you declare your love over the telephone to a recorded announcement. (13)

There is an inevitable clash in the lives of rational beings because they can engage in (Cartesian) doubt. On the one hand, there is a pragmatic necessity to be serious and, on the other hand, we can always step back from this pragmatic seriousness so as to survey our lifespan—however long—from the outside (Nagel 1991, 13, 18, 21). It is crucial to notice, however, that the absurdity of life, according to Nagel, depends on what he calls a view of ourselves *sub specie aeternitatis*, from a fixed point outside of time and outside the bounds of temporal asymmetry.

Nagel's fascination with a view *sub specie aeternitatis* (1991, 15, 23, 134, 204–5) is odd in that it presupposes the divine point of view outside of time found in classical theism, a point of view criticized by Whitehead and especially by Hartshorne, who has, in effect, spent a whole lifetime attacking it and trying to defend a suitable replacement in terms of his view of God as temporally everlasting rather than as eternal. It is unfortunate that Nagel does not engage himself with process thought here. His view of himself *sub specie aeternitatis* is bothersome, not only because it is defended in ignorance of its most formidable critics, but also because it conflicts with Nagel's own view of time as asymmetrical in his essay "Death." The view of time as asymmetrical conflicts with the view *sub specie aeternitatis* because in the latter there is no lesser degree of determination with respect to the "future" than there is with respect to the "past." It should also be noted that Nagel's view *sub specie aeternitatis* cannot escape criticism on the ground that he uses this device hypothetically rather than metaphysically when it is considered that he tries to do a great deal of intellectual work with this hypothetical device. It must be admitted, however, that there is a difference between Nagel's *hypothetical* divine point of view and, say, Hartshorne's concentration on theism as a *metaphysical* position.

Nagel is intent on distinguishing his view of the absurd from that of Camus. The latter's view consists in a histrionic and heroic collision between the self and a recalcitrant world. But for Nagel the absurd consists in a collision within ourselves (1991, 17, 22, 137). When we step back from temporal pursuits so as to see our lives from the perspective of eternity (whatever that means: in the backward step does Nagel really mean that we can see what will happen to us in the future?), we need not abandon our pursuits because of their futility, but we will return to them with at least a grain of salt (19). After we see the absurdity of our beliefs:

> we will take them back, like a spouse who has run off with someone else and then decided to return; but we regard them differently. . . . It is useless to mutter: "Life is meaningless; life is meaningless . . ." as an accompaniment to everything we do. . . . What sustains us, in belief as in action, is not reason or justification, but something more basic than these. (20)

This more basic element, if I understand Nagel correctly, is Humean custom or, perhaps, Bergsonian intuition or Jamesian animal faith (Nagel 1991, x, 65). We pursue our everyday, pragmatic tasks with custom and intuition on our side *until* we take the backward step, see ourselves *sub specie aeternitatis*, and are then confronted with the absurd. The nonhistrionic response to the absurd which is Nagel's hallmark is, perhaps, punctuated by periods of alarm. These can be ameliorated either by not taking the backward step and living our lives as if temporal asymmetry were the case *simpliciter*, as is the case in the lives of animals, or by reducing our beliefs and our pursuit of things, as in certain forms of religious asceticism. But there is not much need to reduce ourselves completely to the level of animality or to become ascetics if the absurd tension is one of the most normal things about human beings in general, as Nagel thinks (21, 23).

C. FREEDOM-DETERMINISM

The major problem noticed thus far with Nagel's thought is his assumption—he offers no arguments here—that we *can* view our lives *sub specie aeternitatis*, that we *can* see our lives from some perspective which is temporally symmetrical such that our present relation to the future is just as determinate and free of contingency as is our present relation to our past. It is precisely this assumption which makes it possible to say that absurdity is the status quo for most humans. The same problem surfaces in Nagel's treatment of the freedom-determinism issue, which I will treat through a series of contrasts. That is, Nagel adopts temporal symmetry in two ways: through a view *sub specie aeternitatis* and through his occasional defense of determinism.

On the one hand, in "Moral Luck" Nagel correctly notes (in a Peircian way) that there is a key role for chance or moral luck in one's moral life, as is illustrated in the following examples:

> Someone who was an officer in a concentration camp might have led a quiet and harmless life if the Nazis had never come to power in Germany. And someone who led a quiet and harmless life in Argentina might have become an officer in a concentration camp if he had not left Germany for business reasons in 1930. . . . Ordinary citizens of Nazi Germany had an opportunity to behave heroically by opposing the regime. They also had an opportunity to behave badly, and most of them are culpable for having failed this test. But it is a test to which the citizens of other countries were not subjected, with the result that even if they, or some of them, would have behaved as badly as the Germans in like circumstances, they simply did not and therefore are not similarly culpable. . . . [T]he mercy of fate. . . . We judge people for what they actually do or fail to do, not just for what they would have done if circumstances had been different. (26, 34)

And Nagel correctly argues that the best one can do, given the asymmetricality of time, is to say *in a conditional way* in advance how a moral verdict will depend on the results. For example:

> If one negligently leaves the bath running with the baby in it, one will realize, as one bounds up the stairs toward the bathroom, that if the baby has drowned one has done something awful, whereas if he has not one has merely been careless. Someone who launches a violent revolution against an authoritarian regime knows that if he fails he will be responsible for much suffering. . . . I do not mean that *any* action can be retroactively justified by history. Certain things are so bad in themselves, or so risky, that no results can make them all right. . . . The judgment after the fact follows from an hypothetical judgment that can be made beforehand, and it can be made as easily by someone else as by the agent. (1991, 30–31)

On the other hand, in this essay Nagel exaggerates the degree to which the past limits our possible courses of action in the future; only a fraction of life is under one's control, he thinks (28), a claim which strikes me as an exaggeration. Regarding the above mentioned examples Nagel states that:

> It is tempting in all such cases to feel that some decision must be possible, in the light of what is known at the time, which will make reproach unsuitable. . . . But this is not true . . . how things turn out determine what he has done. (29–30)

The culprit here, once again, is a view of life *sub specie aeternitatis*, a view which is at odds with the very notion of future contingency, as the later St. Augustine and Calvin realized:

> If one cannot be responsible for consequences of one's acts due to factors beyond one's control, or for antecedents of one's acts that are properties of temperament not subject to one's will, or for the circumstances that pose one's moral choices, then how can one be responsible even for the stripped-down acts of the will itself, if *they* are the product of antecedent circumstances outside of the will's control? Everything seems to result from the combined influence of factors. . . . the *inevitable* result of those antecedent circumstances. . . . [T]he self which acts and is the object of moral judgment is threatened with dissolution by the absorption of its acts and impulses into the class of events. (35–36—my emphasis)

In effect, Nagel has returned to the same sort of "inevitable" tension treated above regarding the absurd. Here the tension is between our strong sense of moral agency, on the one hand, and, on the other, the claim that this agency is undermined by the backward step wherein we take a view of our lives from the perspective of "eternity":

> the idea of agency is incompatible with actions being events, or people being things. But as the external determinants of what someone has done are gradually exposed . . . it becomes gradually clear that actions are events and people things. (37)

Nagel is committed to a belief in human freedom, but it is a belief which is (absurdly) undermined by the strong connection between viewing a human life *sub specie aeternitatis* and determinism. According to process philosophers, the view *sub specie aeternitatis* entails determinism in that in order for there to be human freedom there would have to be undetermined possibilities regarding the future, possibilities precluded by a view which sees the future not as a region of determinables but as already determinate in the mind of an omniscient knower in the classical theistic sense of "omniscience."

Nagel's ability to draw subtle philosophical distinctions is not in question from the process point of view. His treatment of a human subject's immersion in a body and of the domination of the person by body in "Sexual Perversion" is brilliant (47–48), as is his defense of an idiosyncratic version of moral "absolutism" which avoids some of the defects in Kantian deontology (60). But, once again, in "War and Massacre," he takes a backward step away from a prohibition of doing certain things regardless of results and finds that sometimes one *has no choice* but to do terrible things. That is, Nagel once again resigns himself to a dilemma, this time between "absolutism" and utilitarianism; the world may not only be the sort of place which fosters absurdity in human beings, it may be positively evil such that utilitarian resolution to moral problems (where innocent people, say, can be killed) may, at times, be our only real option (Nagel 1991, 56, 67, 73–74, 88).

Like Whitehead and Hartshorne, Nagel is a critic of idle abstractions, as in the abuse of political concepts by public leaders so as to depersonalize the ruthless acts they perform which would never be tolerable in private life. Political leaders very often have too much of a concern for *detached* utilitarian results as opposed to what one is really in the act of *doing* at a particular moment (77, 82–87). Likewise Nagel is instructive regarding why an unequal distribution of social rewards is not justified by possession of talent (100):

> Perhaps voluntary differences in effort or moral differences in conduct have some bearing on economic and social desert. But they are features in which most people do not differ enough to justify very wide differences in reward . . . people with different talents do not thereby deserve different economic and social

> rewards. They may, however, deserve different opportunities to exercise and develop those talents. (97-98)

Yet Nagel's defense of freedom and of *efforts* to ameliorate social injustices is, characteristically, only one side of the coin. The other side has on it the face of a determinist who believes that the effect of human effort in any form is negligible and that injustice cannot be avoided. And when we do make efforts to make the world a better place we must sometimes tolerate lying as a means to that end because, presumably, if the world is sometimes an evil place then (a crude version of?) utilitarianism is, at times, preferable to "absolutist" prohibitions against lying (1991, 97, 100, 104).

In effect, Nagel is only half a process philosopher; that is, only half of him is committed to temporal asymmetry. The other half presupposes a view of human beings *sub specie aeternitatis*, a view which has been traditionally (and disastrously for religion, according to Hartshorne) reserved for God. It is this eternalistic view (or better, the imagined possession of it) which encourages Nagel to take absolute determinism and the absurdity of human life seriously. The half of Nagel that is appealing from a Whiteheadian or Hartshornian perspective, however, is very appealing. For example, Nagel's liberalism presupposes the abandonment of determinism, as does the liberalism of Whitehead and Hartshorne. Nagel claims that natural and social *contingencies* which are not deserved—talent, early environment, class background—should not be rewarded. This is a most agreeable claim to process thinkers like Whitehead and Hartshorne, as is his claim that one is required to love his/her neighbor as oneself, but only as much as one loves oneself when one looks at oneself with fair detachment, so as to avoid selfishness as it is criticized by process thinkers (Nagel 1991, 119, 126).[2]

Fair detachment, however, is a far cry from *sub specie aeternitatis*. Consider Nagel's sharp refusal to take up Derek Parfit's suggestion that the cause of equality would be served well by the dissolution of temporally extended individuals into experiential sequences, a view which has at least *some* similarities to the process view of human identity. Although Nagel insists that his view does not *depend* on a theory of strict personal identity through time it does *employ* such a theory (Nagel 1991 [1979], 120, 124–25, 205; see Parfit 1973). Process thinkers are opposed to two sorts of symmetricality regarding human identity. First, they are opposed to a theory of pure external relations (as in Hume or Russell or in certain Buddhists), whereby the present is just as *unrelated to the past* (or, in different terms, is just as externally related to the past) as it is to the future. Second, they are opposed to a theory of pure internal relations, as in the view *sub specie aeternitatis*, whereby the present is just as much *internally related to the future* as to the past. A third view, whereby human beings are internally related to the past but externally related to the future, is defended by process thinkers. Nagel looks like an asymmetrical, process thinker when he criticizes the second view.

In "The Fragmentation of Value" Nagel makes it clear that moral decisions are sometimes difficult because the probability of different outcomes of the possible causes of action is unknown, but we are nonetheless able most of the time to figure out what we ought to do through a consideration of our temporal asymmetry. For example, having received parental care in the past when we were helpless obligates us to be concerned about the future contingencies which may affect our parents. Or again, the justification for finishing a project to a large extent depends on how much time and energy we have put into it thus far such that the project not be in vain. As we look toward future contingencies in light of past actualities we are well served, he thinks, to hold up Aristotelian *phronēsis* rather than moral absolutism or moral perfectionism as our model. There is nothing defeatist in this admission; rather it is based on the realization that our ability to resolve conflicts may extend beyond our capacity to discover general principles to cover the future as well as the past and present (Nagel 1991 [1979], 128–31, 135). Yet Nagel takes away with one hand what he gives with the other. He sees in ethics the same sort of "inevitable" clash that he sees in the absurd (131, 133). In the following quotation note the phrases "extended through time," "simultaneously," "everyone at once," and, of course, "*sub specie aeternitatis*":

> The capacity to view the world simultaneously from the point of view of one's relations to others, from the point of view of one's life extended through time, from the point of view of everyone at once, and finally from the detached viewpoint often described as the view *sub specie aeternitatis* is one of the marks of humanity. (134)

D. THE MIND-BODY PROBLEM

The unity of the self which human beings sometimes experience is, as Nagel notes, nothing substantial in that it is in some way a case of integration of parts (163). But what exactly is integrated? Nagel is rather forcefully opposed to physicalistic reductionism, as the following quotation indicates (165–66, 188):

> If physicalism is to be defended, the phenomenological features must themselves be given a physical account. But when we examine their subjective character it seems that such a result is impossible. The reason is that every subjective phenomenon is essentially connected with a single point of view, and it seems inevitable that an objective, physical theory will abandon that point of view. . . . Most of the neobehaviorism of recent philosophical psychology results from the effort to substitute an objective concept of mind for the real thing, in order to have nothing left over which cannot be reduced. If we acknowledge that a physical theory of mind must account for the subjective character of experience, we must admit that no presently available conception gives us a clue how this could be done. (167, 175)

Nagel asks a series of questions to help us appreciate this concept of subjectivity based on a "point of view": what is it like to be a bat?, what is it like to be another person? (170), and, the process philosopher would add, what was it like to be "myself" at five years old at my birthday party when my friends arrived? If life is cumulative I am a partially different self at each moment. At times Nagel comes close to Whitehead's and Hartshorne's variety of panpsychism:

> Reflection on what it is like to be a bat seems to lead us, therefore, to the conclusion that there are facts that do not consist in the truth of propositions expressible in a human language. We can be compelled to recognize the existence of such facts without being able to state or comprehend them. (171)

We are definitely not the only instances of subjectivity in the world if even a bat has a *psychē*, but Nagel is *sometimes* open to the possibility that even beings far "below" bats (cells?) have protomental properties:

> To imagine something perceptually, we put ourselves in a conscious state resembling the state we would be in if we perceived it. To imagine something sympathetically we put ourselves in a conscious state resembling the thing itself. . . . We can pursue a more objective understanding of the mental in its own right. At present we are completely unequipped to think about the subjective character of experience without relying on the imagination—without taking up the point of view of the experiential subject. (176, 178)

Nagel's conclusion that panpsychism (i.e., the belief that the basic constituents of organic and inorganic matter have either mental properties or the ability to engage in self-motion) should, at the very least, be seen as just as much a live hypothesis as reductionistic materialism and dualism is based on four premises: (*a*) a living organism is a complex material system; (*b*) physicalistic reductionism does not adequately explain certain mental phenomena in living organisms; (*c*) these phenomena—for example, feelings—are real; and (*d*) these phenomena cannot "emerge" out of physical phenomena (1991, 180–81). Without attempting to assess the strength of Nagel's argument here, it is crucial to notice that it is at least compatible with the arguments of Whitehead and Hartshorne, who are perhaps the two most prominent panpsychists in twentieth century philosophy. It is unfortunate that Nagel does not refer to them at all in his essay "Panpsychism." Some interesting questions arise here: If Nagel had read Whitehead and Hartshorne carefully would he have suggested that the common basis for mind and matter is neither alone but rather some basic constituents which share in both categories (like

Whitehead's mental pole and physical pole?) (Nagel 1991 [1979], 179, 185, 188)? Would Nagel have ended up with an "inevitable" clash among bodies of evidence regarding brain bisection, which militates against the unity of consciousness, and one's experience of unity of consciousness (161)? Would Nagel have defended the deterministic hypothesis that true causes *do* provide necessary and sufficient conditions for their effects—though some causes are probabilistic, he thinks—thereby calling into question the panpsychist thesis that the basic constituents in nature are not determined by necessary and sufficient conditions but are partially self-moving, mindlike pulses of energy (186–87)?

In any event, Nagel's view seems to be that if there are three basic options regarding the mind-body problem (dualism, physicalistic reductionism, and panpsychism), then continued problems with the first two options should at least lead us to take seriously the third option, largely neglected by analytic philosophers, but not by Whitehead or Hartshorne. Whiteheadians and Hartshornians should be grateful for Nagel's introduction of the issue of panpsychism into analytic discourse, but they will probably find it amusing to see Nagel grope regarding issues that process philosophers such as Peirce, Bergson, Whitehead, and Hartshorne have dealt with extensively for over a century. Nagel is genuinely confused as to how to really push the case for panpsychism (193):

> As for panpsychism, it is difficult to imagine how a chain of explanatory inference could ever get from the mental states of whole animals back to the proto-mental properties of dead matter. It is a kind of breakdown we cannot envision, perhaps it is unintelligible. Presumably the components out of which a point of view is constructed would not themselves have to have points of view. (How could a single self be composed of many selves?) (194)

Or again:

> Panpsychism in this sense does not entail panpsychism in the more familiar sense, according to which trees and flowers, and perhaps even rocks, lakes, and blood cells have consciousness of a kind. (194–95)

A fruitful dialogue might begin when process philosophers read Nagel and the authors who have influenced him—Wittgenstein, Parfit, Rawls, Kripke, and others—and when Nagel and his admirers read Bergson, Whitehead's *Science and the Modern World* and *Process and Reality*, and Hartshorne's *Creative Synthesis and Philosophic Method* and *The Divine Relativity*. In the first quotation above it should be noted that the reason why Nagel cannot "envision" panpsychism properly is that he (oxymoronically) associates "proto-mental properties" with "dead matter." And in the second quotation Nagel is unaware of the careful attention process philosophers have paid to the fallacies of composition and division. Trees and rocks as aggregates are not at all sentient or protomental even if their microscopic constituents are; and we need not infer the insentience or immobility of the parts from the inertness of the whole. The uniqueness of animals (including human beings) is their ability, through their central nervous systems-brains, to collect together at a higher level the feelings of microscopic individuals: Hurt my cells (say through intense heat) and you hurt *me*.

I would like to reiterate that the primary purpose of the present section of the chapter is not to argue that Nagel would be a better philosopher if he succumbed to the principles of Whitehead and Hartshorne, although I must admit that there is some of this in the present section of the chapter. Rather, I am trying: (1) to point out the surprising parallels between Nagel's philosophy and process philosophies elaborated by Whitehead and Hartshorne; (2) to indicate why, *on Nagel's own principles*, he should take Whitehead and Hartshorne seriously; and (3) to indicate why the "inevitable" clashes in Nagel's thought are avoidable in that they largely rely on an unargued for conception of temporal symmetry which makes possible his version of a backward step out of time and into eternity.

There is further evidence in favor of these three theses from the final essay in *Mortal Questions*, "Subjective and Objective." Here Nagel defends the process commonplace that there are necessary but not sufficient conditions for agency (1991 [1979], 197). The sufficient conditions for agency are largely supplied by decisions of the agent itself, hence process thinkers tend to think of "creativity" as a transcendental, applicable to Creator and creatures alike. Can even the greatest conceivable knower—God—know what cannot logically be known? The greatest conceivable knower would know all past actualities as actual and all future contingencies that can presently be known *as contingent* (although Whitehead's God admittedly has more extensive knowledge of the future than Hartshorne's). To claim to know a contingency as actualized is a type of presumption. That is, not even God can view the world *sub specie aeternitatis*. And Nagel at one point indicates the implausibility of human beings achieving such a view:

> The only alternative to these unsatisfactory moves is to resist the voracity of the objective appetite, and stop assuming that understanding of the world and our position in it can always be advanced by detaching from that position. . . . Perhaps the best or truest view is not obtained by transcending oneself as far as possible.

Objectivity is inadequate as a comprehensive ideal. (214) To the extent that this is Nagel's view we can understand why he says the following about the problem of personal identity, wherein external (objective) treatments of the problem leave something crucial out:

> The problem is usually presented as a search for the conditions that must obtain if two experiential episodes separated in time are to belong to a single person. Various types of continuity and similarity—physical, mental, causal, emotional—have been considered and they all seem to leave an aspect of personal identity unaccounted for . . . a submerged internal aspect of the problem which is left untouched by all external treatments. (199-200)

Unfortunately, Nagel does not stop here in that, from the perspective of eternity, everything seems determined, all the decisions of agents melt into "events" with necessary and sufficient conditions. Indeed, at one point Nagel does not even find the very concept of agent causation intelligible (198). His usual view is a bit weaker: There is a clash between a person viewed from the inside (agent causation) and from the outside (events seen *sub specie aeternitatis*)

(204). The opposition between agent-centered morality and life viewed *sub specie aeternitatis* is, in Nagel, a stalemate:

> because each of the points of view claims dominance over the other, by virtue of inclusion. The impersonal standpoint takes in a world that includes the individual and his personal views. The personal standpoint, on the other hand, regards the deliverance of impersonal reflection as only a part of any individual's total view of the world. (205–6)

The question which should be asked is: *How* should the point of view of a particular individual with a past and, it is to be hoped, a future be transcended? One way would be to enter imaginatively into other subjective points of view (in previous moments of one's own life, in the lives of other human beings, or in the lives of either a bat or a God), efforts which, however difficult, make perfect sense to me. But how much sense can be made of Nagel's attempt to transcend temporality altogether, to aim at a representation of what is external to *every* specific point of view (207–9)?

E. CONTINUITY IN NAGEL'S PHILOSOPHY

Nagel's most recent books do little to ameliorate the criticisms from a process point of view of his thought in *Mortal Questions*. The view of oneself from the outside, from nowhere, or from the perspective of objectivity, is still equated with a view *sub specie aeternitatis*. The phrase *sub specie aeternitatis* is still used often,[3] as are certain euphemisms: the objective view "at full strength," a "timeless standpoint," a "comprehensive viewpoint," the "frame of all existence," and a transcendence of time and place.[4] Nagel is correct in trying to avoid solipsism, but in order to do so do we need objectivity based on a stance *sub specie aeternitatis* (as if that were possible)? Nagel himself admits (1987, 69) that even a high degree of impartiality, much less a view from eternity (from nowhere), would make one a "terrifying saint." Nagel is both a defender and a critic of objectivity. His understandable fear regarding objectivity is that if we regarded our lives exclusively from without we would develop an indifference to them which, from the internal points of view with which we lead our lives, would be frightful.

Nagel's philosophy can be seen as centering on one problem: How to combine the perspective of a particular person in the world with an objective view of that person and of that world. This is, in fact, a serious problem, and there is nothing objectionable in Nagel's response to it as long as his objectivity retains, as it sometimes does, "a temporal sense." And there is nothing objectionable to Nagel's commitment to some sort of strongly impersonal morality if it is only such a morality which can enable us to curb our selfish tendencies.[5] But he is premature in claiming that we do not at present have the conceptual tools available to resolve the tension between subjectivity and objectivity (in ethics, in questions regarding the meaning of life, in the freedom-determinism debate, etc.). The tension is irresolvable only when the subjective tendency is pushed toward solipsism or when the objective tendency is pushed, as Nagel often pushes it, toward an unrealizable, eternalistic standard. The fundamental idea behind the objective impulse is that there is something defective both in egoism and in anthropocentrism, but in order to avoid these overly narrow points of view it is not immediately clear that we must, as Nagel alleges, abandon the very notion of a (temporal) point of view so as to accrue the advantages of objectivity. Nagel is partially aware of the problems associated with a view *sub specie aeternitatis*: "The truth-conditions of tensed statements can be given in tenseless terms, but that does not remove the sense that a tenseless description of the history of the world (including the description of people's tensed statements and their truth values) is fundamentally incomplete."[6] It is quite an understatement to say that the major difficulty with making tensed statements from the perspective of eternity is that such statements will be incomplete. As theological debate for centuries has indicated, it is nothing short of mysterious (in the pejorative sense of the term, I think) as to how one can remain *sub specie aeternitatis* while one understands or talks about beings in time: Only an unmoved mover, whatever that might be, could be impassible with respect to the temporal beings which it knows or talks about.

At times Nagel speaks as though he could really apprehend the world as centerless (i.e., he could apprehend it from no particular view at all) in that it is possible, he thinks, to be outside all points of view. At other times he admits that one cannot be entirely free of temporal asymmetricality or of some particular view or other. Rather, on the latter alternative the view from eternity (from nowhere) represents a *possible* development toward a universal conception as opposed to a parochial one. But the understandable goal of detaching oneself progressively from one's subjective point of view so as to form a procession of more abstract views is quite different from having as one's goal a latent objective realm which is *completely* outside of time and hence outside the region of future contingency. Nagel's supposed progress toward this ultra-abstract goal leads him to flirt with determinism and actually to be seduced by the notion that a rational life is necessarily absurd. Even if the liberation of the dormant objective "self" is always fragmentary, as Nagel thinks it is, and even if the pursuit of objectivity can be pushed to excess so as to eliminate altogether the insistency of subjective drives, as Nagel admits, there is still something objectionable about the claim that an approach to life *sub specie aeternitatis* is one of the key factors involved in rational human existence. Even when this approach is only seen as asymptotic, it nonetheless is powerful enough to convince Nagel that life would be absurd *if* seen from eternity, and if our future "contingencies" were really mapped out for us. I am claiming that Nagel's secular Augustinianism or Calvinism creates entirely unnecessary problems.[7]

It should be reiterated that Nagel tries to preserve the rivalry between the subjective and objective views rather than to assert the hegemony of the latter. But as a consequence of this rivalry Nagel denigrates the asymmetrical theory of time as a merely subjective constituent of the whole. What is needed from Nagel is: (1) at the very least, a serious consideration of Bernard Williams' claim that the view *sub specie aeternitatis* is a very poor one for human life because each of us always starts and ends in the middle of things; and (2) more importantly, a serious consideration of those twentieth century thinkers who have most carefully criticized the Parmenidean tendency, especially evident in theological circles from Boethius to Kant, but also found in a major way in analytic theists, to assume that objectivity requires a God's eye view of time *in the sense that* God is assumed to be *sub specie aeternitatis*. To ignore these critics altogether, as Nagel has done, makes it too easy for him to argue for his favorite theses.[8] As it now stands, Nagel's use of the view *sub specie aeternitatis* has what *he* calls "the faintly sickening odor of something put together in the metaphysical laboratory."[9]

F. ON TAKING POLYTHEISM SERIOUSLY

One of the ways to combat some of the practical problems created by the classical theistic view of God as *sub specie aeternitatis* is to explore in a preliminary way the importance of polytheism for any adequate contemporary philosophical or theological anthropology or theory of the moral life. This exploration will largely consist in an engagement with the thought of Stephen R. L. Clark, an Anglican philosopher who nonetheless defends a qualified version of polytheistic Neoplatonism. Eventually we will see the benefits of taking polytheism seriously and the danger in taking it too seriously.

Human identity is a fragile thing even on a moderate view. Three views of the relationship between temporal relations and human identity can be distinguished, as we have seen. One extreme view suggests that all temporal relations are external. That is, the present self is not internally affected by "its" past self, nor is it affected by "its" future self. This "drops of experience" view (defended by Hume, Russell, and some Buddhists) in effect is a denial of a self enduring through time. At the other extreme is the classical theistic (Leibnizian and at times Nagelian) view that all temporal relations are internal. That is, the present self is *substantially* the same through time in that both past and future phases of itself are explicitly or implicitly contained in it, and this largely due to an expansive belief in divine omniscience with respect to the future. A moderate view in between these two extreme symmetrical views is the much more plausible asymmetrical view: One is internally affected by one's past but externally related to the future. According to this view, the past provides necessary but not sufficient conditions for the precise character of the present phase of one's self. We are causally affected by our past but we can only anticipate the future through probability estimates: on this view human identity is (accurately, I think) left in a rather fragile state with respect to the future.

Belief in the asymmetrical view of human identity is conducive to a William Jamesian healthy-mindedness in religion in that when melancholia interrupts healthy-mindedness it is possible for a partially new self (James' twice-born self) to come to be. But this view also alerts us to an important question: How is it that we are not always changing, always trading in our old identity, but in some sense acquire a stable character? Both the breakdown and the preservation of human identity must be incorporated in any adequate theory of human identity. Clark, relying on Wordsworth, puts the matter this way:

> We are more likely to fear this breakdown, and so defend ourselves against it more fiercely and rigidly . . . if we think that our chosen identity is indeed an attempt to freeze a wave of the sea, to make solid sculptures out of butter on a warm day. We shall be less fearful of collapse if we conceive that the sea itself is the real shaper of our standing wave, that it was the former identities that were the momentarily aggregated flotsam that the waves have swept away. A stable identity, in short, is likely to be one which is believed to be the manifestation of an underlying reality . . . in touch with "something far more deeply interfused." Those who believe that their identities are maintained by their own endeavors, by their own disciplined insistence on being as they were, are very likely not to last the course. (1986, 74; see also James 1985)

In effect, Clark is claiming that human identity in some way or other depends on divine identity.

Both political and religious liberals like myself and political and religious conservatives like Clark recognize that *both* continuity and change are problems, but Clark, although he usually adheres to the asymmetrical view, thinks that the modern tendency to switch identities as we do clothes has led moral philosophers and theologians to prefer a smorgasbord of values, a wardrobe of differing costumes. The conservative classical theistic emphasis on divine eternity, as opposed to, say, the liberal process theologians' emphasis on divine change, has consequences for philosophical anthropology and the moral life. Both Clark and I want a balance between continuity and change, yet he sees the latter as the greater danger. Hence he thinks it crucial to emphasize that activity of an expected kind serves as a code to others to summon up one identity or god rather than another. Nonetheless:

> the sudden emergence of a forgotten self—an emergence made easier by social ritual and the consumption of a mild drug (usually alcohol)—may be experienced as a joyful rediscovery or an humiliating possession by something quite at odds with waking values. . . . Religion is the collective noun for all such practices, whereby our changing selves may move in time to some unknown tidal motions, without driving us insane. (1986, 77)

These passing moods and styles of action are sometimes hostile to each other. In this contest between alien powers each must be given due respect; this is the lesson to be learned from polytheism (1986, 76).

Clark is correct in rejecting both of the symmetrical views of human identity, even if he sometimes leans (like Nagel) in the direction of the classical theistic, substantial view of the self. But in general he notices the inadequacies of a view of the self as substantial in the sense that the I "has" momentary moods. The ego is more of a demand or a postulate than a plain discovery; it is something which we can see *beneath* the many moods and personalities which play themselves out in everyday life. There is some truth to the familiar criticism that the ancient Greeks had no clear conception of the unity of the human subject. But there is also some truth in the polytheistic belief that each "individual" is a medley of competing parts and loyalties; this truth is corroborated by the fact that contemporary readers do not find Homer's heroes altogether unlike contemporary human beings. Further, the moods and styles encountered by the ego cannot be mortal, as the Greeks knew, because they are confronted again and again not only in the life of the ego but also in the lives of other egos, and they cannot be resisted: "Those who try to proclaim their own immunity to Aphrodite find that she is raised up against them" (1986, 79).

Religious experience is an entry into the world of religious tradition; it consists in being seized by the inwardness of such tradition. Only those who misunderstand this inwardness go out of their way to insist that there is really no Aphrodite. She *is* a real presence or mood in the world, and religious tradition is built out of this and other presences. Some of the things which we think are unreal or dreams are in fact drowsy awakenings to the real (1986, 222–23). It is a crucial feature in many religions that the phenomenal universe is the actualization in time of an ideal project that is best grasped as a cosmic community (a World-Soul) united in love (i.e., by Aphrodite). On this view human beings can be seen in at least two different lights: There is the ordinary life of competitive individualism and material interest and there is the "original" life of divine conciliarity. We can blaspheme Aphrodite, for example, through alcoholism or through academic infighting. But avoiding such blasphemy does not necessarily mean that we should naively preach that Aphrodite is, or even could be, ubiquitous:

> The ancients reminded us that even when kissing our child we should remember that she too is mortal. . . . That hard advice is now seen as a betrayal of "love," a refusal to be besotted, as if such love were the only real thing in an empty world. (S. Clark 1989, 24–25)

Ares is also alive and well in the contemporary world, and a primary devotion to him is certainly to be denigrated:

> Those who fight for killing's sake, the servants of Ares, are as dangerous to us all as the followers of Ouranian Aphrodite. . . . Our problem, as it has always been, is to require the gods to take their proper place. (1989, 114–15)

Ares and Aphrodite are the most hated of the Olympians because both can ruin our lives:

> Ares . . . is not just a devil, any more than Aphrodite: our fear of him is not unlike the terror that in other ages made Aphrodite into the great Temptress; our professions of pacific virtue are as

> hypocritical as the double standards of past sexual morality; our good liberal contempt for fighting men is as understandable, and as damaging to all, as older contempt for women. . . . Perhaps we should ask ourselves why we are so ready to assume the worst of those who would die for us? (1989, 117)

As I pacifist I am not entirely convinced by Clark's case in favor of reverence due to Ares, but it must be admitted that *if* Aphrodite stands for a syrupy sentimentalism or an unpragmatic anaesthesia then *some* other god is needed to counteract her influence (see Dombrowski 1991).

Apollo, conceived as methodical reason, also has his place in religion, but he is not supreme in the cosmos, not even when he appears in the guise of a manipulative type of science:

> What is lacking in this age of the world is the sense that there is some existing pattern in which each proper impulse finds its place. . . . Those who have lost their memory of the one comprehensive order are at the mercy of whatever passion, mood, or fairy chances to drink them up. (S. Clark 1989, 33–35)

The Greek symbol for this comprehensive order was Zeus, who stood for the intelligibility which needed preservation if human life was not to revert to fratricidal chaos in that the service of one god at the expense of another was quintessential blasphemy in the Olympian religion (S. Clark 1986, 78–79). But how much order or continuity can we expect?

There is something to be learned from the ancient Greek view that only the gods are singleminded, hence human life tends to be unsystematic. Even if one organizes the major deities into a pantheon there are still *kers* (the spirits of spite and reprisal) and the furies to contend with. That is, classical theistic Jews, Christians, and Muslims might be premature in assuming that the almighty God of the bible necessarily possesses the philosophical attribute "omnipotence" as the term is used by classical theists (see OO). Although Zeus required that gods and mortals know their respective places, and that they not revolt against Themis, or what was proper, he did not have *total* control, a fact which was best symbolized by the presence of Dionysus.

The task is now, as it was then, to discover an orderly system without resorting to force in the effort to create it. Human knowledge itself insures that this will be a difficult project:

> This "discovery," so to call it, of the possibility of an orderly world-system in which each god has a part to play, and which the demands of different roles were not settled simply by resort to force. . . . This "knowledge of good and evil" was what, in Greek thought, prevented human beings from becoming gods: precisely because they could look before and after, and discriminate, they could not be unselfconsciously absorbed in any single role or mood. (1986, 80)

Here Clark sounds like Nagel. It was part of the Greek genius at moderation to fail to conclude that Dionysus was "the natural man," human nature as it would be if the hegemony of Apollo were broken. Dionysus is not "the natural man" so much as he is a natural possibility. The temporary destruction of Zeus' or Apollo's Olympian order, a destruction symbolized by Dionysus, should be accepted as a moment in life rather than as a defeat (1986, 81; see also Otto 1978). That is, along with W. F. Otto we should militate against the view that the Olympian deities are a band of brigands: Polytheism in its Olympian variety is an attempt to provide a structure for the moods and roles of social humanity and an attempt to convince us that we are vulnerable fragments of a cosmos with its own beauty.

Despite the fact that Christianity is a protest against Olympian religion, it is also, as is well known, a type of Dionysian revivalism. It is important that mysticism and/or enthusiasm remain parts of organized religions so as to prevent a deleterious reification of established order. It is worth remembering that it was not only Jesus who was seen by Hellenized Jews and Christians as similar to Dionysus, but also Yahweh. Eventually, however, Yahweh, God the Father, and Allah were seen as strictly Apollonian and transcendent. Clark is instructive in the way he points out the need for balance in Olympian religion, Christianity, and Buddhism alike:

> Charismatic revivalists . . . succeed only in establishing new patterns of worship and hymnody, so that bourgeois congregations

> sing words that take their meaning from the last revival. "Come Holy Ghost . . . " how many in the congregation really intend to speak in tongues? . . . How many Buddhists, for that matter, really test themselves upon the nonexistence of the self, and seek to realize the Unborn? Like the Olympians, Christians and Buddhists have (to some extent) achieved a synthesis: their ceremonial order does contain a reference to That beyond all orders, and a vocabulary that stands ready for the next revivalist. (S. Clark 1986, 87)

In addition to the synthesis of enthusiastic aliveness in religion and a ceremonial order which refers to some sort of transcendence there is the synthesis of sequential *Nous* and the nonsequential One:

> Stable and continuing religious traditions neither wholly abjure nor wholly endorse "the world." . . . Zeus, Father of Gods and Men, was identified by neo-Platonic theorists—almost the last philosophers to take ordinary religious forms seriously as matter for philosophical inquiry—with *Nous*, the ordering intellect and the order it discloses. This was not the ultimately real, the One. . . . But the One and *Nous*, though distinct, were not diverse: *Nous* itself had its being only from the One, as ceremonial usage and sacred history stem, in their beginnings, from the unnamed that lies beyond all ceremonial. (S. Clark 1986, 88)

In effect, the Abrahamic religions follow some of the Neoplatonists in believing that the partial order imposed by Zeus (*nous*) must be explained in terms of some more ultimate principle. But then one is led to wonder if *this* explanation in terms of an omnipotent deity makes any sense philosophically (say in terms of the theodicy problem, etc.) and if it really helps to explain why we still experience such insistent multiplicity in our lives. A phenomenological account of religious identity, I would allege, can at best recognize *patterns* among the very real Olympians that influence us. Each god may be a strict actuality with no unrealized possibilities, but the whole system of gods and mortals must contain a great deal of contingency as the latter confront the former in the course of time. In any event, it is perhaps more accurate to say that birds court each other *because* of

Aphrodite than it is to say that the obsessional desire of birds *is* Aphrodite. The danger Clark sees (1986, 91–92) is that if we do not refer to the gods to explain phenomena then they will too easily be viewed as poetic fictions, fictions which may well be part of a vision of how things should be; that is, they will implicitly be part of a new, antireligion religion.

Olympian religion is also very helpful in distinguishing pollution from sin. One may inadvertently be polluted, as in the case of Oedipus, when one does something which conflicts with impersonal (usually cosmic) law. By way of contrast, religions of the book tend to treat the penalties of sin as the response of a personal God. But when the innocent suffer we are led to take Olympianism especially seriously (in the effort to obtain a rationally defensible Judaism, Christianity, or Islam) in that some events appear to be the case independent of any decision made by God. Pollution plays *some* role in Judaism, Christianity, and Islam, as in the people with whom Jesus consorted, who had not so much committed moral errors as they had been outcasts from Israel; that is, they had incurred pollution. One of the general goals of religion is something like Hindu *mokṣa*, deliverance from both pollution and sin:

> In morality no-one is to be blamed or punished who is not personally responsible for a crime. . . . Pollution, on the other hand, is only partly deserved, and may be removed by another's action. . . . In our own, partly secular, tradition the usual conjunction of "holiness" and dirt was cancelled by the aphorism that "Cleanliness is next to godliness," which has in its turn gone so far toward idealizing the ritual antisepticism of the world of white-coated doctors, plastic-wrapped meat, and vaginal deodorants as to elicit a youthful rebellion in favour of "naturalness," a largely romantic effort to be at one with the usual processes of nature. (1986, 108–9, 112)

The gods constantly pass through our mind's eye for us to accept or reject or ignore: "To know them is to share experience with them, to live with their life" (S. Clark 1984, 192–93). One of the gods that might pass before us appears as the thought that we are being, or might deservedly be, punished for our wrongs. And this god may well be an obsessional demon (1984, 196, 209). Polytheism teaches that there are, for lack of better words, angels as well as devils. The plurality of these beings runs counterpoint to belief in divine unity; or better, divine unity and the multiplicity of gods (i.e., moods, pulls, temptations, desires) are like centripetal and centrifugal forces in equilibrium:

> Faith in Divine Unity amounts to faith in the intelligibility of things, that there is a single pattern, the Logos. . . . That faith was represented for Hellenes, especially the neo-Platonists, in the figure of Zeus. . . . [T]he Logos is not now evident to us. Rational polytheists deplore the tendency of monotheists to imagine unity too soon. . . . [E]very mode and mood of our being, of the world's being, should be acknowledged as a fact, and as something to be "welcomed." (1984, 212–13)

But in our age the problem, from Clark's conservative point of view, is not so much that God (the One or *Nous*-Zeus) has been forgotten altogether as that there has been a triumphant, hegemonic return of the ancient deities. The problem is not so much that we do not take polytheism seriously as that we take it *too* seriously.

The liberal, process theism that I have been defending in this book can be designated as a dipolar theism: God necessarily exists and remains steadfastly good *in the midst of* all of the divine and creaturely changes. Hence there is no necessary conflict between this view and the Clarkian one wherein a qualified polytheism is used as a device to criticize the contemporary denigration of divine (or marital) endurance *simpliciter.* Or again, there is a sense in which liberal believers like myself can agree with Clark that the radical desacralizing and deconstruction of received order is merely fashionable chatter. Liberal believers, too, believe that God endures and that in the midst of all of the changes in my life it is still, in a sense, *my* life.

Pure polytheism would consist in the radical plurality and incommensurability of value preferred by some secularists. In this light polytheism is largely propaedeutic to an appreciation of the whole; it is a prelude to an exposition of belief in an Abrahamic or Neoplatonic One which in some sense includes the lives of the many. To take polytheism seriously, rather than to take it too seriously, is to refuse to see any huge gap between it and Christianity. For example, the God-man or the Logos is not *sui generis* in Christianity:

> Plotinus, who was certainly as great a philosopher and spiritual leader as Hellenic civilization ever produced, remarked that Pheidias' statue of Olympian Zeus was what Zeus would look like if He did indeed "take flesh and dwell among us" (*Enneads* 5.8.1). (S. Clark 1989, 178)

Secular theorists of human identity have unwittingly become polytheistic in their acceptance of multiple and often contradictory ideals and in their moral claim that it is not always possible to do right without at the same time doing dreadful wrong. It is difficult to criticize contemporary polytheism, however, because its defenders do not think of themselves as polytheists. But the invisible world of the gods is not so ethereal that it is trivial. There are undeniable forces in the world, half-glimpsed visions or absent-minded absorptions in memory or fable, which constitute a sort of divine immanence. But it is precisely the "once-upon-a-time" character of these forces which should lead us to consider, by way of contrast, the reality of divine unity. The gods may be evoked by music, poetry, and love; and to disprove their existence one needs to do more than dredge Loch Ness:

> The argument is a metaphysical one, about the proper description of our experience and the correct metaphysical guess about the ground of that experience . . . an appropriate metaphorical description of certain states of spiritual being. If a broadly spiritist metaphysics is ultimately found to be false, then there have never really been any (gods); but in that case there have never "really" been any human persons either. If there are persons, then there are at least some spirits weirdly mingled with the material. And if there are some, what reason is there to deny that there are also others, perhaps of a larger and more alien kind? (S. Clark 1987, 352–54)

In sum, my exploration of polytheism in this section of the chapter has consisted in the following steps:

1. The asymmetrical view of time, which is a moderate view between two extremes, leaves human identity in a fragile state.
2. But it does not leave it in a more fragile state than it is in reality, contra the classical theistic, substantialist thesis.
3. Any adequate theory of human identity must account for both continuity and change.
4. To the extent that change is a necessary feature of human identity (as it is even for Clark) polytheism must be taken seriously.
5. But Clark may be correct that polytheism is taken *too* seriously in contemporary culture.
6. Hence the effort to discover the underlying unity to one's life, an effort integrally connected to the effort to understand divine unity, is crucial.
7. But a phenomenology of one's personal experience indicates that this unity can only be partial in that Aphrodite and Ares, Apollo and Dionysus, the furies, and various spirits of spite and reprisal and memory still pull us in different directions.
8. And the theodicy problem, among others in the philosophy of religion, insures that the sort of stability which would be provided by a classical theistic, omnipotent deity will continue to be difficult to defend.
9. Hence we will have to rest content within the Abrahamic religions with only a partial refutation of polytheism. (Even Jesus was on several occasions tempted.)
10. And this is exactly what we should expect: Neither the "one" nor the "many" in the problem of the one and the many can be wished away.

G. ASYMMETRICAL RELATIONS, IDENTITY, AND ABORTION

Thus far in this chapter I have tried to show, through a consideration of the philosophies of Nagel and Clark, the practical defects of a view of the human self based on a theory of pure internal temporal relations, a view held, in different ways and with different language, by most classical theists, including analytic classical theists. In the remainder of this chapter I will deal with these practical defects practically (not a redundancy) through a treatment of an issue in applied ethics that is of interest to almost all theists: abortion. Once again, we will see the superiority of Hartshorne's approach to this issue to the classical theistic one.

Philosophical opponents of abortion usually base their opposition on the claim that the fetus is a human person, or at least that it has the potential to be a human person, hence it is murder, or something close to murder, to abort it. This claim, in turn, is based on a logic of symmetrical relations whereby human identity can be attributed to a being whether it is viewed in its transition from past to present *or* if it is viewed in its transition from present to future. In this last section of the chapter I will freely use Hartshorne's thought to criticize opponents of abortion. Specifically, I will criticize this use of symmetrical temporal relations, a use which has (surprisingly, given the attention abortion has received from philosophers) largely been ignored by scholars.

I will present my view as a mean between two undesirable extremes: (1) The classical theistic view (which is often used to support opposition to abortion) is that all events in a person's life are *internally* related to all the others, such that implicit in the fetus are all the experiences of the adult, and this due to God's eternal "foreknowledge" of everything that is to happen to the fetus. An equally disastrous view is (2) in that, although this view would permit abortion, it provides insufficient grounds for showing respect for even an adult human being. This is the view of Hume or Russell that, strictly speaking, there is no personal identity because each event in "a person's life" is *externally* related to the others. Despite the obvious differences between these two views they are both symmetrical, as I will show.

Let us consider the defects in the classical theistic view first. "If I was already 'myself' in childhood, still *that* self did not have and never can have my adult knowledge" (WM, 18–19). That is, in its memories the adult has its childhood, but no child can have its adulthood. There is a partial but not a complete identity between a child and any adult. Classical theism's theory of unqualified identity fails to take into consideration these implications of temporal becoming for human identity. Do young persons really identify themselves with the elderly persons they *may* eventually become? Hardly.

If one supposes that a person is simply one reality from before birth until death (or after), then one is in effect denying that with each change in life we have a partly new concrete reality; one would be implying that there is a strictly identical reality with merely new qualities. But, contra the classical theistic view, to say that Mary is "the same person" day after day and year after year is primarily to say that she does not become Jane. This leaves open the possibility that Mary on Friday and Mary on Monday are somewhat different realities, both quantitatively (one is older than the other) and qualitatively (Mary on Monday has actually had experiences over the weekend which Mary on Friday could only imagine) (OO, 104–5). The "identity" between the two Marys is real, but it is an abstract reality rather than any concretely lived experience. That is, genetic identity is a nonstrict identity, as opposed to the classical theist's (and the opponent of abortion's) theory of strict identity.

A nonstrict identity is composed of two or more successive concrete actualities with partly identical and partly differing qualities. It makes sense to claim that a person in a later state includes that person in an earlier state, *but not vice versa*. For example, only I remember my past in the inward way in which I remember it, although even I remember it vaguely and partially. The point is that I-now cannot be adequately described without mentioning my past, but (in distinction to the opponents to abortion) I-then could have been (could only have been!) adequately described without mentioning I-now.

The fact that one's past self is in some significant sense "another" self should not be underestimated, especially when the issue of abortion is considered (CS, 8). To claim that a person is an identical entity through time containing successive accidental properties is really a misleading way of describing an individual enduring through change. Successive states are not so much "in" the identical entity as it is in them (CS, 20). At a given moment a human being is definite, and he is definite in his history up until that point, but until he dies his future is at least partly indefinite, even with respect to the immediate future, and perhaps largely indefinite with respect to the distant future. If it makes sense to say, as it obviously does, that this human being could have had a somewhat different career up until the present, then he is a partly indefinite entity. That is, a human being is not, in spite of the classical theistic view, the same as his career. The latter is an abstraction in comparison with the concreteness of lived experience (CS, 23).

There is a certain bias in the history of philosophy, as we have seen, from which it has painfully tried to free itself: the favoring of one pole of conceptual contrasts at the expense of the other pole. Being has traditionally been preferred to becoming, identity at the expense of diversity, and so on. (CS, 44; LP, 17). The prejudice in favor of being as opposed to becoming is related to the theory of strict identity. If all events in a person's life are real together, say in the mind of the classical theistic God, then the totality of events simply is, with being and not becoming as the inclusive concept. The classical theistic view of human identity I am here criticizing clearly exhibits this bias. The hope of defenders of this view has been that by attacking the idea of a partially changing identity one could make secure the true reality or true being of an individual. An unintended consequence of this view is that it leads to determinism. If the future is just as internally related to the present as is the past (i.e., if the present is just as much affected by the future as by the past) then what are normally called future contingencies merely refer to our ignorance of what is already in the cards (CS, 174). It is no accident that the strict identity view is often based on the theory that God knows with absolute assurance the outcome of future contingencies, a theory which traditionally, and understandably, has run up against the objection that such *absolutely certain* knowledge would eliminate the possibility of future contingencies. On the theory of strict identity, all change consists in attaching predicates to a strictly identical subject (or substance) which endures throughout the succession of predicates. This seems to imply that substances are eternal in that, being changeless, they are incapable of creation or destruction unless, of course, they are created or destroyed by divine miracle, an implication actually welcomed or at least implied by some who are opposed to abortion in the miracle of God breathing a soul into a fertilized egg (CS, 180).

The ordinary use of personal pronouns and nouns is perfectly compatible with the process, nonstrict view of identity I am defending. I am I and not any other person (CS, 183). The series of experiences of which I have intimate memory contains no members of your series. It is not true that only defenders of strict identity can explain the persistence of character traits, whereas event pluralists who defend nonstrict identity can only give grudging recognition to these traits. Identity is not so much in dispute as its analysis or symmetrical-asymmetrical structure. Obviously, I am in some sense numerically the same person I used to be, but it is equally obvious that in some sense I am a different person, even numerically different in that I have *more* past experiences as constituents of who I am. It is my present, however, which contrasts itself with my past, not the other way around. The old reality enjoyed or suffered no contrast with what came later; at best it vaguely anticipated what came later. "Life is cumulative, and hence asymmetrical in its relatedness" (CS, 184). The classical theistic view stumbles in viewing self-identity as merely numerical oneness, with at most a plurality of qualities, a single noun with many adjectives (LP, 120).

Genetic identity is a special strand of the causal order of the world, and rests on the same principle of inheritance from the past as does causality in general. Even the unconscious memories of our earliest moments form part of our individual natures. Once one is born, or perhaps even as a *developed* fetus (to be explained later), the particular events which prolong one's existence are additions to a personal sequence (CS, 185). By way of contrast, classical theistic strict identity implies (but this implication is seldom admitted) that nothing a person does or that happens to that person could have been otherwise (CA, 160). I am alleging that in order to avoid the untoward implications of the classical theistic view one needs to posit the concrete determinate actuality in the present (which in some way preserves its past) as that which "has" properties (CA, 168).

Although I will show in detail below the connection between asymmetrical temporal relations and the issue of abortion, I would like to introduce this connection briefly here through a consideration of Aristotle. Tracing the conception of the human person as substance back to Aristotle is a commonplace in philosophy, but it would be a mistake to think that Aristotle saw the future careers of individuals as definite. That is, Aristotle did not need a doctrine of preestablished harmony because he believed in at least a partly indeterminate future not known in minute detail by God. Even a well-informed Aristotelian like I. M. Bochenski has been willing to admit that reality, even human reality, consists in a (personally ordered) series of events (CA, 86–87). The technical jargon of process philosophy can be seen as an attempt to dot each i and cross each t of Aristotelian concepts like *dynamis, energeia*, and future contingency. An individual career (i.e., an event sequence), once begun, has the potentiality for later prolongations. But it is an open question in Aristotle scholarship whether it is better to say that the actualization of a potency is contained in the potency or that the potency is contained in the actualization. If the present is more than the past (i.e., if reality is cumulative for Aristotle) there is a new whole of determinations in the present and the latter alternative is more accurate. Events are capable of being superceded by what is more than they are, for example, an infant self does *not* contain the adult phases of itself, nor does the fetal "self" contain the infant phases of "itself."

It is significant to note that Aristotle was not opposed to abortion (nor was Plato—see Carrick 1985), and that his theory of fetal development even influenced thinkers like Saints Augustine and Thomas Aquinas, who were opposed to abortion. It has been convincingly argued,[10] I think, that Augustine and Thomas were opposed to abortion due to the view that abortion was a perversion of the true purpose of human sexuality. Their opposition to abortion was *not* due to a belief that the fetus in the early stages of pregnancy was a person. Both Augustine (through the influence of the Stoics) and Thomas maintained the Aristotelian belief that the fetus went through stages of development and *gradually* developed into a person. The fetus goes from a vegetative to a sentient state, and then the human child eventually develops rationality. Augustine refers to the fetus in the early stages of pregnancy as a seed (*semina*) or a cutting (*tale*) or a sprout (*germen*) which is pruned (*deputo*) in abortion.

Obviously, I am not trying to offer anything like an adequate treatment of Aristotle's or Augustine's or Thomas' views on fetal development or abortion. Rather, I am trying to use these thinkers to illustrate how odd, and how indefensible, contemporary classical theistic opposition to abortion is. If I am not mistaken, there are two significant ways in which one can philosophically argue against abortion. One consists in the *perversity* view and the other in the *ontological* view. The former, defended by Augustine and Thomas, is taken seriously these days only by a few fundamentalist religious believers who think that abortion is a perversion of the true function of sexuality, which is solely, or at least primarily, to have children within marriage. The latter view, which *is* taken seriously by many contemporary theists, is defective for all of the reasons I cite in this section of the chapter. The view that it is wrong to abort the fetus due to the ontological status of the fetus (even in the early stages of pregnancy) as a human person is based on what I have above called the theory of strict, temporally symmetrical identity. Joseph Donceel refers to this view as "Cartesian" because, in place of Aristotle's (and Augustine's and Thomas's) view that the *psychē* and body organically develop *together* in the fetus, the contemporary opponent of abortion usually relies on the view that a *psychē* worthy of as much moral respect as that found in a sound-minded adult can instantaneously appear in the microscopic speck of matter called a fertilized egg. This Cartesian view (which Aristotle, Augustine, and Thomas would, I think, have found ridiculous) implies that psyche and body are separate entities altogether and that they can mature without any organic connection with each other. Contemporary classical theistic opponents of abortion are thus Cartesians in spite of themselves and have abandoned, ironically enough, the more moderate positions of Saints Augustine and Thomas Aquinas.

The reasonableness of the theory of nonstrict, temporally asymmetrical identity can be seen when it is contrasted with a second extreme, but equally symmetrical, view. Hume, Russell, and some

Buddhists have overstated the nonstrictness of genetic identity by claiming that all temporal relations are external, hence strict identity theorists can rightly fear this view (OO, 105). But before showing what is defective in the theory of purely external relations, I would like to indicate its grain of truth. The theory of purely internal relations starts with a correct intuition regarding the need to explain the persistence of character traits, but it grossly overemphasizes the personal continuity needed to preserve these traits. Likewise, the theory of purely external relations (in Buddhism, especially) starts with the legitimate insight that the qualification of personal identity allows for at least partial identity with others. The "no soul, no substance" doctrine of the Buddhists enables us to understand the Pauline claim that we are members one of another. That is, self-love and love of others are on much the same footing and neither makes much sense without the other (OO, 107–8), especially when it is realized that my previous self is to some degree an other self from the one I am now.

From this insight, however, defenders of external relations like Russell show no more hesitation than classical theists regarding the acceptance of symmetrical relations. If events in nature are mutually independent, then nature is analogous to a chaos of mutually independent propositions (CS, 83). The defender of asymmetry (who views a present person as internally related to his past but as externally related to "his" future) finds it odd to see Russell attacking those who have little or no use for anything but internal relations. And it is equally odd to see partisans of purely internal relations trying to refute Hume or Russell (CS, 96).

One defect in the theory of purely external relations is that we do in fact usually talk as though events depend on what happens before but not on what happens afterwards; we do talk as though asymmetry is the case. This in itself does not refute a Hume or a Russell, but it should lead defenders of purely external relations to wonder if believing in events as dependent both ways (i.e., present dependent on past and present dependent on future) is necessarily worse than believing in events as independent both ways (CS, 147, 213). There is also the familiar difficulty of preserving moral responsibility for one's past actions if one is not internally related in some way to those actions.

Consider the following clever and, I think, devastating example from Hartshorne:

> One may parody the prejudice of symmetry as follows: Suppose a carpenter were to insist that if hinges on one side of a door are good, hinges on both sides would be better. So he hangs a door by hingeing it on both sides, and it then appears that the hinges cannot function, so that the door is not a door but a wall. "We'll fix that," says another carpenter, and removes all the hinges. So now the door is again not a door, but a board lying on the floor. This is how I see the famous controversy about internal and external relations. (CS, 216)

The classical theist is one example of the first carpenter. More complications set in when it is realized that a symmetrical theory of purely internal relations leads to an unworkable monism, whereas a symmetrical theory of purely external relations leads, as Russell realized, to a radical pluralism. Russell's mistake was in assuming that one *had to be* either an absolute monist or an absolute pluralist and that one could not benefit from the strengths of internal and external relations. Defense of purely internal relations leads to the erroneous conclusion that we can *only* expect what laws governing the internal relations will allow, and the view which emphasizes purely external relations *should* lead to the conclusion that at each moment anything could conceivably happen next (LP, 174). Speaking of Russell, Hartshorne makes the following observation, which was alluded to in the Introduction to the present book:

> The combination of extreme causal determinism and extreme pluralism (lack of any internal relations connecting the constituents of reality) repeated the most bizarre feature of Hume's philosophy. The combination violently connects and violently disconnects the constituents of reality. (CA, 156)

Most who use the contemporary slogan "respect for life" seem unaware of the vast gulf in quality between experiences open to a fetus compared to experiences possible for a walking, talking child, not to mention the mother of the fetus. The question should be, respect for life on what level? A single human egg cell is alive, but it has no experiences like those of an adult, or a child, or even of an animal with a central nervous system (see Dombrowski 1988b). Augustine did well by comparing the fetus in the early stages of pregnancy (before the development of the central nervous system, which, as we now know, makes sentiency possible) to a plant. No egg cell, fertilized or not, can simply turn itself into a truly human individual (with sentience as a necessary condition for the truly human). Only years of attention can do that. Just as we need a mean between extremes regarding temporal relations—avoiding both the classical theistic theory regarding pure internal relations, where all events in a person's life are interdependent, and the antimetaphysical pluralism of the early Wittgenstein and Russell, where all things are mutually independent—we also need a mean between injudicious extremes regarding respect for life (WM, 4–5).

If to be a person in the fullest sense is to be conscious, rational, and have a moral sense, then a fetus is, *at best*, a probability of a person, hence those who equate abortion with murder are engaging in demagoguery. A probability of something is not that something, especially when the probability can only be realized with considerable effort and sacrifice on the part of others (WM, 59–60). I am *potentially* the president of the United States, but I do not insist that "Hail to the Chief" be played when I enter the room. I will *probably* be a grandfather some day, yet at 42 and with more than a few grey hairs appearing, I nonetheless think it is premature to call be "Grandpa."

It changes the whole quality of life to learn that there are murderers about, but the embryo is not bothered by, nor is it even conscious of, the fact that there are abortionists about. "The human value of the embryo is essentially potential and future, not actual and present" (WM, 125). The functioning which it does *actually* exhibit is nothing especially exalted when compared to other beings, even a great many nonhuman beings. Of course, even the potentiality of a fetus has some value, but *this* value (even plants have some value) is nothing absolute and should be weighed against the values of those—especially the mother—actually functioning at a much higher level (i.e., at the level of sentiency, at the very least, if not at the level of rationality). Indeed, as some "pro-lifers" notice, the aborted fetus could have turned out to be a genius, but this is not the same as actually being a genius. The aborted fetus could have also turned out to be a murderer. It is unclear, to say the least, how one can make the status of a presentient cluster of cells more or less exalted by considering what it *might* eventually become (WM, 126).

Randolph Feezell (1987) comes close to the view of abortion I am defending here.[11] Although my criticism is primarily directed against strict identity theory based on a strong view of divine omniscience with respect to the future (which is connected with what Feezell calls the conservative view of abortion), it also has implications for Feezell's moderate view, which criticizes the casual attitude some (he calls them liberals) may have toward the fetus, which is a "soon to be actual" person (1987, 47). At times, Feezell is careful to refer to the fetus as a future (i.e., a possible) person, and then attempts to attribute rights to the fetus on that basis. But this attempt, I suggest, is only successful when Feezell almost imperceptibly slips into the strict identity (i.e., conservative or classical theistic) view. Consider his claim that "the death of the fetus is a severe misfortune for *the person* whose possibilities have been negated" (1987, 46—my emphasis; note that here Feezell does not say "future person"). He also says that "at conception a unique chromosomal combination occurs, and that is the basis for speaking of some identifiable *potentiality* which *will be born* and *will develop* into that person whose history we must *now* morally consider" (1987, 44–45—my emphasis).

My criticisms are as follows: If the fetus is a potential (i.e., a future person), as Feezell sometimes admits, why should we grant it rights *now*? To say that it should have rights now because it *definitely* will be born and *definitely* will develop into an infant is to subtly slip into the strict identity theory based on symmetrical temporal relations. That is, if Feezell had said that the fetus *may* eventually be born and that it will *perhaps* develop into a person a more accurate (from the point of view of asymmetry) description of the fetus' mode of existence would be given, such that there would be less of a tendency to treat the fetus as a bearer of rights. Feezell is correct that fully actual persons are the subjects of misfortune (1987, 45), but I am not convinced that potential persons, because they exist in space and have a history, are also (albeit in a "weaker sense") subjects of misfortune. The question is: What *sort* of actuality does the historical being in question have? Rocks also occupy space and have a historical route of occasions making up their careers. Feezell is also correct in pointing out (as is Nagel) the asymmetry we are willing to adopt regarding prenatal nonexistence and posthumous nonexistence (1987, 43). We are not unhappy about the former, but it makes perfect sense to be bothered about the latter. I do not think that death simply as such is an evil, but it does make sense to grieve over a premature or ugly or violent death of a sentient being. But these types of death bother us because an actual person who was capable of receiving violence or who actually had hopes for the future (hopes which existed in the present) was cut down. In the end, however, Feezell's moderate view (which leans toward the conservative view) is not too much different in practical effect from my or Hartshorne's moderate view (which leans toward the liberal view) in that I am only delivering a carte blanche for abortion in the early stages of pregnancy and pointing out that the fetus in the later stages of pregnancy has a moral status analogous to that of an animal, a status which I think deserves considerable attention on our part.

A view similar to Feezell's is defended by Don Marquis (1989), who, like Feezell, is worried that the fetus' valuable future is lost in abortion. However, Marquis admits that abortion is morally permissible when it occurs so early in pregnancy that the fetus is "not yet definitely an individual" with a future. He is not clear regarding when this occurs; nor is he clear about when it becomes legitimate to refer to the life of a fetus as *its* life. In short, a moderate defense of the permissibility of abortion early in pregnancy may very well be compatible with an opposition to abortion that is not absolute, as in the cases of Feezell and Marquis.

The fetus is obviously alive, as is grass, and it is obviously human *in the sense that* it has human parents and has a human genetic structure. But if what I have said regarding asymmetrical relations and human identity is correct, the primary moral question becomes: When does an individual human life become as valuable as the life of an animal? And the secondary question becomes: When does an individual human life become more valuable than that of a "mere" animal? My response to the first question is: around the fourteenth week of pregnancy, when a central nervous system, and hence sentiency per se, develops. A response to the second question is much more difficult to make (OO, 99–101). Not even an infant reasons in any sense equally with, or beyond the capacity of, dogs, apes, or porpoises (WM, 33), although even the infant is enormously superior to a fertilized egg in many morally relevant respects: levels of sentiency, consciousness, fear, and so on (OO, 55). From the fact of infant inferiority, however, we should not be driven in a Michael Tooley–like direction[12] toward the moral permissibility of infanticide, but rather toward the protection of the lives of animals. They are *actually* sentient and it is a fundamental moral axiom to claim that no being that can suffer ought to be forced to suffer gratuitously.[13]

The point I am trying to make here is not only that a fetus in the early stages of pregnancy is not a moral agent, but also that it must go through a certain period of development to reach the threshold of moral patiency, that is, sentiency per se. Only after sentience per se (as opposed to microscopic "sentiency") is acquired can we even begin to compare fetuses to other beings who are not moral agents but who are moral patients: the comatose, nonhuman animals, and so on. It is difficult, if not impossible, to imagine how we could consistently generalize the claim that nonsentient beings (i.e., beings who may have sentiency in their microscopic parts but which, lacking a central nervous system, are, as wholes, insentient) have rights. For example, if such (vegetative) beings have rights, then human beings would likely starve in that they would have little, if anything, to eat. The equal value of the possible and the actual "is not an axiom that anybody lives by or could live by" (OO, 101). Even on strictly anthropocentric grounds it is not an axiom with any pragmatic value.

Although not in itself an argument against the opponent of abortion, nor an argument in favor of infanticide, the following consideration by Hartshorne indicates the counterintuitiveness of the theory of strict identity:

> In nearly every society until recent centuries it was taken for granted that killing of human adults is a vastly more serious matter than even infanticide (if the latter is done by the parent or

> parents). This is enough to show that the idea of a fetus as a person in the full sense is not so plainly true that it can be used as a noncontroversial premise for political or moral conclusions. (OO, 101)

Equally problematic is the adjective "innocent" used of fetuses, a term which has at least two senses. It may very well be the case that we ought not to kill the innocent not because they are guiltless but because they are not harming us at this time; that is, there are such things as "innocent threats." Thus, if a fetus poses no harm to the pregnant woman it is innocent in this sense of the term. However, the usual sense of the term contrasts with "guilty" or "culpable." Only if those who saw abortion as morally permissible had ever claimed that fetuses were wicked and ought to be punished could the innocence of the fetus be a moral consideration (OO, 102). In this second sense of the term, the "innocence" of the fetus is like that of the animals: an incapacity to distinguish right from wrong but a capacity to experience pain. Here fetal innocence deserves consideration *once it has achieved* this capacity but not before (OO, 102–3).

A classic case of human beings becoming entangled in their own language is exhibited when opponents of abortion ask: How would you have liked it if your mother had aborted you? An adequate response would presuppose a responsible use of pronouns. I would neither have liked nor disliked the abortion because before the development of sentiency per se there would have been no "I" at all, and for some time after the development of sentiency there would have been fetal "innocence" but only a tenuous selfhood at work (OO, 103).[14] Once again, an understanding of the theory of asymmetrical relations is what enables us to see that:

> The "pro-life" literature is mostly a string of verbally implied identifications of fertilized egg cell with fetus, of fetus with infant, infant with child, child with youth, youth with adult. I repeat, any cause is suspect which ignores or denies distinctions so great. . . . I have respect for the fetus as . . . a wondrous creation . . . it is capable of eventually, with much help from relatively adult persons, becoming first an infant (and then a child). . . . We are all human *individuals* long before we are *persons* in the value sense of actually thinking and reasoning in the human

> fashion. Even in dreamless sleep as adults, we are not actually functioning as persons; but this does not abolish the obviously crucial difference between a fetus whose potentiality for rational personhood requires at least many months of help by actual persons to be actualized even slightly, and a sleeping adult who has already functioned as a person for many years and who has made many plans for what it will do in its waking moments, perhaps for years to come. (OO, 112, also 116–17)

During the first weeks of pregnancy an embryo is but a colony of cells, "itself" as a whole not much of an individual at all. Those who are offended by the claim that cows or chimps (OO, 13; WM, 49; see Hartshorne 1978) deserve more respect than the fetus in the early stages of pregnancy usually resort to a type of question-begging which Peter Singer calls "speciesism": The human fetus in the early stages of pregnancy deserves moral respect just because it *is* human. To avoid begging the question as to *why* the embryo deserves moral respect, the classical theistic opponent of abortion (who typically ignores Saints Augustine and Thomas Aquinas on *this* issue) usually resorts to something like what I have called the theory of strict identity based on a symmetrical theory of temporal relations. And if, as I have tried to show, this latter theory (and other symmetrical theories) has more defects than its asymmetrical alternative, then opposition to abortion is, at the very least, questionable.[15]

No doubt defenders of strict identity will conflate the asymmetrical view with the theory of purely external relations by claiming that both theories make human identity too fragile. My response to this claim is, in a strange way, a sympathetic one. In the theory of purely external relations there is no real human identity through time, whereas in the asymmetrical view there is a human identity, but it is fragile. But it is not "too" fragile. The asymmetrical view leaves human beings, in contrast to God, "as fragile as they are and not a whit more" (CA, 87).

NOTES

INTRODUCTION

1. See Hume's view that it is meaningless playing with words to say there is a mind that thinks, wills, and loves yet this mind is wholly simple and immutable, in *Dialogues Concerning Natural Religion*, ed. N. K. Smith (Oxford: Clarendon Press, 1935), 197.

2. See my "Theism as the Cause of Agnosticism: The Case of the Darwinian James Rachels," *Ultimate Reality and Meaning* 18 (1995), 275–288.

1. MUST A PERFECT BEING BE IMMUTABLE?

1. I am referring to his paper titled "Analytic Themes in Whitehead's Metaphysics," presented to the Eastern Division of the APA in 1987.

2. My criticisms of Stump, Kretzmann, and Mann apply as well to the earlier work of Geach and Ross, writers who also assumed that God is immutable. See Geach, 1977, 22, and Ross 1969, 63, although Ross is quick to point out that there are nonetheless contingent attributes that God has, but they are not due to any agent other than God; I will return to Ross later in the book. I will not be treating nonanalytic Thomists in this article, e.g., those like Norris Clark, who have indeed entered into debate with process theists.

3. I have especially relied on Hartshorne's PS in this chapter, a work which contains many of Hartshorne's views found in his other books.

4. See Kretzmann 1966; Martin 1976; and Moskop 1984.

5. I realize this is an assumption on my part, nor is it made with equanimity. Also, my treatment of divine attributes below should give special treatment to Mann, who conflates the divine nature with the divine attributes. Finally, I admit that the permanence-change contrast is used both as an instance of a noninvidious contrast and as a generic heading for all of the other instances of noninvidious contrasts listed.

6. For Hartshorne, God must be as great as possible at any particular time, or else God would not be the greatest being. But new moments bring with them new possibilities for greatness, which God must realize in the best way possible if God is the greatest, or better, the unsurpassable. This means that God is greater than any being who is not God, but God can always, must always, surpass previous instances of divine greatness. It does not mean that God's earlier existence was inferior, because it was at that particular time the greatest conceivable existence, the greatest existence logically possible, and greater than any other being. Regarding the term "perfect" in the title to this chapter, it should be noted that Hartshorne sometimes avoids this term because many assume it to be a synonym for pure actuality or immutability. Hence he sometimes prefers "greatest conceivable being," etc.

7. This does not mean that there are no historical roots to Hartshorne's dipolar theism. See his PS and IO. Also see an excellent article by Leonard Eslick, "Plato as Dipolar Theist," *Process Studies* 12 (1982): 243–51.

8. Let me emphasize once again that the purpose of Mann's article is to show that God as simple and immutable can also be a person. The question I am asking is: Why should we assume that God is immutable *in every respect*? The purpose of the article by Stump and Kretzmann is to elucidate the concept of eternity, but in their elucidation they indicate the same assumption as Mann's. Also, the reader who is interested in Hartshorne's treatment of the theodicy problem,

God as creator, divine power, etc., can easily find his thoughts on these matters. God is not a watered down divinity in Hartshorne's thought. For example (contra Mann, Stump, and Kretzmann), God as a perfect knower would not have to mean that God would eternally know every actuality, but rather could mean that God would know what can be known; God's omniscience means that God would perfectly know actualities as actualities, and future contingencies as contingencies. To "know" a future contingency as an actuality is to know imperfectly. Just as there is no highest number, there are some values, such as knowledge, which do not admit of a maximum in a temporally changing world. See Carr-Wiggin 1984, where the author admits that God's failure to change would be for the worse, yet God may still be immutable in the sense that God is always omniscient and perfect, at time-1 and time-2, etc. Another article that criticizes Stump and Kretzmann is by Delmas Lewis (1984). Also see Zeis 1984 and Shields 1987. However, for a defense of immutability, see Kondoleon 1984.

9. See Hartshorne's EA. It is clear from Plantinga's *The Nature of Necessity* (Oxford: Oxford University Press, 1974) and other works that he is somewhat familiar with Hartshorne's work on the ontological argument, but there is no written evidence of which I am aware that Plantinga is very much interested in Hartshorne as a process theist.

10. I will deal with Swinburne on divine embodiment later in this book.

11. Also see my "Hartshorne and Plato" in The Library of Living Philosophers series, Lewis Hahn, ed., *The Philosophy of Charles Hartshorne* (LaSalle, Ill.: Open Court, 1991).

12. Plantinga's views on divine immutability rely heavily on Wolterstorff, 1975. Richard Creel also seems to rely on Wolterstorff. See Creel 1986. Also see a fine review of this book by James Keller in *Process Studies* 15 (1986): 290-296.

13. Again, see my "Hartshorne and Plato" as well as the conclusion to the present chapter.

14. See my article titled "An Anticipation of Hartshorne: Plotinus on *Daktylos* and the World-Soul," *The Heythrop Journal* 29 (1988): 462–67.

15. See More, 1921. The position that identifies the form of the good with God relies on the Neoplatonic (actually the neo-Aristotelian) interpretation popular in late antiquity.

16. Other factors enter into the reluctance of some to abandon divine immutability, e.g., the classical theistic tradition of male bias in theology, which favors a rigid God devoid of emotion; and the classical theistic tendency to think in substantial rather than in process terms, a tendency which should be as antiquated in theology as it is in geology, biology, and physics. Also see Mavrodes, 1988, 114–15, who points out that the Incarnation is beneath the dignity of God as conceived by classical theists. So much the worse for this conception of God, he thinks.

2. METHOD AND POLAR EQUALITY IN DIPOLAR THEISM

1. See Gale 1991; Helm 1988; Wierenga 1989; and any of a number of books by D. Z. Phillips.

2. References to Lequier can be found in several of Hartshorne's books. Also see the indices in his books regarding Nicholas Berdyaev, G. T. Fechner, et al.

3. Hartshorne had accidentally met Lovejoy as early as Hartshorne's days at Harvard in the 1920s. He informs us that he read Lovejoy's books and a few of his articles with keen interest because Lovejoy "really wrestled" with the history of ideas. Further, he claims that Lovejoy, who was not a vulnerable man, nonetheless was a man whom every sane person would think of highly. See DL, 341, 392.

4. Later in the book in response to Durrant these seven cases will be expanded into fifteen.

5. The focus of this chapter has forced me to ignore much of what is good in Gunton's book: his description of Hartshorne's doctrine on relations is extremely good, his treatment of the difference between God's abstract pole and our abstract description of God is very good, etc.

6. Gunton has not totally escaped the less than desirable connection between classical theism, on the one hand, and militarism and ecological rapacity, on the other.

7. Ward 1974, 158. Also see Brian Leftow (1991, 34–35), who dismisses Hartshorne's thought because of the "strange" modal thesis that possibility and necessity are modes of time and process, e.g., the supposedly "strange" view that "always" entails "absolute necessity."

8. These words are spoken by the Eleatic Stranger in the *Sophist* 247e.

9. Whitehead 1961 [1933], 119–22, 129.

10. Whitehead 1938, 162–63.

11. 1938, 92, 112, 126, 132.

12. Whitehead 1961 [1933], 83, 154, 158–59, 166, 275–76.

13. See Whitehead 1957 [1925], 234–35. Also see 1954, 217.

14. See Christian 1959, 246, 252, on the importance of the mingling of forms in Whitehead, even if the form when seen *in itself* does not mingle; but a form is not so much a one-in-itself as a one-as-being (as power).

15. See also Eslick 1955, 42–44, 46–48.

16. Eslick 1953, 17. Also see my "Being *Is* Power," 1995.

17. See Lowe 1962, 27. Also see the many references to Plato in *Dialogues of Alfred North Whitehead*. Lowe is sceptical as to whether as many of Whitehead's ideas can be traced back to Plato as Whitehead thought could be, see 253–54, 268. The present book is meant in part to defend Whitehead's intuitions regarding Plato. Also see Lowe 1962, 45–46, 327, 339.

18. See Griffin 1989, 26–27, 30. Also see Davis 1989, in the same volume, and Fiddes 1988. Fiddes differs in many respects from Griffin, but nonetheless in many other ways supplements Griffin's case.

3. DIVINE EMBODIMENT

1. Hartshorne's thoughts on the World-Soul and the divine body are scattered throughout his many books; see the indices to MV, PS, RS, CS, IO, OO, among others.

2. *Optics*, query 28.

3. Swinburne relies here on Harrison 1973–74.

4. Here Swinburne relies on Danto 1965.

5. See *Summa Theologiae* I.8; and *Summa Contra Gentiles* III. 68.7–8.

6. The identity of S2 across the equation S1:S2::S2:S3 is essential for my thesis in this section of the chapter. *Any* analogy is an effort to move from something we understand well to something we see through a glass darkly. We have no alternative but to interpret subhuman reality (S1) and superhuman reality (S3) through the only samples of reality we know directly: ourselves as embodied animals. The task is to use our own experience to bridge the gap between ourselves, on the one hand, and lesser or greater beings, on the other, without anthropomorphic orgies. See Thomas Nagel, "What Is It Like To Be a Bat?," in 1991 [1979]; and Collins 1947.

7. Swinburne 1979, 105. Although the Greeks did not know about cells, they did know about nerves (*neura*). See Solmsen 1961, 150–67, 169–97.

8. Wainwright cites *On the Truth of the Catholic Faith*, I, tr. A. Pegis (Garden City, NY: Doubleday Image Books, 1955), ch. 20, numbers 33, 37.

9. Mohr 1985. It is only Mohr's treatment of the World-Soul that I am criticizing from his otherwise excellent book. See pp. 171–77 on the World-Soul. Also see pp. 178–83 on soul, pp. 53–84 on time and eternity, pp. 85–98 on flux and space, and pp. 158–70, 184–88 on theodicy.

10. I am not sure what Mohr means when he criticizes various commentators on the *Timaeus* (Cornford, Cherniss, Archer-Hind, Herter, and Rosen) by saying that they offer "(unneeded) charitable attempts to dismiss Plato's thought from Christian thought and more generally as attempts to reduce the number of unfashionable theological commitments in Plato's cosmology" (1985, 40). Is Mohr agreeing with Plato's theological commitments or disagreeing with them?

11. Once again, see my "Hartshorne and Plato" on the ontological argument.

12. See Cornford 1963, 39. He claims that in the divine soul of the universe is a divine reason, the latter symbolized by the Demiurge. Also see AW, 4–5 and IO, 70–71.

13. Wolfson1934, I:358–60. Mohr does not explicate the relationship between the Demiurge and the World-Soul, but states only that the division between the two is more than mythical. Are they two gods for Mohr? Or if only one God, how are they related? Mohr is also unsure as to why the World-Soul must succumb to the bodily world. The dipolar logic of Hartshorne's theism is especially helpful here.

14. DR, 79–80; MV, 52. Hartshorne relies on Demos (1939), 120–25, who agrees that God is dipolar for Plato because reality is dipolar, and who suggests that God and the forms are abstractions from one complex fact of patterned activity, a view which is not exactly Hartshorne's but is close to it.

15. PS, 58–59. In addition to the standard texts where Aristotle discusses the gods, consider *De anima* 406b, where he appears to criticize Plato's attempt in the *Timaeus* to think of the World-Soul animating the spatial magnitude of the body of the world.

16. See Cornford 1923; and Bovet 1902.

17. Solmsen details how Xenophanes and Aeschylus partially prepared the way for Plato by indicating that God (Plato's Demiurge) was pure mind who acted without physical effort (1942, 43); Euripides at times thought of God in cosmic terms (46); Anaxagoras and Diogenes of Apollonia dealt with an intelligent organizer of the world—anything which serves its purpose as well as a bodily organ cannot be the work of *Tyche* (1942, 50–51); etc. This groping for a cosmic deity as opposed to a political one was characteristic of several pre-Socratic thinkers; a philosophical "science" was taking over the lead in the the search for a new divine principle. This concept of God as cosmic was not threatened by political upheaval, and hence philosophy of nature was the chief potential source for new religious beliefs. Plato criticized the gods in the construction of the Republic so as to make room for the World-Soul/Demiurge in the *Timaeus*. Also see 1942, 92, on Thales.

18. See William Goodwin, ed., *Plutarch's Morals* (Boston: Little, Brown, and Co., 1870), III:133, "Whether the World Be an Animal." Also see the following studies: (*a*) Barnes 1979, 196, where in Empedocles the cosmic sphere is given a divine status. (*b*) Robinson 1968, 77, attests to the Pythagorean belief in the World-Soul. (*c*) Burnet 1930, 49, 75, gives the sources (including Aristotle) for holding that Thales and Anaximenes believed in the World-Soul. (*d*) Kahn 1981, 11, 171, 208, 268, 275, 278, 337, contrasts human learning of many things (*polymathia*), on the one hand, with the divine wisdom of the World-Soul, on the other, which is found in several forms in Heraclitus: *hen to sophon*, universal *logos*, cosmic *gnōmē*, and *kyberman panta*. The very idea of a cosmos leads to a belief in a cosmic God, the contemplation of which largely constitutes human wisdom; we are partial constituents of cosmic order. Heraclitus sometimes personified the cosmic principle as Zeus, and at other times viewed it as a rarefied, all-pervading presence, like ether, a view which was later made famous by the Stoics. Kahn also details approximations of the World-Soul in Xenophanes, Anaxagoras, and Empedocles.

19. This discomfort is not found in Hartshorne nor in Lovelock 1984, which is on the scientific plausibility of something similar to the World-Soul, but of a nondivine sort.

20. See Cornford (1959, 28), who, contra Mohr, emphasizes that the World-Soul as a *zoon* must be self-moved if only because it was a commonplace in antiquity that animals were self-moved.

21. For two good summaries of the doctrine of the World-Soul in the *Timaeus*, see Guthrie 1978, 5:292–99; and Shorey 1933, 332–35.

22. Two noted scholars I do not find helpful in the understanding of the World-Soul are P. E. More (1921, 89, 113, 116–17, 172, 223), who wavers as to whether or not the World-Soul is a God; and Vlastos (1975, 25–27, 29, 31), who, when the question is asked, "Why does the cosmos have a soul?," responds by saying that the Form of a Living Creature has a soul. In effect, if I understand Vlastos correctly, the main reason why Plato talked about the World-Soul was to have a model for the Demiurge to create other (presumably human) souls. But this interpretation fails to take Plato's

religiosity seriously, for it implies that the *telos* of the World-Soul is to contribute to us; it is to commit the theological error of putting the creature above the Creator. I seriously doubt if Plato would have wanted this.

23. This word is from Friedlander (1958, I:31; III:328, 348, 365, 436), who sees this respiritualization of law, art, and nature as the central task of Plato's life; hence Plato can be said to return to Thales' notion that "all things are full of gods." Friedlander is also instructive regarding the similarity between the individual and God; e.g., in the *Gorgias* (505e) Plato indicates that there is not only a soul for the cosmos but also that there is something like a cosmos or wholeness for the individual soul. That is, the best humans reflect the World-Soul in that their common principle is the *agathon*. If the world is, as Friedlander notes many contemporary thinkers believe, a mere machine then the appearance of a leaf or a caterpillar would be "miraculous."

24. Very helpful on the *constancy* of the world's organic functioning as due to the World-Soul is Hans-Georg Gadamer (1980, 140–46, 164–67), who notices that an animal, even a divine animal, differs from a plant because it can relay back to itself all the stimulations of sense experience. That is, the World-Soul integrates the scattered multiplicity of the bodily, an integration which is similar to that found in Anaxagoras and Xenocrates. Gadamer is also helpful in the defense of Hartshorne's version of Platonic theodicy in that the second, "bad" World-Soul of the *Laws* cannot be taken literally; a second "World" Soul would entail a third to unify the first two into a cosmos, etc. Cf. Solmsen 1942, 147n.18.

25. One problem with using male pronouns in reference to the World-Soul is that the World-Soul can be seen, as was noted earlier, as an attempt to preserve the best in the Great Mother tradition in religion which existed before the bifurcation between Father Sky God and Mother Earth Goddess, a bifurcation which gradually tilted toward Father Sky God, out of which the God of classical theism grew.

26. Regarding the *Timaeus*, my debt is enormous to A. E. Taylor's classic, *A Commentary on Plato's Timaeus* (1928, 77–78, 80, 82,

103, 105, 124, 255–56). Among Taylor's worthwhile points I would like to emphasize is his belief that the World-Soul (God) is far more important in the *Timaeus* than in the *Republic* largely because it is a key part of a new cosmology without matter (an indirect way of saying that Plato was a panpsychist). Taylor also indicates that the language of God (here the Demiurge) putting soul into the body of the world is obviously not to be taken literally. God—*aristē psychē*—is transcendent and immanent, i.e., dipolar. The former makes it difficult to call Plato's God pantheistic, the latter makes it difficult to limit God in an Aristotelian-Thomistic way. It is no surprise that Taylor uses Whitehead to criticize monopolarity, as in his criticism of viewing soul as "substance."

27. Findlay (1974, 375), is instructive regarding the World-Soul in Plotinus. Here the World-Soul is an unquiet faculty (as in Hartshorne's claim that it receives influence from *all* creatures), like Martha busy over many things (*polypragmōn*—III.7.2), in contrast to the One. Hartshorne supplements Findlay's insights. The Greeks—Plato, Aristotle, and Epicurus among them—realized that any possible world must involve a multiplicity of individuals, each making their own decisions, hence there is an aspect of real chance in what happens (OO, 15). Unfortunately, this notion of chance was not sufficiently synthesized by Plato with the atomism of Leucippus and Democritus (IO, 16). It is perhaps this failure which accounts for the monopolarity of the neoplatonists in their interpretation of Plato. In a way, Plotinus reaffirms Plato's "three aspects of the ultimate" in the *Timaeus*: the Forms, (especially the Form of the Good), the Demiurge, and the World-Soul. These appear in Plotinus as the One, Intellect (*nous*), and the Plotinian World-Soul. But Plotinus has a (necessitarian) logical principle for the progression from the One to the World-Soul. (Cf. Whittemore 1966.) Plotinus's ontolatry differs from Plato's belief in a World-Soul because the self-motion of soul is replaced by a conception of soul with a merely "accidental and superficial motility," a motility derived in an Aristotelian way from body rather than from the soul's own nature. Plotinus at least enhanced Plato's aesthetic argument for God, and he rightly viewed Plato's forms as essentially "objects for Nous," but for the most part

his monopolarity detracted from an appreciation of Plato's greatest insights (PS, 211–12, 221). Hartshorne finds it "comic" to watch Plotinus trying to prove that without unity and simplicity we cannot understand the multiple and complex. How true!, but without plurality, contrast, and complexity there is "no unity, beauty, goodness, value, or reality" (CS, 121). Finally, see Moreau 1939, 75ff.

28. Origen, *On First Principles*, tr. G.W. Butterworth (Gloucester, MA: Peter Smith, 1973), 17, II.1.3.

4. ALSTON AND MORRIS ON THE CONCEPT OF GOD

1. In addition to Plato and Bergson, Hartshorne cites Milton Munitz regarding the impossibility of absolute nothingness. See *The Mystery of Existence* (New York: Appleton-Crofts, 1965).

2. Ford 1974, 1973. Ford's view is more complex than Alston indicates. At times Ford has agreed with Alston and at times Ford has agreed with something like Hartshorne's view: God is to be conceived in terms of an unending series of successive temporal unifications of the world.

5. DESCRIBING GOD

1. James Ross, "On Proofs for the Existence of God," *The Monist* (1970). In "An Impasse on Competing Descriptions of God" Ross is not only softening his criticisms of process thought found in "On Proofs for the Existence of God" but also in a review that appeared in 1970 in the *Journal of the American Academy of Religion* of John Cobb's *God and the World* (Philadelphia: Westminster, 1969). Also see an analytic theist who seems at times to lean toward a Hartshornian view of God: Van Inwagen, 1988.

2. Durrant relies here on Elizabeth Anscombe and Peter Geach 1961. The lone article from Hartshorne that Durrant relies on to develop his criticisms is "The God of Religion and the God of Philosophy," in *Talk of God*, ed., G. N. A. Vesey. (London: Macmillan, 1969).

3. See my *St. John of the Cross: An Appreciation* (Albany: SUNY Press, 1992), in which Hartshorne is used to provide a better metaphysical basis for understanding mystical experience in Christianity than the basis provided by classical theism.

4. See an excellent article by Nancy Frankenberry, "Hartshorne's Method in Metaphysics," in PC. But Frankenberry overstates her case at one point (p. 299) when she claims that Hartshorne's method contains only a minimal pragmatic aspect. Here regarding mysticism, regarding the pragmatic necessity of human freedom (à la William James), etc., Hartshorne constantly makes philosophical judgments based on pragmatic criteria. Likewise, I do not think it is true to say that logical considerations overshadow phenomenological ones in Hartshorne (PC, 307–8). His repeated concern for the religious experiences of mystics should not be overlooked; see Hartshorne's "Mysticism and Rationalistic Metaphysics," *The Monist* 59 (1976): 463-469. It is just as true to say that Hartshorne's method consists in experience seeking understanding as it is to say that it consists in understanding seeking exemplification in experience.

5. See A. N. Whitehead, *Religion in the Making* (New York: Macmillan, 1926): 123, 144. Also see Bergson, *The Two Sources of Morality and Religion*, 255: "The mystics unanimously bear witness that God needs us, just as we need God."

6. THE CONCEPT OF GOD AND THE MORAL LIFE

1. Nagel's view here has implications, as he notes, regarding abortion. A fetus in the early stages of pregnancy, *before* the development of a central nervous system, can hardly be said to suffer a misfortune when aborted.

2. See Nagel 1970. Also see R. Morris 1991 on Whitehead's and Hartshorne's liberalism.

3. Thomas Nagel, *The View from Nowhere* (Oxford: Oxford University Press, 1986), 88, 130–31, 199, 212, 214.

4. Ibid., 4, 134, 138, 187, 212.

5. *The View from Nowhere*, 3, 8, 132, 190.

6. Ibid., 59; also 10, 18, 27.

7. Ibid., 63, 82–83, 85–86, 91, 210.

8. Ibid., pp. 163, 199, 214, 228. Also see my "On Why Patriotism Is Not a Virtue," *International Journal of Applied Philosophy* 7 (1992): 1–4, on the political consequences of Nagel's view *sub specie aeternitatis*.

9. Ibid., 49. Also see Feezell (1984), who criticizes Nagel's notion of absurdity not only because his notion of objectivity fails as a necessary condition for a rational human life, but also because his notion of subjectivity fails. Also see a forthcoming volume by Randall Auxier on the correspondence between Hartshorne and the personalist Brightmen.

10. See my "St. Augustine, Abortion, and *Libido Crudelis*," *Journal of the History of Ideas* 49 (1988): 151–56. And see Joseph Donceel's articles on abortion and Thomas Aquinas, e.g., the one in *Abortion in a Changing World* (New York: Columbia University Press, 1970).

11. Feezell 1987. I should note at this point that throughout this chapter I have assumed a strong connection between: (*a*) belief in divine knowledge in minute detail and with absolute assurance of what will happen in our future; and (*b*) determinism. Obviously many analytic theists do not see such a strong connection; having read extensively in this area, it still seems to me that (*a*) entails that whatever we do is (logically) determined to be the same as what God already knows in minute detail and with absolute assurance we are going to do. For a summary of recent work in this area, see Fischer 1992. It should be noted that Nagel and Feezell, who are not classical theists, nonetheless inherit some of the traditional problems associated with classical theism.

12. Michael Tooley, "Abortion and Infanticide," *Philosophy and Public Affairs* 2 (1972): 37–65. Tooley is correct in searching for a morally relevant threshold for moral patiency, but it is by no means clear why he so casually rejects (or how he could reject!) sentiency as such a criterion. Is he really willing to claim that a being which can experience suffering does not have the right not to have suffering inflicted on it gratuitously?

13. See my *The Philosophy of Vegetarianism* (Amherst: University of Massachusetts Press, 1984).

14. See my "Starnes on Augustine's Theory of Infancy," *Augustinian Studies* 11 (1980): 125–33.

15. For a summary of some of the scientific research which supports the view that the fetus is not a prepackaged human being (e.g., even something so relatively simple as a fingerprint arises at least in part due to chance events not present in a fertilized egg), see Charles Gardner, "Is an Embryo a Person?," *The Nation*, 13 November 1989.

Bibliography

Adams, Robert M. 1987. *The Virtue of Faith and Other Essays in Philosophical Theology.* Oxford: Oxford University Press.

Alston, William. 1951. "Whitehead's Denial of Simple Location." *Journal of Philosophy* 48 (1951): 713–20.

———. 1952. "Internal Relatedness and Pluralism in Whitehead." *Review of Metaphysics* 4 (1952): 535–58.

———. 1964. *Philosophy of Language.* Englewood Cliffs, NJ: Prentice-Hall.

———. 1964b. "The Elucidation of Religious Statements." In *Process and Divinity: The Hartshorne Festschrift.* LaSalle, IL: Open Court.

———. 1984. "Hartshorne and Aquinas: A Via Media." In *Existence and Actuality: Conversations with Charles Hartshorne.* Chicago: University of Chicago Press. Repr. in *Divine Nature and Human Language* (Ithaca: Cornell University Press, 1989).

Anscombe, Elizabeth and Peter Geach 1961. *Three Philosophers: Aristotle, Aquinas, Frege.* Oxford: Blackwell.

Aquinas, St. Thomas. See Thomas Aquinas, St.

Aristotle. 1941. *The Basic Works of Aristotle.* Ed. McKeon New York: Random House.

Audi, Robert. 1986. *Rationality, Religious Belief and Commitment.* Ithaca: Cornell University Press.

Barnes, Jonathan. 1979. *The Presocratic Philosophers.* London: Routledge and Kegan Paul.

Bergson, Henri. 1911. *Creative Evolution.* Tr. Mitchell. New York: Holt. Originally published in 1907.

———. 1977 [1932]. *The Two Sources of Morality and Religion.* Tr. by Brereton. Notre Dame: University of Notre Dame Press.

Bovet, Pierre. 1902. *Le Dieu de Platon d'après l'ordre chronologique des dialogues.* Geneve.

Bracken, Joseph. 1991. *Society and Spirit: A Trinitarian Cosmology* Selinsgrove, PA: Susquehanna University Press.

Burnet, John. 1930. *Early Greek Philosophy.* London: Black.

Carr-Wiggin, Robert. 1984. "God's Omnipotence and Immutability." *The Thomist* 48 (1984): 44–51.

Carrick, Paul. 1985. *Medical Ethics in Antiquity.* Boston: D. Reidel.

Christian, William. 1959. *An Interpretation of Whitehead's Metaphysics.* New Haven: Yale University Press.

Clark, Stephen R. L. 1984. *From Athens to Jerusalem.* Oxford: Clarendon Press.

———. 1986. *The Mysteries of Religion.* Oxford: Basil Blackwell.

———. 1987. "How to Believe in Fairies." *Inquiry* 30 (1987).

———. 1989. *Civil Peace and Sacred Order.* Oxford: Clarendon Press.

Clarke, D. S. 1987. "Whitehead and Contemporary Analytic Philosophy." *Process Studies* 16 (1987): 26–34.

Clarke, W. Norris. 1979. *The Philosophical Approach to God.* Winston-Salem, N. C.: Wake Forest University Press.

Collins, James. 1947. *The Thomistic Philosophy of the Angels.* Washington, DC: Catholic University of America Press.

Cook, Robert. 1987. "God, Time and Freedom." *Religious Studies* 23 (1987): 81–94.

Cornford, F. M. 1923. *Greek Religious Thought.* London.

———. 1959. *Plato's Timaeus.* Indianapolis: Bobbs-Merrill.

———. 1963. *Plato's Cosmology.* London: Routledge and Kegan Paul.

Creel, Richard. 1986. *Divine Impassibility.* Cambridge: Cambridge University Press.

Danto, Arthur. 1965. "Basic Actions." *American Philosophical Quarterly* 2 (1965): 141–48.

Davies, Brian. 1983. "A Timeless God?" *New Blackfriars* 64 (1983): 215–24.

Davis, Stephen. 1989. "Why God Must Be Unlimited." In *Concepts of the Ultimate*, ed. Tessier. New York: St. Martin's.

Demos, Raphael. 1939. *The Philosophy of Plato.* New York: Scribner's.

Dombrowski, Daniel. 1980. "Starnes on Augustine's Theory of Infancy." *Augustinian Studies* 11 (1980): 125–33.

———. 1984. *The Philosophy of Vegetarianism* Amherst: University of Massachusetts Press.

———. 1988. "St. Augustine, Abortion, and *Libido Crudelis.*" *Journal of the History of Ideas* (1988): 151–56.

———. 1988b. *Hartshorne and the Metaphysics of Animal Rights.* Albany: SUNY Press.

———. 1988c. "An Anticipation of Hartshorne: Plotinus on *Daktylos* and the World-Soul." *The Heythrop Journal* 29 (1988): 462–67.

———. 1991. *Christian Pacifism.* Philadelphia: Temple University Press.

———. 1992. *St. John of the Cross: An Appreciation.* Albany: SUNY Press.

———. 1992b. "On Why Patriotism Is Not a Virtue." *International Journal of Applied Philosophy* 7 (1992): 1–4.

———. "Being Is Power." 1995. *American Journal of Theology and Philosophy* 16 (1995): 299–314.

———. "On Theism as the Cause of Agnosticism." *Ultimate Reality and Meaning* 18 (1995): 275–288.

Donceel, Joseph. "Immediate Animation and Delayed Hominization." *Theological Studies* 31 (1970): 76–105.

Durrant, Michael. 1973. *The Logical Status of "God."* London: Macmillan.

———. 1992. "The Meaning of 'God'." *Philosophy*, supplement 31 (1992): 71–84.

Edwards, Rem. 1981. "Kraus's Boethian Interpretation of Whitehead's God." *Process Studies* 11 (1981): 30–34.

Eslick, Leonard. 1953. "The Dyadic Character of Being in Plato." *Modern Schoolman* 31 (1953).

———. 1955. "The Platonic Dialectic of Non-Being." *New Scholasticism* 29 (1955).

———. 1982. "Plato as Dipolar Theist." *Process Studies* 12 (1982): 243–51.

Esser, M. 1910. "Finden sich Spüren des ontologischen Gottesbeweises vor dem Heiligen Anselm?" Jahrbücher für Philosophie und spekulative Theologie 29 (1910).

Feezell, Randolph. 1984. "Of Mice and Men: Nagel and the Absurd." *Modern Schoolman* 61 (1984): 259–65.

———. 1987. "Potentiality, Death, and Abortion." *Southern Journal of Philosophy* 25 (1987): 39–48.

Fiddes, Paul. 1988. *The Creative Suffering of God.* Oxford: Clarendon Press.

Findlay, J. N. 1974. *Plato: The Written and Unwritten Doctrines.* New York: Humanities Press.

Fischer, John Martin. 1992. "Recent Work on God and Freedom." *American Philosophical Quarterly* 29 (1992): 91–109.

Ford, Lewis. 1973. "Whitehead's Differences from Hartshorne." In *Two Process Philosophers.* Tallahassee, FL: American Academy of Religion.

———. 1974. "The Non-Temporality of Whitehead's God." *International Philosophical Quarterly* (1974).

———. 1978. *The Lure of God: A Biblical Background for Process Theism.* Philadelphia: Fortress Press.

Frankenberry, Nancy. 1991. "Hartshorne's Method in Metaphysics." In *The Philosophy of Charles Hartshorne*, ed. Hahn. LaSalle, IL: Open Court.

Friedlander, Paul. 1958. *Plato.* New York: Pantheon.

Gadamer, Hans-Georg. 1980. *Dialogue and Dialectic.* New Haven: Yale University Press.

Gale, Richard. 1991. *On the Nature and Existence of God.* Cambridge: Cambridge University Press.

Gardner, Charles. 1989. "Is an Embryo a Person?" *The Nation*, 13 November 1989.

Geach, Peter. 1977. *Providence and Evil.* Cambridge: Cambridge University Press.

Gilroy, John. 1989. "Hartshorne and the Ultimate Issue in Metaphysics." *Process Studies* 18 (1989): 38–56.

Gowen, Julie. 1987. "God and Timelessness: Everlasting or Eternal?" *Sophia* 26 (1987): 15–29.

Griffin, David Ray. 1989. "Reply: Must God Be Unlimited?" In *Concepts of the Ultimate.* ed. Tessier. New York: St. Martin's.

Gunton, Colin. 1978. *Becoming and Being: The Doctrine of God in Charles Hartshorne and Karl Barth.* Oxford: Oxford University Press.

Guthrie, W. K. C. 1978. *A History of Greek Philosophy.* Cambridge: Cambridge University Press.

Hack, R. K. 1931. *God in Greek Philosophy to the Time of Socrates.* Princeton: Princeton University Press.

Harrison, Jonathan. 1973–74. "The Embodiment of Mind, or What Use is Having a Body." *Proceedings of the Aristotelian Society* 74 (1973–74): 33–55.

Hartshorne, Charles. 1923. "An Outline and Defense of the Argument for the Unity of Being in the Absolute or Divine Good." Ph.D. dissertation, Harvard University, 1923.

———. 1941. *Man's Vision of God.* New York: Harper and Brothers.

———. 1948. *The Divine Relativity.* New Haven: Yale University Press.

———. 1953a. *Reality as Social Process.* Boston: Beacon Press.

———. 1953b. *Philosophers Speak of God.* Chicago: University of Chicago Press.

———. 1962. *The Logic of Perfection.* LaSalle, IL: Open Court.

———. 1967a. *A Natural Theology for Our Time.* LaSalle, IL: Open Court.

———. 1967b. *Anselm's Discovery.* LaSalle, IL: Open Court.

———. 1969. "The God of Religion and the God of Philosophy." In *Talk of God*, ed. Vesey. London: Macmillan.

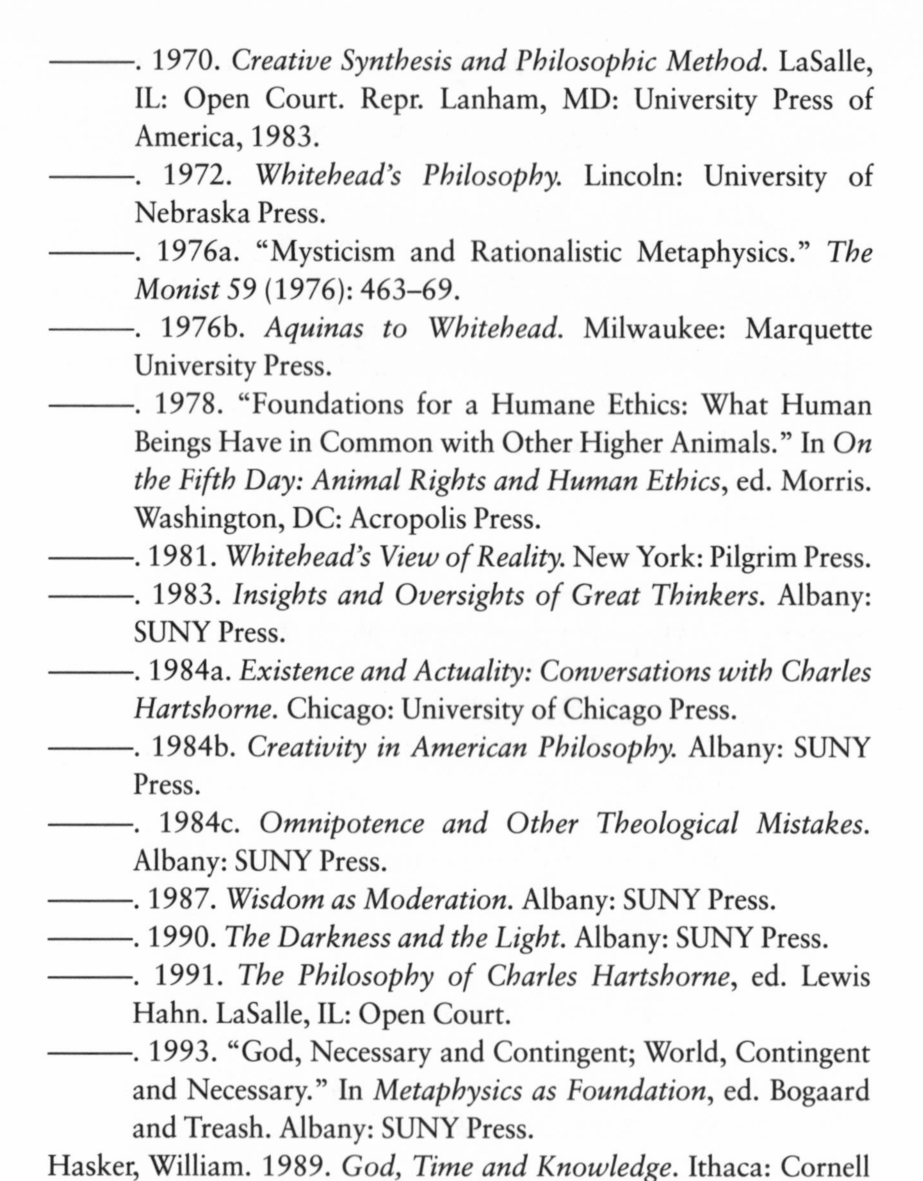

———. 1970. *Creative Synthesis and Philosophic Method.* LaSalle, IL: Open Court. Repr. Lanham, MD: University Press of America, 1983.

———. 1972. *Whitehead's Philosophy.* Lincoln: University of Nebraska Press.

———. 1976a. "Mysticism and Rationalistic Metaphysics." *The Monist* 59 (1976): 463–69.

———. 1976b. *Aquinas to Whitehead.* Milwaukee: Marquette University Press.

———. 1978. "Foundations for a Humane Ethics: What Human Beings Have in Common with Other Higher Animals." In *On the Fifth Day: Animal Rights and Human Ethics*, ed. Morris. Washington, DC: Acropolis Press.

———. 1981. *Whitehead's View of Reality.* New York: Pilgrim Press.

———. 1983. *Insights and Oversights of Great Thinkers.* Albany: SUNY Press.

———. 1984a. *Existence and Actuality: Conversations with Charles Hartshorne.* Chicago: University of Chicago Press.

———. 1984b. *Creativity in American Philosophy.* Albany: SUNY Press.

———. 1984c. *Omnipotence and Other Theological Mistakes.* Albany: SUNY Press.

———. 1987. *Wisdom as Moderation.* Albany: SUNY Press.

———. 1990. *The Darkness and the Light.* Albany: SUNY Press.

———. 1991. *The Philosophy of Charles Hartshorne*, ed. Lewis Hahn. LaSalle, IL: Open Court.

———. 1993. "God, Necessary and Contingent; World, Contingent and Necessary." In *Metaphysics as Foundation*, ed. Bogaard and Treash. Albany: SUNY Press.

Hasker, William. 1989. *God, Time and Knowledge.* Ithaca: Cornell University Press.

Helm, Paul. 1988. *Eternal God.* Oxford: Clarendon Press.

Hume, David. 1935. *Dialogues Concerning Natural Religion.* Ed. N. K. Smith. Oxford: Clarendon Press.

James, William. 1985. *The Varieties of Religious Experience.* Cambridge MA: Harvard University Press.

Johnson, J. Prescott. 1963. "The Ontological Argument in Plato." *The Personalist* 44 (1963): 24–34.

Kahn, Charles. 1986. *The Art and Thought of Heraclitus.* Cambridge: Cambridge University Press.

Katz, Steven, ed. 1978. *Mysticism and Philosophical Analysis.* London: Sheldon Press.

———, ed. 1983. *Mysticism and Religious Traditions.* New York: Oxford University Press.

Keller, James. 1986. Review of Creel in *Process Studies* 15 (1986): 290–96.

Kenny, Anthony. 1976. "Divine Foreknowledge and Human Freedom." In *Aquinas*, ed. Anthony Kenny. Notre Dame: University of Notre Dame Press.

King-Farlow, John. 1963. "Could God Be Temporal?" *Southern Journal of Philosophy* 1 (1963): 21–28.

Kneale, W. 1961. "Time and Eternity in Theology." *Proceedings of the Aristotelian Society* 61 (1961): 87–108.

Kondoleon, Theodore. 1984. "The Immutability of God: Some Recent Challenges." *The New Scholasticism* 58 (1984): 293–315.

Kretzmann, Norman. 1966. "Omniscience and Immutability." *Journal of Philosophy* 63 (1966): 409–21.

Kraus, Elizabeth. 1979. *The Metaphysics of Experience: A Companion to Whitehead's Process and Reality.* New York: Fordham University Press.

Kuntz, Paul. 1988. "Whitehead the Anglican and Russell the Puritan: The Traditional Origins of Muddleheadedness and Simple-mindedness." *Process Studies* 17 (1988): 40–44.

Leftow, Brian. 1991. *Time and Eternity.* Ithaca: Cornell University Press.

Lewis, Delmas. 1984. "Eternity Again: A Reply to Stump and Kretzmann." *International Journal for Philosophy of Religion* 15 (1984): 73–79.

———. 1987. "Timelessness and Divine Agency." *International Journal for Philosophy of Religion* 21 (1987): 143–59.

———. 1988. "Eternity, Time and Tenselessness." *Faith & Philosophy* 5 (1988): 72–86.

Loomer, Bernard. 1976. "Two Conceptions of Power." *Process Studies* 6 (1976): 5–32.

Lovejoy, A. O. 1917. "On Some Conditions of Progress in Philosophical Inquiry." *The Philosophical Review* 26 (1917): 123–63.

Lovelock, James. 1984. *Gaia.* Oxford: Oxford University Press.

Lowe, Victor. 1962. *Understanding Whitehead.* Baltimore: Johns Hopkins University Press.

Lucas, George. 1988. "'Muddleheadedness' versus 'Simplemindedness': Comparisons of Whitehead and Russell." *Process Studies* 17 (1988): 26–39.

———. 1989. *The Rehabilitation of Whitehead.* Albany: SUNY Press.

Mann, William. 1983. "Simplicity and Immutability in God." *International Philosophical Quarterly* 23 (1983): 267–76.

Marquis, Don. 1989. "Why Abortion Is Immoral." *The Journal of Philosophy* 86 (1989): 183–202.

Martin, R. M. 1976. "On God and Primordiality." *Review of Metaphysics* 29 (1976): 497–522.

Mavrodes, George. 1988. *Revelation in Religious Belief* Philadelphia: Temple University Press.

McFarland, Thomas. 1969. *Coleridge and the Pantheist Tradition.* Oxford: Clarendon Press.

Mesle, Robert. 1983. "Aesthetic Value and Relational Power." *Process Studies* 13 (1983): 59–70.

Mohr, Richard. 1985. *The Platonic Cosmology.* Leiden: Brill.

Moltmann, Jurgen. 1985. *God in Creation.* San Francisco: Harper & Row.

More, P. E. 1921. *The Religion of Plato,* Princeton: Princeton University Press.

Moreau, Joseph. 1939. *L'Ame du monde de Platon aux Stoiciens.* Paris.

Morris, Randall. 1991. *Process Philosophy and Political Ideology.* Albany: SUNY Press.

Morris, Thomas. 1986. *The Logic of God Incarnate*. Ithaca: Cornell University Press.

———. 1987. *Anselmian Explorations*. Notre Dame: University of Notre Dame Press.

Moskop, John. 1984. *Divine Omniscience and Human Freedom*. Macon, GA: Mercer University Press.

Munitz, Milton. 1965. *The Mystery of Existence* New York: Appleton-Century-Crofts.

Nagel, Thomas. 1970. *The Possibility of Altruism*. Oxford: Oxford University Press.

———. 1986. *The View from Nowhere*. Oxford: Oxford University Press.

———. 1987. *What Does It All Mean?* Oxford: Oxford University Press.

———. 1991 [1979]. *Mortal Questions*. Cambridge: Cambridge University Press.

Nelson, Herbert. 1987. "Time(s), Eternity, and Duration." *International Journal for Philosophy of Religion* 22 (1987): 3–19.

Oakes, Robert. 1977. "Classical Theism and Pantheism: A Victory for Process Theism?" *Religious Studies* 13 (1977): 167–74.

———. 1987. "Does Traditional Theism Entail Pantheism?" In *The Concept of God*, ed. Morris. Oxford: Oxford University Press.

Ogden, Schubert. 1984. "The Experience of God: Critical Reflections on Hartshorne's Theory of Analogy." In *Existence and Actuality: Conversations with Charles Hartshorne*. Chicago: University of Chicago Press.

Origen. 1973. *On First Principles*. tr. G. W. Butterworth. Gloucester, MA: Peter Smith.

Otto, W. F. 1978. *The Homeric Gods*. Salem, NH: Ayer.

Owen, H. P. 1971. *Concepts of Deity*. London: Macmillan.

Padgett, Alan. 1992. *God, Eternity and the Nature of Time*. New York: St. Martin's.

Parfit, Derek. 1973. "Later Selves and Moral Principles." In *Philosophy and Personal Relations*, ed. Montefiori. London: Routledge and Kegan Paul.

Pike, Nelson. 1970. *God and Timelessness*. New York: Schocken.

———. 1992. *Mystic Union: An Essay in the Phenomenology of Mysticism*. Ithaca: Cornell University Press.

Phillips, D. Z. 1988. *Faith after Foundationalism*. London: Routledge.

Plantinga, Alvin. 1967. *God and Other Minds*. Ithaca: Cornell University Press.

———. 1974. *The Nature of Necessity*. Oxford: Oxford University Press.

———. 1980. *Does God Have a Nature?* Milwaukee: Marquette University Press.

Plato. 1973. *The Collected Dialogues of Plato*. Ed. Hamilton and Cairns. Princeton: Princeton University Press. Also the Greek ed. of Burnet.

Plotinus. *Enneads*. Loeb ed. Cambridge, MA: Harvard University Press.

Plutarch. *Plutarch's Morals*. Ed. William Goodwin. Boston: Little, Brown, and Co., 1870.

Popper, Karl. 1972. *Objective Knowledge*. Oxford: Clarendon Press.

Prior, A. N. 1962. "The Formalities of Omniscience." *Philosophy* 37 (1962): 114–29.

Robinson, J. M. 1968. *An Introduction to Early Greek Philosophy*. New York: Houghton Mifflin.

Ross, James. 1969. *Philosophical Theology*. New York: Bobbs Merrill.

———. 1970. "On Proofs for the Existence of God." *The Monist* (1970).

———. 1977. "An Impasse on Competing Descriptions of God." *International Journal for Philosophy of Religion* 8 (1977): 233–49.

Rorty, Richard. 1979. *Philosophy and the Mirror of Nature*. Princeton: Princeton University Press.

Shields, George. 1987. "Davies, Eternity, and the Cosmological Argument." *International Journal for Philosophy of Religion* 21 (1987): 21–37.

Shorey, Paul. 1933. *What Plato Said*. Chicago: University of Chicago Press.

Simons, John. 1989. "Eternity, Omniscience and Temporal Passage." *Review of Metaphysics* 42 (1989): 547–68.

Smart, Ninian. 1965. "Interpretation and Mystical Experience." *Religious Studies* 1 (1965): 75–87.

Solmsen, Friedrich. 1942. *Plato's Theology.* Ithaca: Cornell University Press.

———. 1961. "Greek Philosophy and the Discovery of the Nerves." *Museum Helveticum* 18 (1961): 150–67, 169–97.

Soskice, Janet Martin. 1985. *Metaphor and Religious Language.* Oxford: Clarendon Press.

Stace, Walter. 1960a. *Mysticism and Philosophy.* Philadelphia: Lippincott.

———. 1960b. *The Teachings of the Mystics.* New York: New American Library.

Stump, Eleonore and Kretzmann, Norman. 1981. "Eternity." *The Journal of Philosophy* 78 (1981): 429–58.

Swinburne, Richard. 1968. "The Timelessness of God." *Church Quarterly Review* (1968): 323–37, 472–86.

———. 1977. *The Coherence of Theism* Oxford: Oxford University Press, 1977.

———. 1979. *The Existence of God* Oxford: Oxford University Press, 1979.

———. 1981. *Faith and Reason* Oxford: Oxford University Press, 1981.

Taylor, A. E. 1928. *A Commentary on Plato's Timaeus.* Oxford: Clarendon Press.

Thomas Aquinas, St. 1955. *On the Truth of the Catholic Faith: Summa Contra Gentiles.* Tr. A. Pegis. Garden City, NY: Doubleday Image Books.

———. 1964–81. *Summa Theologiae.* Blackfriars ed. New York: McGraw-Hill.

Tomlinson, J. L. 1982. "Divine Sempiternity and Atemporality." *Religious Studies* 18 (1982): 177–90.

Tooley, Michael. 1972. "Abortion and Infanticide." *Philosophy and Public Affairs* 2 (1972): 37–65.

Tracy, David. 1985. "Analogy, Metaphor, and God-Language: Charles Hartshorne." *Modern Schoolman* 62 (1985).

Van Inwagen, Peter. 1988. "The Place of Chance in a World Sustained by God." In *Divine and Human Action.* Ed. Morris. Ithaca: Cornell University Press.

Vitali, Theodore. 1977. "The Peircian Influence on Hartshorne's Subjectivism." *Process Studies* 7 (1977): 238–49.

Vlastos, Gregory. 1975. *Plato's Universe.* Seattle: University of Washington Press.

Wainwright, William. 1987. "God's Body." In *The Concept of God,* ed. Morris. Oxford: Oxford University Press.

Ward, Keith. 1974. *The Concept of God.* New York: St. Martin's.

———. 1982. *Rational Theology and the Creativity of God.* Oxford: Blackwell.

Whitehead, A.N. 1926. *Religion in the Making.* New York: Macmillan.

———. 1938. *Modes of Thought.* New York: Macmillan.

———. 1954. *Dialogues of Alfred North Whitehead.* Boston: Little, Brown.

———. 1957 [1925]. *Science and the Modern World.* New York: Macmillan.

———. 1961 [1933]. *Adventures of Ideas.* New York: Free Press.

———. 1978 [1929]. *Process and Reality,* corrected ed. New York: Free Press.

Whittemore, Robert. 1966. "Panentheism in Neo-Platonism." *Tulane Studies in Philosophy* 15 (1966): 47–70.

Wierenga, Edward. 1989. *The Nature of God.* Cambridge: Cambridge University Press.

Wolfson, H. A. 1934. *The Philosophy of Spinoza.* Cambridge, MA: Harvard University Press.

Wolterstorff, Nicholas. 1975. "God Everlasting." In *God and the Good,* ed. Orlebeke. Grand Rapids, MI: Eerdmans.

Zaehner, R. C. 1961. *Mysticism, Sacred and Profane.* New York: Oxford University Press.

Zagzebski, Linda. 1991. *The Dilemma of Freedom and Foreknowledge.* Oxford: Oxford University Press.

Zeis, John. 1984. "The Concept of Eternity." *International Journal for Philosophy of Religion* 16 (1984): 61–71.

Index of Names

Adams, Robert M., 144
Aeschylus, 225
Alston, William, ix, 2, 4–5, 8, 25, 77–81, 84–85, 89, 91, 94, 118, 121, 125–137, 139–141, 143–144, 147–148, 159–163, 229
Ammonius Saccas, 113
Anaxagoras, 225–227
Anaximenes, 226
Anscombe, Elizabeth, 171, 229
Anselm, St., 19, 25, 153
Aristotle, 4–5, 9–10, 12, 21, 36–37, 40, 47, 59, 64, 68–69, 89, 91–92, 99, 106–108, 111–112, 140, 150–151, 184, 208–209, 225–226, 228
Audi, Robert, 144
Augustine, St., 3, 12, 21, 27, 60, 68, 139, 181, 192, 208–209, 212, 217, 231–232
Auxier, Randall, 231

Barnes, Jonathan, 226
Barth, Karl, 54, 140
Berdyaev, Nicholas, 73, 222
Bergson, Henri, 10, 43, 47, 55, 131, 179, 187–188, 229–230
Bochenski, I. M., 208
Boethius, 3, 7, 12, 17, 32–33, 133, 135–136, 193
Bovet, Pierre, 225
Bracken, Joseph, 93
Burnet, J., 105, 226

Calvin, John 181, 192
Camus, Albert, 34, 178
Carrick, Paul, 208
Carr-Wiggin, Robert, 221
Christian, William, 151, 223
Clark, Norris, 219
Clark, S. R. L., 6, 193–203
Clarke, D. S., 174
Cobb, John, 229
Collins, James, 224
Cook, Robert, 7, 29
Cornford, F. M., 100, 224–226
Creel, Richard, ix, 3, 8, 13–14, 30–35, 37, 39, 125, 134, 139–140, 143–144, 148, 221
Cusanus, Nicholas, 9

Danto, Arthur, 224
David of Dinant, 28
Davis, Stephen, 73–74, 223
Democritus, 228
Demos, Raphael, 225
Derrida, Jacques, 42
Descartes, Rene, 43, 46, 178, 209
Dewey, John, 146
Diogenes of Apollonia, 225
Donceel, Joseph, 209, 231
Durrant, Michael, 5, 8, 143, 149–155, 157, 160, 222, 229

Edwards, Rem, 135–137
Einstein, Albert, 18
Empedocles, 226
Epictetus, 33
Epicurus, 47, 228

Eslick, Leonard, 36, 68, 70–71, 220, 223
Esser, M., 104
Euripides, 225

Fechner, Gustav, 47, 222
Feezell, Randolph, 213–214, 231
Feuerbach, Ludwig, 1, 162
Fiddes, Paul, 223
Findlay, J. N., 109, 228
Fischer, John Martin, 231
Ford, Lewis, 93, 134, 229
Frankenberry, Nancy, 230
Frege, Gottlob, 149, 154
Freud, Sigmund, 1
Friedlander, Paul, 227

Gadamer, Hans Georg, 227
Gale, Richard, 39, 222
Gardner, Charles, 232
Geach, Peter, 32, 154, 171, 219, 229
Griffin, David Ray, 73–74, 223
Gunton, Colin, ix, 4, 8, 14, 39–40, 50, 52, 58–64, 73, 121, 143–144, 148, 222–223
Guthrie, W. K. C., 226

Harrison, Jonathan, 224
Hegel, G. W. F., 46, 60
Helm, Paul, 3, 7, 39, 222
Heraclitus, 70, 226
Hobbes, Thomas, 28
Homer, 195
Hume, David, 1–2, 34, 46, 47, 83, 87, 105, 179, 184, 193, 204, 209–211, 219

James, William, 10, 146, 179, 194, 230
Jesus, 1, 18, 75, 117, 198, 200, 203
John of the Cross, St., 10, 146, 165–169, 230
Johnson, J. Prescott, 104

Kahn, Charles, 226
Kant, Immanuel, 1, 47, 55, 71, 104–105, 166–167, 182, 193
Katz, Steven, 165–170
Keller, James, 221
Kondoleon, Theodore, 221
Kraus, Elizabeth, 135
Kretzmann, Norman, 3, 7, 13–14, 17–19, 22, 26–27, 29–30, 32, 219–221
Kripke, Saul, 188
Kuntz, Paul, 2

Leftow, Brian, ix, 7, 29, 223
Leibniz, Gottfried, 193
Leucippus, 228
Lequier, Jules, 10, 40, 222
Lewis, Delmas, 221
Locke, John, 67–68
Loomer, Bernard, 74–75
Lovejoy, A. O., 4, 40–50, 222
Lovelock, James, 226
Lowe, Victor, 223
Lucas, George, ix, 2, 13, 173–174
Lucretius, 176

Mann, William, 3, 13–17, 22, 26–27, 29–30, 32, 128, 219–221
Marquis, Don, 214
Martin, R. M., 19, 220
Marx, Karl, 1
Mavrodes, George, 222
McFarland, Thomas, 121–122
McKeon, Richard, 47
McTaggert, J. M. E., 7
Mesle, Robert, 75
Mill, John Stuart, ix, 167
Mohr, Richard, 5, 78, 93–97, 112, 224–226
Moltmann, Jurgen, 5, 78, 92–93
Montague, W. P., 10
More, P. E., 222, 226
Moreau, Joseph, 229
Morris, Randall, 230
Morris, Thomas, 5, 8, 121, 137–141, 144, 148
Moskop, John, 19, 220
Munitz, Milton, 229

Nagel, Thomas, 6, 174–193, 195, 198, 203, 214, 224, 230–231
Newton, Isaac, 82, 88
Nietzsche, Friedrich, 1

Oakes, Robert, 5, 91
Ogden, Schubert, 163
Otto, W. F., 198
Origen, 78, 113, 116–119, 229

Padgett, Alan, 7
Parfit, Derek, 183–184, 188
Parmenides, 36, 70, 103–104, 192
Paul, St., 27, 117, 125, 210
Peirce, C. S., 29, 47, 53, 146, 165, 180, 187
Pfleiderer, Otto, 10

Pheidias, 202
Phillips, D. Z., 3, 39, 222
Philo, 1, 68
Pike, Nelson, 19, 165, 167–169
Plantinga, Alvin, 3, 13–14, 26–30, 34, 221
Plato, 4–5, 10, 28, 31, 35–38, 40, 44, 47, 54, 59–61, 65–74, 78, 85–86, 88–89, 91–114, 116–117, 119, 130–131, 145, 201, 208, 221, 223–229
Plotinus, 55, 64, 78, 113–117, 119, 202, 222, 228–229
Plutarch, 28, 108, 226
Popper, Karl, ix, 6, 47, 50
Pythagoras, 109, 226

Quine, W.V.O., 122

Rachels, James, 219
Rawls, John, 188
Robinson, J. M., 226
Rorty, Richard, 41–42
Ross, James, ix, 2, 5, 8, 143–149, 157, 159–160, 162, 171, 219, 229
Royce, Josiah, 42
Russell, Bertrand, 2, 46, 152, 173, 184, 193, 204, 209–212
Ryle, Gilbert, 80

Scotus Erigena, John, 9
Shields, George, 221
Shorey, Paul, 226
Singer, Peter, 217
Smart, Ninian, 167
Socinus, Faustus, 10, 47
Solmsen, Friedrich, 5, 78, 107–112, 116, 224–225, 227
Soskice, Janet Martin, 152
Spinoza, Baruch, 1, 9–10, 60, 71, 93, 122–124
Stace, Walter, 166–170
Stengel, Casey, 75
Strawson, Peter, 14
Stump, Eleanore 3, 7, 13, 17–19, 22, 26–27, 29–30, 32, 219–221
Swinburne, Richard, 4–5, 7, 28–30, 56, 77–78, 81–91, 118, 131–132, 221, 224

Taylor, A. E., 227–228
Teresa of Avila, St., 10, 146, 170
Thales, 225, 227
Thomas Aquinas, St., 3, 12, 15, 17, 19–22, 29, 33, 37, 51, 56, 64, 78, 84, 89, 91, 125, 133–136, 145–146, 148, 162, 165, 208–209, 217, 224, 228, 231
Tooley, Michael, 215, 231
Tracy, David, 93, 164–165

Van Inwagen, Peter, 229
Varisco, Bernardino, 10
Vitali, Theodore, 146
Vlastos, Gregory, 226
Voltaire, 1

Wainwright, William, 5, 91, 224
Ward, Keith, 5, 7, 64–65, 90–91, 223
Whitehead, Alfred North, 2, 10, 13, 31, 37–38, 47, 49, 60–63, 66-69, 71, 77–78, 93, 111, 115, 133–136, 140, 153, 173–174, 178, 182–183, 185–189, 219, 223, 228, 230
Whittemore, Robert, 228
Wierenga, Edward, 39, 222
Williams, Bernard, 192
Wittgenstein, Ludwig, 20, 188, 212
Wolfson, Harry, 101, 225
Wolterstorff, Nicholas, 30, 32, 221
Wordsworth, William, 34, 43, 194

Xenocrates, 227
Xenophanes, 225–226

Zaehner, R. C., 167
Zeis, John, 221